D1488358

THE MENTAL REPRESENTATION OF TRAIT AND AUTOBIOGRAPHICAL KNOWLEDGE ABOUT THE SELF

Advances in Social Cognition, Volume V

THE MENTAL REPRESENTATION OF TRAIT AND AUTOBIOGRAPHICAL KNOWLEDGE ABOUT THE SELF

WITHDRAWN

Advances in Social Cognition, Volume V

Edited by
THOMAS K. SRULL
ROBERT S. WYER, JR.
University of Illinois, Urbana—Champaign

Lead Article by
Stanley B. Klein and Judith Loftus

LEA LAWRENCE ERLBAUM ASSOCIATES, PUBLISHERS
1993   Hillsdale, New Jersey   Hove and London

Copyright 1993 by Lawrence Erlbaum Associates, Inc.
All rights reserved. No part of this book may be reproduced in
any form, by photostat, microform, retrieval system, or any other
means without the prior written permission of the publisher.

Lawrence Erlbaum Associates, Inc. Publishers
365 Broadway
Hillsdale, New Jersey 07642

Library of Congress Cataloging-in-Publication Data

Advances in Social Cognition

ISSN 0898-2007
ISBN 0-8058-1310-1 (cloth)
ISBN 0-8058-1312-8 (paper)

Printed in the United States of America
10   9   8   7   6   5   4   3

Contents

Preface

This is the fifth volume of the *Advances in Social Cognition* series. From its inception, the purpose of the series has been to present and evaluate new theoretical advances in all areas of social cognition and information processing. An entire volume is devoted to each theory, thus allowing it to be evaluated from a variety of perspectives and permitting its implications for a wide range of issues to be considered.

The series reflects the two major characteristics of social cognition: the high level of activity in the field and the interstitial nature of the work. Each volume contains a target chapter that is chosen because it is timely in its application, novel in its approach, and precise in its explication. This is then followed by a set of companion chapters that examine the theoretical and empirical issues the target chapter has raised. These latter chapters are written by authors with diverse theoretical orientations, representing different disciplines within psychology and, in some cases, entirely different disciplines. Target authors are then given the opportunity to respond to the comments and criticisms of their work, and to examine the ideas conveyed in the companion chapters in light of their own. The dialogue created by such a format is highly unusual but, we believe, extremely beneficial to the field.

Public debates are interesting and informative but they require a special group of people if they are to be productive. In this respect, we want to thank the many people who agreed to participate in the project. Most of all, we owe a considerable debt to Stan Klein and Judith Loftus. Their work represents some of the most sophisticated and carefully constructed that social cognition has to offer. In their target article, Klein and Loftus consider several ways in which trait and behavioral knowledge about oneself might be represented in memory. They then report a series of studies that they believe are effective in assessing whether people retrieve specific exemplars or abstract trait summaries for use in making trait judgments of themselves. The authors conclude that behavioral exemplars play a far smaller role in the representation of trait knowledge than is often assumed.

The commentators have played an equally important and difficult role. They were asked to prepare chapters that were critical but fair, and ones that were detailed but well reasoned. Readers will find that each of them is insightful, thought provoking, and an important contribution in its own right; as a group, they address issues cutting across social, cognitive, personality, clinical, and developmental psychology. We want to extend our sincere appreciation to each of the commentators for being so analytical and clear.

Finally, we want to acknowledge the invaluable assistance of Lawrence Erlbaum Associates. Larry's personal support and encouragement of the *Advances* series, as well as the continuing commitment of his staff to producing a high quality series of volumes, is deeply gratifying. It is a pleasure to work with them.

Thomas K. Srull
Robert S. Wyer, Jr.

1 The Mental Representation of Trait and Autobiographical Knowledge About the Self

Stanley B. Klein
Judith Loftus
University of California, Santa Barbara

If there is one topic on which we all are experts, it is ourselves. Psychologists depend on this expertise, as asking people questions about themselves is an important means by which they gather the data that provide much of the evidence for psychological theory. Personal recollections play an important role in clinical theorizing; people's thoughts, feelings, and beliefs provide the principle data for attitudinal research; judgments of one's traits and descriptions of one's goals and motivations are essential for the study of personality.

Yet despite their long dependence on self-report data, psychologists know very little about this basic resource and the processes that govern it. Consider, for instance, a judgment about one's traits, a common request in personality and social research. Most people can answer a question like "Are you cooperative?" in less than 3 seconds. But how do they do it? What determines our responses to questions about the self? How is knowledge about the self represented in memory? Sadly, psychology has little to offer in answer to these questions.

This lack of understanding is particularly striking when one considers how far psychology has come in understanding the representation and utilization of knowledge in domains other than the self. Cognitive psychologists have proposed and tested models describing the mental representation of words (e.g., Morton, 1969), sentences (e.g., J. Anderson, 1976), categories (e.g., Medin & Smith, 1984; Rosch, Mervis, Gray, Johnson, & Boyes-Braem, 1976) scripts, (e.g., Schank & Abelson, 1977), and stories (e.g., Graesser, 1981; van Dijk & Kintsch, 1983). Social psychologists have tested representational models of emotions (e.g., Clark & Fiske, 1982), attitudes (cf. Pratkanis, Breckler, & Greenwald, 1989), social stereotypes (e.g., Andersen & Klatzky, 1987), groups (e.g., Park & Hastie, 1987), and impression formation (e.g., Hamilton, 1989; Klein &

Loftus, 1990a; Wyer & Srull, 1989). Yet, despite the importance of the self as a concept in psychology, virtually no empirically tested representational models of self-knowledge can be found.

Recently, however, several theoretical accounts of the representation of self-knowledge have been proposed (for recent reviews, see Higgins & Bargh, 1987; Kihlstrom et al., 1988; Klein & Kihlstrom, 1986; Wyer & Srull, 1989). These models have been concerned primarily with the factors underlying a particular type of self-knowledge—our trait conceptions of ourselves. The models all share the starting assumption that the source of our knowledge of the traits that describe us is memory for our past behavior. They disagree, however, about the role of individual behaviors in the representation of that knowledge. Specifically, some models argue that knowledge of our traits is represented at the level of individual behaviors exemplifying those traits, and that responses to questions about one's traits must be "computed" from a consideration of relevant behaviors in memory. Other models, however, argue that trait self-knowledge also can be represented in abstract form. Specifically, they propose that traits that a person considers central to his or her self-concept will be represented abstractly, and that questions regarding those traits may be answered by directly accessing the abstract representation.

The distinction separating these proposals is one that has emerged from the cognitive literature on categorization. One view holds that knowledge of a category is a summary representation abstracted from experience with multiple exemplars of that category (e.g., Homa & Chambliss, 1975; Posner & Keele, 1968; Rosch, 1975). Thus, a summary representation includes those properties that are characteristic of the category. According to this view, a determination of whether a particular object is an instance of a given category will be based on the perceived similarity of the object to the summary representation of the category in memory. For example, deciding whether a penguin is a bird will depend on the similarity of "penguin" to the summary representation of the category "bird" (i.e., whether "penguin" possesses some criterial number of properties characteristic of birds).

A second view, however, denies abstraction, and proposes instead that the mental representation of a concept consists solely of the separate representations of its known exemplars (e.g., Brooks, 1978; Hintzman, 1984, 1986, 1988; Hintzman & Ludlam, 1980; Medin & Shaeffer, 1978; Nosofsky, 1987). According to this view, the determination of whether an object is an instance of a particular concept will be based on the similarity of the object to known *exemplars* of the concept in memory. Thus, judging whether "penguin" is an instance of the concept "bird" will involve retrieving from memory known exemplars of birds and comparing "penguin" with them.

The issue for self-theorists concerns our knowledge of the constellation of traits that describe us, and the role of known exemplars—one's past behaviors—in the representation of that knowledge. The question is whether knowledge of one's traits is abstracted from behaviors relevant to those traits and represented in memory in summary form, or whether it consists simply of the separate representations of one's trait-relevant behaviors. Among the current models of self, however, the debate is not strictly between these opposing positions—all of the models agree that exemplars are important for judgments of at least some traits. The argument is about whether trait knowledge is represented exclusively at the level of exemplars, or whether some abstraction occurs as well.

In this chapter, we first review the available models of the processes underlying trait self-descriptiveness judgments. Although these models appear quite different in their basic representational assumptions, exemplar and abstraction models sometimes are difficult to distinguish experimentally (for a recent review, see Barsalou, 1990). We next present a series of studies using several new techniques that we believe are effective for assessing whether people recruit specific exemplars or abstract trait summaries when making trait judgments about themselves. On the basis of these studies, we conclude that specific behavioral exemplars play a far smaller role in the representation of trait knowledge than previously has been assumed. Finally, we discuss the limitations of social cognition paradigms as methods for studying the representation of long-term social knowledge, and we explore the implications of our research for both existing and future social psychological research.

TWO VIEWS OF TRAIT SELF-DESCRIPTIVENESS JUDGMENTS

The Pure Exemplar View

Exemplar-based theories of the self-judgment process reflect the view that our knowledge of our traits is inseparable from specific autobiographical memories (e.g., Bellezza, 1984; Bower & Gilligan, 1979; Groninger & Groninger, 1984; Locksley & Lenauer, 1981; Matlin, 1989; Warren, Chattin, Thompson, & Tomsky, 1983). Although the details of these theories differ, they have in common the proposal that trait self-knowledge consists of the representations in memory of individual autobiographical episodes. According to this view, a judgment of whether a trait is self-descriptive is made by retrieving memories of behaviors relevant to the trait and computing the similarity of the trait to the behaviors retrieved. Thus, to decide whether one is cooperative, one would retrieve from memory behaviors relevant to cooperation and determine whether there is a match between those behaviors and "cooperative." Retrieving behaviors such as my agreement to participate in a department project, should lead me to decide that "cooperative" is self-descriptive. (Consistent with this proposal, Bower and Gilligan, 1979, noted that subjects asked to judge trait adjectives for self-descriptiveness report that they often retrieve specific autobiographical incidents to do so.)

Some of the original formulations of the pure exemplar view (e.g., Hampson, 1982a; Locksley & Lenauer, 1981) were based on an extention of Bem's (1967, 1972) theory of self-perception. Bem proposed that our knowledge of our own thoughts, feelings, and other internal states is inferred from observing our behavior and the circumstances in which it occurs. For example, a person will infer that he is hungry if he is enthusiastically eating a large meal. The idea that we infer our current internal states from currently observed behaviors suggested to some self-theorists that we also may infer our knowledge of whether a trait is self-descriptive from *memories* of past behaviors (see also Chaiken & Baldwin, 1981; Fazio, Effrein, & Falender, 1981; Salancik & Conway, 1975; Schlenker & Trudeau, 1990).

The Dual Exemplar/Summary View

In contrast to the pure exemplar view, a number of investigators have argued for both exemplar and summary representation of trait knowledge about the self (e.g., Bower & Gilligan, 1979; Cantor & Kihlstrom, 1987; Chew, 1983; Kihlstrom & Cantor, 1984; Kihlstrom et al., 1988; Mancuso & Ceely, 1980; Markus, 1977, 1980; Wyer & Gordon, 1984; Wyer & Srull, 1986). According to this view, the self-descriptiveness of a trait can be determined *either* by computations performed on trait-relevant autobiographical memories, or by directly accessing summary knowledge of one's traits in memory. It is assumed that summary representations will be accessed if they exist, and that autobiographical retrieval and similarity computation will be performed only when a trait is not represented in summary form. The existence of a summary representation of a given trait is thought to imply that the trait is central to a subject's self-concept (e.g., Kihlstrom & Cantor, 1984; Kihlstrom et al., 1988).

As we have noted, the models just described are primarily theoretical and have not been subjected to thorough empirical testing. In general, these models of the self have been difficult to test because the available methodologies that have been used to study the representation of exemplar and summary knowledge in other domains do not easily transfer to the study of knowledge about the self. For example, Medin, Altom, Murphy (1984) presented an elegant paradigm for assessing the contributions of exemplar and prototype information to nonsocial classification. The paradigm requires that subjects either learn category prototypes and exemplars concurrently, learn prototypes first and then exemplars, or learn exemplars only. Smith and Zarate (1990) successfully adopted the same procedure to study social judgments. The paradigm is inappropriate for studying knowledge of self, however, because self-knowledge is well-developed, and thus cannot be manipulated in the way the paradigm requires.

The paradigms typically used in research on the representation of trait knowledge about other people (i.e., person memory) are similarly inappropriate for the study of self. They explore the representation of trait knowledge about others by examining subjects' recall of a list of behaviors, each of which has been designed to exemplify a particular trait, and all of which ostensibly were performed by a "target" person. Principles governing the representation of trait knowledge about others are inferred from the effects on subjects' recall of experimental manipulations of the stimulus behaviors. Clearly, this approach would not work for studying trait knowledge about the self, as knowledge of one's own traits is developed over a lifetime, and experimental control over its acquisition, therefore, is not possible.

In short, the traditional laboratory paradigms for studying social categorization and person memory—presenting carefully designed stimuli under controlled conditions, and testing their effects over short time periods—are not appropriate for testing the representation of long-term knowledge about the self. We have found, however, that we can get around some of the problems inherent in studying the representation of self-knowledge by examining the time subjects take to access preexperimental knowledge about the self in memory. In the next section, we describe a series of studies that use response latencies to test an assumption common to the trait self-judgment models we have presented—that judgments are mediated by retrieval of behaviors from autobiographical memory.

INVESTIGATIONS OF THE SELF-JUDGMENT PROCESS

The Task-Facilitation Paradigm: An Overview of the Experimental Design

Our initial tests of exemplar-based models of the self-judgment process used a task-facilitation paradigm in which subjects performed two tasks in succession for a single stimulus trait (e.g., Klein, Loftus, & Burton, 1989, Experiment 2). The paradigm was based on the following premise: If, in the process of performing the first task, information relevant to performing the second task is made available, then the time required to perform the second task should be less than if that information were not available (e.g., Collins & Quillian, 1970; Macht & O'Brien, 1980). Thus, one way to determine the degree to which two tasks require, and thereby make available, similar information is to examine the degree to which performing the first task reduces the time required to perform the second. The reduction in performance time should be greatest when the information overlap between the first and second tasks is relatively large, and should be least when the overlap is relatively small.[1] In the extreme case, when the first and second tasks are identical, the reduction in time required to perform the second should be maximal.

---

[1]Interestingly, Malt (1989) independently proposed a technique based on similar ideas for diagnosing the contributions of exemplars and abstractions to nonsocial category judgments.

We used three tasks in our experiments: A *descriptive* task, which required subjects to judge a stimulus trait word for self-descriptiveness; an *autobiographical* task, which required subjects to retrieve from memory a specific incident in which they manifested the stimulus trait; and a *semantic* task, which required subjects to generate a definition for the stimulus trait. A trial consisted of performing two tasks in succession, an initial task and a target task, on the same trait adjective. All possible combinations of the three task types (descriptive, autobiographical, and semantic) were used, giving us nine initial task–target task pairs. This allowed us to examine target task response latencies for all three tasks as a function of initial task performed. The assignment of trait adjectives to the initial task–target task combinations (eight adjectives each) and the order in which the task combinations were presented were randomized across subjects.

Each trial began with the appearance on a computer screen of a cue word for the initial task. The cue was either DESCRIBES (for the descriptive task), REMEMBER (for the autobiographical task), or DEFINE (for the semantic task). After 1 second, a trait adjective appeared below the cue and a timer was started. Both words remained on the screen until the subject indicated by pressing a key that he or she had completed the initial task. The timer then stopped, response latency was recorded, and the initial task cue was removed, leaving the stimulus trait on the screen. After a 1-second pause, the cue word for the target task (DESCRIBES, REMEMBER or DEFINE) appeared on the screen and the timer was reactivated. Again, the cue and the trait adjective remained on the screen until the subject indicated that he or she had completed the target task. The timer then stopped and target task response latency was recorded. There was then a 2-second delay before the beginning of the next trial.

We specifically did not request that subjects verbalize their responses to any of the tasks. Given the tendency of most people to want to present themselves in socially desirable terms (e.g., Arkin, 1986; Edwards, 1957, 1970; Wiggins, 1973), we feared that asking subjects to report their task responses would increase the chances that self-presentational concerns would influence their responses to the descriptive and autobiographical tasks. For instance, in making a self-descriptiveness judgment, a subject might be reluctant to reveal that a socially undesirable trait (e.g., "immoral") describes him or her. Or, for the autobiographical task, a subject could be uncomfortable about relating an incident in which he or she behaved in a socially undesirable way (e.g., "I remember the time that I stole money from my roommate"). We did not want these concerns to interfere with subjects' latencies to perform the tasks, so we purposely did not require subjects to reveal their responses during the experimental trials; rather, we instructed them to generate responses to the task questions in their heads.

Subjects were told it was important that they perform the tasks accurately and that they indicate immediately when they had completed each task. They also were told that on trials where the target task was the same as the initial task, they need not generate a new response for the target task; rather, they could simply call the original response to mind a second time.

Experiment 1: A Test of the Pure Exemplar Model

If, as a pure exemplar model implies, a self-descriptiveness judgment requires autobiographical information, then two things should occur. First, the reduction in time required to perform an autobiographical target task should be greater when a descriptive task is performed first than when a semantic task is performed first. This is because the autobiographical information required for an auto-biographical task will have been made available during the descriptive task but not during the semantic task. Second, the reduction in time required to perform a descriptive task should be greater when an autobiographical task is performed first than when a semantic task is performed first, because the autobiographical information required for the descriptive task will have been made available during the autobiographical task, but not during the semantic task.[2]

By contrast, if a self-descriptiveness judgment does not require auto-biographical information, then (a) performing a descriptive task first should not lead to a greater reduction in the time required to perform an autobiographical target task than would result from first performing a semantic task; and (b) performing an autobiographical task first should not lead to a greater reduction in the time required to perform a descriptive task than would result from first performing a semantic task.

The mean target task latencies are shown in Fig. 1.1.[3] Consistent with the premise underlying the task-facilitation paradigm—that facilitation of a target task by an initial task is an increasing function of overlap in information required for the two tasks—target task response latencies for all three task types were shortest when the initial task and target task were same. At first glance, this result might seem to indicate that on trials where the initial and target tasks were the same, subjects simply pressed the response key without performing the task a second time. We do not think this is what happened, however, for two reasons. First, the mean target task latencies for these conditions ranged from 1,780

---

[2]It is important to note that we are not arguing that autobiographical memories must be consciously available to exert an influence on subsequent task performance. On the contrary, we share with many exemplar theorists the view that the effects of individual exemplars often will be outside of conscious awareness (e.g., Hintzman, 1986; Kahneman & Miller, 1986; Smith, 1990b). We argue only that if, in the process of performing an initial task, autobiographical memories are activated, these memories will be more easily accessible for subsequent retrieval or for self-descriptiveness judgments than if they had not already been activated.

[3]Analyses of the mean and median response latencies yielded identical patterns of significant results. To facilitate comparisons with latency data reported in previous explorations of self-knowledge (e.g., Keenan & Baillet, 1980; Kuiper & Rogers, 1979), we present the results of analyses on the means.

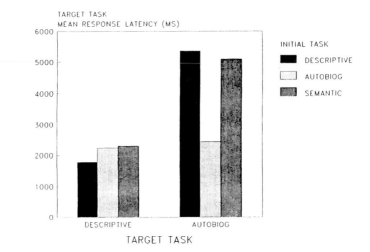

FIG. 1.1.   Target task mean response latencies as a function initial task performed (Experiment 1).

milliseconds to 2,433 milliseconds—much longer than would be expected if subjects had responded immediately without performing a task (e.g., Collins & Quillian, 1970). Second, on trials where both tasks were autobiographical, the mean response time for the autobiographical target task was 2,433 milliseconds. This latency is comparable to autobiographical reactivation times reported in the literature (e.g., Cornoldi, DeBeni, & PraBaldi, 1989), and suggests, therefore, that subjects did, in fact, bring autobiographical incidents to mind a second time.

The facilitation pattern predicted by the pure exemplar hypothesis, however, did not occur. Response latencies for the autobiographical target task were the same, regardless of whether the initial task was descriptive or semantic (see Fig. 1.1). Subjects who initially made self-descriptiveness judgments do not appear to have accessed autobiographical information to do so, as they were no faster to retrieve autobiographical information when it was explicitly requested for the autobiographical task than subjects who initially generated definitions ($Ms = 5,356$ and $5,092$ milliseconds, respectively). Similarly, response latency for the descriptive target task was the same, regardless of whether the initial task was autobiographical or semantic ($Ms = 2,237$ and $2,303$ milliseconds, respectively). Apparently, having autobiographical information available was not particularly useful for making self-descriptiveness judgments, as subjects who retrieved autobiographical incidents before making their judgments were no quicker than those who did not. Thus, the latency data from both target tasks fail to support the view that self-descriptiveness judgments either require or are influenced by autobiographical retrieval.

After completing this experiment, however, we felt that we should consider another possibility. It could be that information overlap between the descriptive and autobiographical tasks—and hence the expected facilitation—is influenced by the extent to which a trait is self-descriptive. Our premise has been that if autobiographical retrieval occurs during self-descriptiveness judgments, then the autobiographical information retrieved should facilitate a subsequent auto-biographical task. This reasoning is plausible for traits that are self-descriptive, because the information subjects retrieve first to judge a trait for self-descrip-tiveness should be similar to the information they need next for the auto-biographical task.

But for traits that are not self-descriptive, the information utilized by the descriptive and autobiographical tasks may not be similar. For example, in judging the trait "introverted" for self-descriptiveness, an extroverted subject might readily recall an incident in which he or she was extroverted, and decide on the basis of this disconfirming evidence that "introverted" is not self-descrip-tive (e.g., Chew, 1983; Klein et al., 1989). For a subsequent autobiographical task, however, this subject must recall an incident in which he or she was in fact introverted. In this case, the information made available by the descriptive task would not overlap with the information required for the autobiographical task; and thus, even though the self-descriptiveness judgment was mediated by auto-biographical retrieval, facilitation of the autobiographical task would not occur.

Another possibility is suggested by the dual exemplar/summary model. Ac-cording to this model, autobiographical retrieval is more important for judgments on some traits than on others: Judgments about traits that are irrelevant to one's self-concept are more likely to depend on autobiographical retrieval than are judgments about traits that are central to one's self-concept (e.g., Bower & Gilligan, 1979; Chaiken & Baldwin, 1981; Kihlstrom & Cantor, 1984; Klein & Loftus, 1990b; Wyer & Srull, 1989). Specifically, traits central in defining the self are assumed to be represented explicitly as part of one's self-knowledge (e.g., Kihlstrom & Cantor, 1984; Wyer & Srull, 1989). Self-descriptiveness judgments about such traits are accomplished by directly accessing the trait's representation in memory (e.g., Bower & Gilligan, 1979; Kihlstrom et al., 1988; Klein et al., 1989). By contrast, traits that are irrelevant to one's self-concept are unlikely to be explicitly represented as part of one's self-knowledge (e.g., Bower & Gilligan, 1979; Kihlstrom & Cantor, 1984). Judging these traits for self-descriptiveness, therefore, would require inferences based on trait-relevant auto-biographical information in memory (e.g., Bower & Gilligan, 1979; Kihlstrom & Cantor, 1984; Kihlstrom et al., 1988).

For example, if the trait "generous" is not one in terms of which a subject typically characterizes him or herself, then to decide whether it is self-descrip-tive, the subject must first retrieve relevant behavioral evidence (e.g., "I re-member giving money to a beggar") from which he or she can infer his or her decision ("I must be generous"). Thus, for irrelevant traits, autobiographical retrieval could mediate self-descriptiveness judgments and facilitation could occur, but it would be difficult to detect if we combined the results for all traits without regard to self-descriptiveness.

If may be premature, then, to reject the exemplar-based models of the self-judgment process on the basis of our failure to find facilitation in Experiment 1. Autobiographical retrieval may, in fact, mediate some self-descriptiveness judgments, but perhaps this becomes apparent only when responses for descriptive, not descriptive, and irrelevant traits are examined separately.

Experiment 2: Does Trait Self-Descriptiveness Affect Facilitation?

Fortunately, there is a straightforward way to increase the sensitivity of our experimental design. In the next experiment (Klein, Loftus, Trafton & Fuhrman, 1992, Experiment 2), we repeated the task-facilitation procedure with a new group of subjects ($N = 29$), but this time we obtained self-descriptiveness ratings for each of the stimulus traits. After subjects completed the experimental trials, they again were presented with each trait and asked to rate it on a 9-point scale marked (1) "extremely unlike me," (5) "irrelevant," (9) extremely like me." These ratings allowed us to sort subjects' response latencies for the 90 stimulus traits into three levels of self-descriptiveness. For each initial task–target task pair (15 trait adjectives per pair), the five traits receiving the highest ratings were placed in the high descriptive category, the five traits receiving the next highest ratings were placed in the medium descriptive category, and the remaining five traits were placed in the low descriptive category. In case of ties where the trait could be assigned to adjacent categories, random assignment was employed.

To ensure that subjects' variability in their use of the full range of the rating scale did not invalidate our assignment of traits to the three categories, we computed the mean ratings for traits in our high, medium, and low descriptiveness categories. These means did indeed reflect scale values consistent with the category headings ($Ms = 8.2$, 6.1, and 4.1, for high, medium, and low, respectively).

The Effects of Trait Self-Descriptiveness on Initial Task Latency

Before discussing the results for the target tasks, we mention several interesting findings that emerged when we examined just the initial task response latencies, as a function of trait self-descriptiveness.

First, as can be seen in Fig. 1.2, our three experimental tasks yielded very different latency functions. The semantic task gave a flat function, indicating that the time required to generate definitions was independent of trait self-descrip-

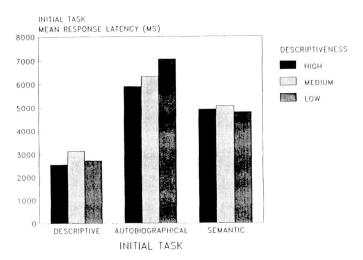

FIG. 1.2.   Initial task mean response latencies as a function of trait self-descriptiveness (Experiment 2).

tiveness. By contrast, the autobiographical task showed a monotonically increasing function: Latencies were shortest for retrieval of autobiographical incidents involving high descriptive traits and longest for retrieval of incidents involving low descriptive traits. Finally, the descriptive task latencies form an inverted "U," with longer latencies for medium descriptive traits than for high or low descriptive traits.

These initial task functions can help resolve several questions about our procedure that are critical to interpreting the results obtained with the task facilitation-paradigm. The first question is whether or not responses to the descriptive and autobiographical tasks were affected by the social desirability of the traits in question. We had attempted to minimize subjects' concerns about self-presentation by not requiring them to report their responses to the tasks. But reducing the effects of self-presentational factors does not necessarily mean that social desirability will not influence subjects' responses. There is evidence, for example, that subjects tend to attribute to themselves personality traits with socially desirable features and to reject those with socially undesirable features, and that this is somewhat independent of the tendency to engage in impression management for self-presentational purposes (e.g., Edwards, 1970). Thus, even when responding only internally, subjects performing the descriptive task might still, rather than access the self-knowledge required for the task, adopt a rule of simply responding "yes" to desirable traits and "no" to undesirable traits (e.g., Edwards, 1957, 1970; Wiggins, 1968). Unfortunately, allowing our subjects to keep their responses private left us unable to monitor whether or not this occurred. In fact, it left open a second question—whether subjects performed the tasks at all.

From the initial task latencies, however, we can see evidence that subjects did, in fact, perform the tasks and that their responses were not influenced by trait social desirability.. First, the latency functions we obtained are comparable to those obtained by researchers who collected subjects' responses at the time of task performance. For example, the inverted "U" function seen with our descriptive task replicates the results of numerous studies in which subjects reported their self-descriptiveness judgments at the time they made them (e.g., Kuiper, 1981; Lord, Gilbert, & Stanley, 1982; Mueller, Thompson, & Dugan, 1986). The monotonically increasing function found for our autobiographical task latencies parallels the findings of Klein and Loftus (1991), who asked subjects to describe in detail autobiographical episodes in which they exemplified each of a list of trait adjectives. The data from that study revealed the same inverse relation between trait self-descriptiveness and latency to retrieve autobiographical incidents. The correspondence of our data with that reported elsewhere for similar tasks suggests that our subjects, although they were not monitored, did perform the required tasks.

Second, when we reanalyzed the initial task data, this time segregating latencies on the basis of social desirability (e.g., Kirby & Gardner, 1972), we were able to see that social desirability was not the basis of subjects' responses to the autobiographical and descriptive tasks. For each initial task–target task pair, we placed the five adjectives with the highest normative social desirability ratings in the high desirability category, the five adjectives with the next highest ratings in the medium desirability category, and the remaining five adjectives in the low desirability category. The resulting latency functions are shown in Fig. 1.3. Here, in contrast to the three different functions in Fig. 1.2, where traits are segregated by self-descriptiveness, we can see that when traits are segregated by normative social desirability, functions for all three tasks are flat. Clearly, then, the original latency functions for the descriptive and autobiographical tasks reflect something other than a tendency to respond to traits simply on the basis of social desirability.

A third methodological question concerns our choice of definition generation as the appropriate control task for our studies. We assumed in choosing it that performing this task would not involve self-knowledge; but although this seemed intuitively plausible, we had no direct evidence in support of our assumption. Fortunately, the initial task latencies as a function of trait self-descriptiveness (see Fig. 1.2) strongly suggest that we were correct. Consistent with findings elsewhere that trait self-descriptiveness has pronounced effects on latency to perform tasks involving self-knowledge (e.g., Ganellen & Carver, 1985; Klein et al., 1989; Kuiper, 1981; Kuiper & Rogers, 1979; Markus, 1977; Mueller et al., 1986), latencies for both the descriptive and autobiographical tasks show strong effects of self-descriptiveness. The semantic task, however, shows no effect. Thus, we conclude that definition generation does not involve information about the self, and therefore serves as an appropriate control.

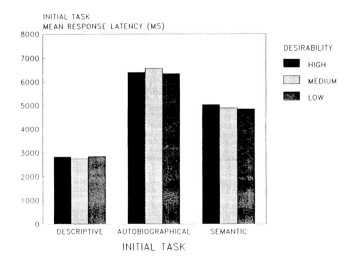

FIG. 1.3. Initial task mean response latencies as a function of trait social desirability (Experiment 2).

Target Tasks: Facilitation Results

The data of primary interest, the joint effects of initial task and trait self-descriptiveness on target task latencies, are shown in Fig. 1.4. Once again, we failed to find the facilitation predicted by exemplar-based self-judgment models. The left panel of Fig. 1.4 shows that regardless of whether the traits fell in the high, medium, or low descriptiveness categories, the time taken to perform a descriptive target task was not differentially influenced by performance of an autobiographical or a semantic initial task. Similarly, the right panel of Fig. 1.4 shows that the time required to perform an autobiographical task was not differentially influenced by previous performance of a descriptive or a semantic task. Thus, contrary to the predictions of the dual exemplar/summary hypothesis, trait self-descriptiveness does not appear to influence facilitation. In fact, if we compare Fig. 1.4 and 1.2, we can see that when latencies are broken down by trait self-descriptiveness, the latency functions for each of the self-target tasks is essentially identical to that of its corresponding initial task: Descriptive task latencies show the inverted "U" pattern and autobiographical task latencies show the monotonically increasing function. In short, the time required to perform the self-target tasks appears completely uninfluenced by the type of task performed initially.

Thus, although this second study was informative about the differential effects of self-descriptiveness on response latency for self-descriptiveness judgments and autobiographical retrieval, it did not give any evidence that self-descriptiveness affects facilitation. Consequently, our failure to find facilitation

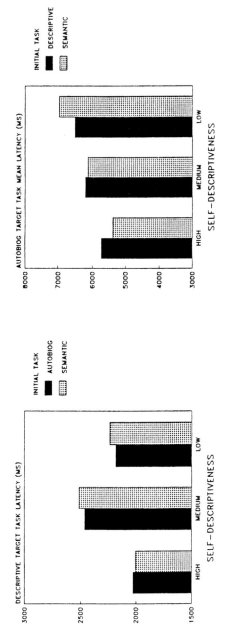

FIG. 1.4. Target task mean response latencies as a function of initial task performed and trait self-descriptiveness (Experiment 2).

in Experiment 1 cannot be attributed to undetected effects of trait self-descriptiveness.[4]

CONVERGING EVIDENCE

Experiments 1 and 2, in failing to find evidence that trait-relevant autobiographical memories are made available during the performance of a descriptive task, argue against the exemplar models of the self-judgment process. Instead, they support a model in which judgments about the self-descriptiveness of trait adjectives are made without reference to behavioral evidence.

The findings from any one paradigm, however, are open to multiple interpretations and vulnerable to the charge that they reflect more the idiosyncracies of the methodology than the behavior of the variables of interest. We therefore decided to continue to test the exemplar view using different methodologies and dependent measures. This "converging operations" approach to hypothesis testing (e.g., Garner, Hake, & Eriksen, 1956; Pryor & Ostrom, 1981; Srull, 1984) is based on the premise that although it is relatively easy to generate alternate explanations for findings from a single experiment, it becomes increasingly difficult to do so when experiments using different paradigms yield the same findings. The next section describes two additional approaches we took toward testing exemplar models of self-judgment.

Experiment 3: Encoding Specificity and Recognition Accuracy

Our first approach was based on the principle of encoding specificity (e.g., Tulving, 1979, 1983). According to this principle, performance on a memory test is an increasing function of the overlap between information stored during encoding and the information present at retrieval. Memory is said to be best when retrieval conditions make available the same information that was available at the time of study (e.g., Tulving, 1983; Tulving & Thompson, 1973).

An experiment by Light and Carter-Sobell (1970) demonstrated this principle in a recognition memory paradigm. In that experiment, subjects were required to remember a list of nouns each of which had more than one distinct meaning. Each noun was presented at study along with a modifier that biased one of the noun's possible meanings (e.g., traffic-*JAM*). The recognition test presented the nouns either alone, with the modifier studied (e.g., traffic-*JAM*), or with a

---

[4]The reader should note that although the task-facilitation paradigm yielded null findings, the failure to find evidence for exemplar effects for self-judgments is not due to an insensitivity of the methods employed. As is seen in Experiment 5, the paradigm provides robust evidence of exemplar effects when the referent is changed from self to other (i.e., one's mother).

modifier biasing a different meaning (e.g., strawberry-*JAM*). The condition in which the information at retrieval matched the information at study (noun with studied modifier) produced the best recognition performance.

In our study, we used the encoding specificity principle to test the implications of the exemplar models of self-judgments for recognition memory (Klein, Loftus, and Plog, 1992). The experiment, an extention of a paradigm developed by Groninger and Groninger (1984), was conducted in two sessions. During the first session, subjects were assigned randomly to one of three study task conditions (semantic, descriptive, or autobiographical), and performed the appropriate task for a list of 30 trait words. After completing the encoding phase, they were told that the second part of the experiment would take place in 2 weeks, but were not told that their memories would be tested.

The second session consisted of 60 trials with 60 stimulus traits. Half of the traits were "old" (presented at study) and half were "new" (not previously presented). Each trial had two parts: Subjects first performed either a semantic, descriptive, or autobiographical task, and then made a recognition judgment in which they decided whether the stimulus trait was one they had seen during the study session. For each subject, old and new trait words were evenly divided among the three tasks, with both the pairing of trait and task and the order of trait presentation randomized across subjects. Thus, for the "old" traits, the task performed at recognition was identical to the task performed at study in one third of the trials.

The encoding specificity principle states that recognition accuracy will be an increasing function of the degree of overlap between information provided at study and information provided at retrieval. We therefore predicted that if autobiographical information is required for self-descriptiveness judgments, recognition accuracy for subjects who perform a descriptive task at study should be higher when the recognition task is autobiographical than when it is semantic. This is because the overlap between the information made available at encoding and at retrieval will be greater between the descriptive and autobiographical tasks than between the descriptive and semantic tasks.

By the same reasoning, recognition accuracy for subjects performing an autobiographical task at study should be higher when the recognition task is descriptive than when it is semantic, because the information made available by the autobiographical study task will have more overlap with the information made available by the descriptive retrieval task than with that made available by the semantic retrieval task.

If autobiographical information is *not* required for a self-descriptiveness judgment, then (a) recognition accuracy for subjects who perform a descriptive task at study should be unaffected by whether the retrieval task is autobiographical or semantic, and (b) recognition accuracy for subjects who perform an autobiographical task at study should be unaffected by whether the retrieval task is descriptive or semantic.

TABLE 1.1
Mean Percentages Correct (Hit Rate
Minus False Alarm Rate) as a Function of Encoding
and Retrieval Conditions (Experiment 3)

Encoding Context	Retrieval Context		
	Autobiog	Descriptive	Semantic
Autobiog	37.89	27.37	30.53
Descriptive	21.05	35.26	24.21
Semantic	31.58	28.42	45.79

Our results can be found in Table 1.1. Recognition accuracy was calculated as the proportion of hits ("old" items correctly identified as "old") minus the proportion of false alarms ("new" items incorrectly identified as "old"). As can be seen, the scores coincide with principle of encoding specificity: Recognition accuracy was best when the task performed at study was the same as the task performed at retrieval.

Once again, however, we found no support for an exemplar model of self-judgments. For words subjected to an autobiographical study task, a descriptive recognition task ($M = 27.37\%$) was no more effective as a retrieval context than was a semantic task ($M = 30.53\%$). For words subjected to a descriptive study task, an autobiographical recognition task ($M = 21.05\%$) was no more effective as a retrieval context than was a semantic task ($M = 24.21\%$).

Experiment 4: Encoding Variability and Free Recall

Our next test of the exemplar model was based on the encoding variability hypothesis (e.g., E. Martin, 1971). According to this hypothesis, there are a number of different ways in which a stimulus can be encoded: For example, the word "bank" can be encoded in terms of its orthography (e.g., typeface, letter form), phonemic attributes (e.g., rhymes with the word "tank"), or various meanings (e.g., "a place for keeping money," "the sloping of a road along a curve"). The encoding variability hypothesis asserts that the more varied the information encoded about a stimulus word, the greater the probability that the word will be retrieved in a later free recall test (e.g., J. Anderson, 1976; E. Martin, 1968, 1971, 1972). Thus, if two encoding tasks make available different types of information about a stimulus word, then better recall will result from performing both tasks during a single presentation of the word than would result from performing either task alone (e.g., Hunt & Einstein, 1981; Klein & Loftus, 1987). By contrast, if two tasks provide redundant information, then performing them both for a single stimulus word should not be more beneficial to recall than performing either one alone (e.g., Klein & Loftus, 1987; K. Klein & Saltz, 1976).

If exemplar models are correct that a self-descriptiveness judgment entails retrieval of autobiographical information, then the information made available by a descriptive task should be similar to that made available by an autobiographical task. Therefore, performing both a descriptive and an autobiographical task for a list of traits should not produce greater recall than performing either task alone. However, if self-descriptiveness judgments do not entail retrieval of auto-biographical information, then the information made available by a descriptive task should not be similar to that made available by an autobiographical task. In that case, performing both a descriptive and an autobiographical task should produce better recall than that obtained with either task alone.

Our next study (Klein et al., 1989, Experiment 4) tested these predictions by comparing the recall of subjects performing both a descriptive and an auto-biographical task during a single presentation of a stimulus word with that of subjects performing only one task or the other. Because it is possible that per-forming both tasks could lead to better recall simply because of the additional processing required to perform two tasks, we also included two other conditions, which served as controls. In these conditions, subjects performed the same encoding task twice on each trial (either two descriptive or two autobiographical tasks). As in Experiments 1 and 2, we instructed subjects who performed the same task twice to go through the process of generating their responses again for the second task. We expected that if the combined descriptive–autobiographical task were to show an increase in recall that resulted from increased processing time, then a similar increase would be seen in the repeated-task conditions.

Table 1.2 shows that the combined encoding tasks (descriptive–auto-biographical) did produce higher recall than either of the single encoding tasks (descriptive or autobiographical). The two repeated task conditions (descriptive–descriptive and autobiographical–autobiographical), however, did not. The failure of the repeated tasks to produce higher recall indicates that the additional processing time involved in performing two tasks cannot account for the success

TABLE 1.2
Mean Number of Words Recalled as a Function of Encoding Task
(Experiment 4)

Encoding Task				
Auto	*Desc*	*Auto-auto*	*Desc-desc*	*Desc-Auto*
11.88a	11.25a	10.94a	10.62a	14.38b

Note: Auto = autobiographical; Desc = descriptive. Cells shar-ing a common subscript do not differ significantly by Newman-Keuls testing ($p < .05$).

of the combined task. Thus, the fact that the combined task condition was successful in increasing recall over the single task conditions indicates that the information made available by the first and second tasks did not overlap. We conclude, then, that if the descriptive and autobiographical tasks do not make available similar information, it is difficult to argue that self-descriptiveness judgments entail autobiographical retrieval.

CONCLUSIONS ABOUT EXEMPLAR MODELS OF SELF-KNOWLEDGE AND THE SELF-JUDGMENT PROCESS

Exemplar models state that self-descriptiveness judgments are computed from a consideration of autobiographical memories. This predicts that judging a trait for self-descriptiveness should enhance the availability of autobiographical information in memory. However, we did not find self-descriptiveness judgments in any of our experiments to have this effect.

These results lead us to two conclusions. First, the representation of self-knowledge in memory differs from the representation described by exemplar models: Specifically, it appears that self-trait knowledge is represented in memory in abstract form. Second, contrary to the predictions of exemplar models, trait-descriptiveness judgments about the self are made by accessing these abstract representations without reference to trait-relevant autobiographical episodes.

IS TRAIT-BEHAVIOR INDEPENDENCE SPECIFIC TO THE SELF?

There is a longstanding debate in social psychology over whether self-knowledge is represented differently from other types of social knowledge. The extent to which self-knowledge has been shown to be richly elaborated and highly organized (e.g., Klein & Loftus, 1988; Markus, 1977; Rogers, Kuiper, & Kirker, 1977) has led many investigators to argue that the self has unique cognitive properties (e.g., Keenan & Baillet, 1980; Kendzierski, 1980; Kuiper & Rogers, 1979; Lord, 1980; Markus & Sentis, 1982). However, others (e.g., Bower & Gilligan, 1979; Greenwald & Banaji, 1989; Kihlstrom & Cantor, 1984; Turner, 1987) maintained that the principles governing the representation of social knowledge should be constant, regardless of the specific subject of that knowledge (e.g., self, others). The sentiment in the literature has seemed to favor the former view, as self-knowledge has been shown to have information-processing consequences that have not been obtained for other types of social knowledge (for a review, see Higgins & Bargh, 1987).

What about our finding that behavioral exemplars are not involved in self-trait judgments? Is this another example of the "special" qualities of self-knowledge, or does it apply in general to judgments about long-term social knowledge? Our next study[5] examined this question; and, as it turned out, the answer we found gave us important insight into the overall question regarding the hypothesized "unique structure" of self-knowledge.

Experiment 5: Trait Judgments About Familiar Others

In this experiment we used the task-facilitation paradigm to examine trait judgments about a person other than the self. We repeated the procedure described in Experiment 2, with one change: This time a subject's mother (rather than the self) served as the target person. Thus, the *Describes* task became "decide whether the presented trait adjective describes your mother" and the *Remember* task became "recall an incident in which your mother's behavior exemplified the presented trait." The *Define* task was unchanged. After completing the latency collection part of the experiment, we presented the 90 trait adjectives again, one at a time, and had subjects rate the traits on a 9-point scale marked (1) "extremely unlike my mother," (5) "irrelevant," and (9) "extremely like my mother."

If the independence of behavioral exemplars and trait judgments is specific to self-knowledge, then we should find support for an exemplar-based judgment model when trait judgments are made about mothers. Subjects should perform a *Describes Mother* task faster when it is preceded by a *Remember Mother* task than when it is preceded by a *Define* task because the *Remember Mother* task should provide the trait-relevant behavioral information needed for the *Describes Mother* task. By similar reasoning, behavioral information made available during a *Describes Mother* task should enable subjects to perform a subsequent *Remember Mother* task more quickly than they would if the initial task were *Define*.

If, however, the failure of the exemplar model to account for self-descriptiveness judgments reflects a general principle of the representation of social knowledge, then an exemplar-based judgment model should also fail to account for trait judgments about others. Using "Mother" as a referent should then yield results that parallel those obtained for the self: We should see no evidence that a descriptiveness judgment activates behavioral information or that activating behavioral information facilitates a descriptiveness judgment. A *Describes Mother* task and a *Define* task should not differentially affect the time needed to perform a *Remember Mother* task; and a *Remember Mother* task and a *Define* task should not differentially affect the time needed to perform a *Describes Mother* task.

Figure 1.5 presents target task latencies as a function of initial task performed. These latencies show a marked difference from the pattern of latencies found in

---

[5]These data represent the combined results of studies by Klein, Loftus, Trafton, and Fuhrman (1992, Experiment 1) and Klein and Loftus (1991). Because these studies had identical patterns of statistically significant results, we present here the aggragate data.

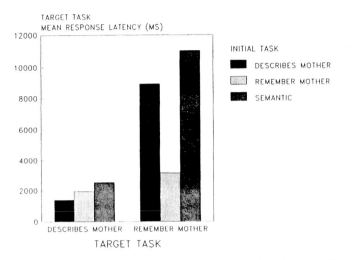

FIG. 1.5.   Target task mean response latencies as a function of initial
task performed (Experiment 5).

our earlier studies, when self served as referent. Subjects were 526 milliseconds
faster to perform the *Describes Mother* target task when it was preceded by a
Remember Mother task than they were when it was preceded by a *Define* task.
Equally striking is the result for the *Remember Mother* target task: Subjects were
2,111 milliseconds faster to remember their mothers' behaviors when they first
judged whether the traits were descriptive of their mothers than they were when
they first generated trait definitions.

These latency data suggest that unlike self-judgments, judgments about one's
mother *are* computed from a consideration of trait-relevant behavioral memories.
This is important, because it shows that our previous failures to find facilitation
were not due to the insensitivity of our paradigm, but rather to the referent being
tested.

We wondered, however, whether the relation between trait judgments and
behaviorial memories of mother might be moderated by subjects' perceptions of
the extent to which traits being judged described their mothers. For example, for
reasons similar to those discussed in Experiment 2, it is possible that behavioral
memories play a greater role when judging traits viewed as atypical of or irrelevant to mother (e.g., traits rated "low" or "medium" in mother-descriptiveness),
than traits viewed as characteristic of mother (e.g., traits rated "high" in mother-
descriptiveness). Accordingly, we next analyzed the target task latencies as a
joint function of initial task and trait descriptiveness. As in Experiment 2, for
each of the initial–target task pairs (15 traits per pair) the five traits receiving the
highest ratings were placed in the high category, the five traits receiving the next
highest rating were placed in the medium category, and the five traits receiving
the lowest ratings were place in the low category.

The latencies for the *Describes Mother* target task, segregated by trait-descriptiveness, are shown in left panel of Fig. 1.6. The effects of initial task on these latencies can be seen to vary as a function of the degree to which the trait was rated as descriptive of mother. For traits falling in the high category, an initial *Remember Mother* task was no more facilitating than an initial *Define* task. By contrast, for traits falling in the medium and low categories, subjects were much quicker to perform the *Describes Mother* task when it was preceded by a *Remember Mother* task than when it was preceded by a *Define* task: Latencies for the medium and low descriptive traits wee shorter by 1,081 milliseconds and 356 milliseconds, respectively, when the initial task was *Remember Mother* than when it was *Define*.

The *Remember Mother* target task latencies, seen in the right panel of Fig. 1.6, present a similar picture. Once again, we found no differential facilitation for traits falling in the high category. But for traits falling in the medium and low categories, we found considerable facilitation. Subjects were faster to remember their mothers' trait-relevant behaviors when they first performed a *Describes Mother* task than they were when they first performed a *Define* task: Latencies for medium and low traits were shorter by 3,405 milliseconds and 2,515 milliseconds, respectively, when the initial task was *Describes Mother* than when it was *Define*.

Does the exemplar model hold for trait judgments about one's mother? Or are these judgments, like those about the self, made without reference to behavioral exemplars? The answer seems to depend on the trait being judged. We found no evidence of facilitation for judgments about traits rated "high" in mother-descriptiveness, which suggests that these judgments were accomplished by accessing abstract trait knowledge about mother in memory. For judgments about traits rated "medium" or "low" in mother-descriptiveness, however, we found considerable facilitation, from which we infer that these judgments were computed from a consideration of trait-relevant behavioral memories about mother.

One way to think about these findings is to consider them in light of recent models of category judgment that include roles for specific episodes as well as summary representations abstracted from a set of related episodes (e.g., Barsalou, 1987, 1988; Busemeyer, Dewey, & Medin, 1984; Elio & J. Anderson, 1981; Estes, 1989; Homa, Dunbar, & Nohre, 1991; Homa, Sterling, & Trepel, 1981; Ross, Perkins, & Tenpenny, 1990). According to these "mixed" models, the type of information recruited for a category judgment is determined primarily by the amount of experience one has with the category. During the early stages of learning about a category, category judgments must be based on episodic information in memory, as too few episodes have been experienced to support the abstraction process (e.g., Homa et al., 1991; Ross et al., 1990). As the number of category-relevant episodes increases, an abstract representation of the category evolves (e.g., Homa et al., 1981; Kolodner, 1984; Ross et al., 1990; Schank, 1982), which then serves as the basis for future judgments (e.g., Homa et al.,

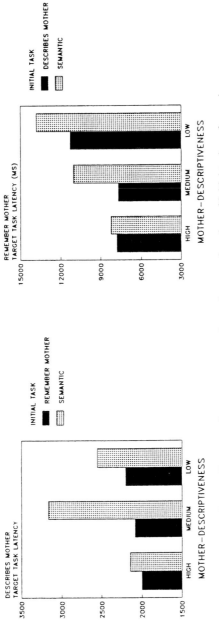

FIG. 1.6. Target task mean response latencies as a function of initial task performed and trait-descriptiveness (Experiment 5).

1981; Homa et al., 1991). Thus, the importance of specific episodes for category judgments decreases as category experience increases.

If one views trait concepts as cognitive categories (e.g., Buss & Craik, 1983, 1984; Hampson, 1982b), this model has a relatively straightforward application to our data. The formation of abstract knowledge of a person's trait characteristics can be seen as depending on sufficient experience with that person's behaviors to support the abstraction process. One's representation of that person will include summary representations of only those traits for which a sufficient number of behaviors have been observed. If, for a particular trait, only a few relevant behaviors have been observed, judging whether or not that trait describes the person will require computation on the basis of those behaviors in memory. However, with greater exposure to trait-relevant behaviors, a summary representation of the trait will be formed. Future judgments can be made on the basis of this abstract trait knowledge, and retrieval of specific behaviors no longer will be necessary. Put simply, the more we know about a person, the more likely we are to have summary trait representations of his or her behaviors (e.g., Monson, Tanke, & Lund, 1980; Sande, 1990; Sande, Goethals, & Radloff, 1988), and the less likely we are to rely on specific behaviors to make trait judgments about him or her. This conception, although similar to the dual exemplar/summary model of self-knowledge described in the introduction to this chapter, is different in that it specifies the amount of trait-relevant experience, rather than trait "centrality," as the primary determinant of whether trait knowledge is represented abstractly or at the level of exemplars.

The data from Experiment 5 are generally consistent with a "mixed" model. Judgments for traits rated "high" in mother-descriptiveness showed no evidence of autobiographical retrieval. Presumably, those traits were ones for which subjects had observed a large number of behaviors, because traits that are highly descriptive are those that are manifested most frequently. Thus, for highly descriptive traits, subjects were likely to have formed summary representations. As a result, they could access these representations and perform the descriptive task without retrieving specific behaviors. Judgments for medium and low descriptive traits showed greater reliance on retrieval of behavioral evidence. This would be expected if subjects had observed fewer behaviors exemplifying these traits: they would be less likely to have formed summary representations of these traits and therefore would be more likely to require behavioral information to make a judgment.

It is important, however, to note that judgments for traits rated "low" in mother-descriptiveness showed slightly less facilitation than did traits rated "medium" in mother-descriptiveness. This is surprising if low descriptive traits are those for which subjects have observed the fewest behaviors. Judgments about these traits should be more likely than judgments about medium descriptive traits to depend on retrieval of behaviors, and they therefore should show more evidence of facilitation.

A possible reason for this oddity is that an alternate strategy exists for making judgments about low descriptive traits. Although these traits are themselves less likely than medium descriptive traits to be represented abstractly, they are more likely than medium traits to be opposites of traits that *are* represented abstractly (i.e., high descriptive traits). The abstract representation of an opposite trait could provide a subject with the information needed to make a judgment about a low descriptive trait (e.g., Park, 1986). For example, in judging whether the trait "rude" describes one's mother, a subject might readily access his or her abstract representation of his or her mother as polite, and decide on this basis that she is not rude. Therefore, a subject could judge a low descriptive trait not only by retrieving relevant behavioral memories, but also by accessing the representation of its opposite, if an opposite is explicitly represented. This mixing of response strategies would dilute the observed facilitation, as only some judgments of low descriptive traits would refer to behavioral evidence. By contrast, medium descriptive traits are less likely to have opposites explicitly represented. Judgments about them should more consistently require behavioral retrieval, which should result in greater observed facilitation.

Thus, for judgments about mother, exemplars appear to be required when the trait being judged is medium or low in mother-descriptiveness, but not when the trait being judged is highly descriptive of mother. Yet we find no evidence that exemplars are involved in judgments about the self, regardless of level of trait descriptiveness. Does this mean that the self operates under wholly different rules from other knowledge bases? Or is it the case that the apparent exemption of the self from exemplar-based processing of trait judgments is the result of the fact that, compared to our experience with others, our experience with ourselves is vast (e.g., Baxter & Goldberg, 1987; Chew, 1983; Sande, 1990; Sande et al., 1988; Smith, 1990a)? Perhaps there are few, if any, trait dimensions for which we have not had sufficient experience to form abstract trait knowledge about ourselves.

THE EFFECT OF EXPERIENCE ON SELF-DESCRIPTIVENESS JUDGMENTS: COULD A "MIXED" MODEL APPLY TO THE SELF?

Experiment 6: The Context Study

In our next experiment we attempted to answer this question by manipulating the amount of experience relevant to a particular self-descriptiveness judgment (Klein, Loftus, Trafton & Fuhrman, 1992, Experiment 3). We did this by specifying a time frame to which subjects should refer when making their judgments. Our goal was to obtain some judgments regarding contexts in which subjects' experience was relatively low. If our previous failure to find evidence of autobiographical retrieval was due to subjects' typically high level of trait-relevant experience, then limiting that experience might increase the importance of auto-biographical memories in the self-judgment process.

Subjects all were first-year undergraduates who had been on campus for only a short time. Thus, the "low-experience" context referred to the time period since they had come to college and the "high-experience" context referred to their lives prior to entering college. We compared response latencies for trait judgments made with reference to the low-experience context to those made with reference to the high-experience context. We predicted that if a mixed model of trait judgment could apply to self-knowledge, then low-experience judgments should show more evidence of autobiographical retrieval than high-experience judgments.

In this experiment, we again used the task-facilitation paradigm, with several modifications. First, our descriptive and autobiographical tasks now included a second cue that specified the context to consider when performing the task. The cue for the low-experience context was "school," which referred to subjects' experience since coming to college; the cue for the high-experience context was "home," which referred to subjects' experience *before* coming to college. The two self-tasks (descriptive and autobiographical) were factorially combined with the low- and high-context cues to create four task-context pairings:

1. The pairing of the autobiographical task with the low-experience context was cued by *Remember School*, which indicated that subjects should restrict their autobiographical retrieval to incidents that occurred since entering college.

2. The pairing of the autobiographical task with the high-experience context was cued by *Remember Home*, which indicated that subjects should restrict their autobiographical retrieval to incidents that occurred prior to entering college.

3. The pairing of the descriptive task with the low-experience context was cued by *Describes School*, which indicated that subjects should judge whether the presented trait described how they saw themselves since entering college.

4. The pairing of the descriptive task with the high-experience context was cued by *Describes Home*, which indicated that subjects should judge whether the presented trait described the way they were prior to entering college.

A second change in experimental design was introduced to keep the experimental cells to a manageable number: Autobiographical retrieval was performed only as an initial task, and self-descriptiveness judgments were performed only as a target task. Cueing for the semantic task was unchanged, and it continued to serve as both an initial and a target task.

These changes resulted in a 3 × 3 factorial design, with initial task (Semantic, Autobiographical-Home, and Autobiographical-School) and target task (Semantic, Descriptive-Home, Descriptive-School) both varied within subjects ($N = 24$). The assignment of trait words to the initial task–target task pairs and the order in which the task pairs were presented were randomized across subjects.

A mixed model of self-judgments makes the following predictions about response latencies for the descriptive target task:

1. When the context for the descriptive task is *Home,* response latencies should be the same, regardless of whether the initial task was *Remember Home, Remember School,* or *Define.* This is because experience of the self at home should be sufficient to have supported formation of abstract trait knowledge; and with this knowledge available, self-descriptiveness judgments will be made without reference to behavioral exemplars.

2. When the context for the descriptive task is *School,* however, response latencies should be shorter when the initial task is *Remember School* than when it is either *Remember Home* or *Define.* This is because in the *School* context, subjects will have had comparatively few trait-relevant experiences. They therefore will be less likely to have formed abstract trait knowledge, and more likely to rely on memories of their behavior at school to decide if traits are self-descriptive. Of the three initial tasks, only the *Remember School* task provides autobiographical information about the self at school. Although the *Remember Home* task would make available trait-relevant behavioral exemplars, this information would be irrelevant to judgments about the self at school. Thus, the *Remember Home* should be no more facilitating than a semantic task to performance of a *Describes School* target task.

The results can be seen in the left panel of Fig. 1.7. As predicted, the time required to perform the *Describes Home* task was not differentially affected by the previous performance of a *Remember Home* task, a *Remember School* task, or a *Define* task. By contrast, the *Describes School* task was performed more quickly when preceded by an initial *Remember School* task than when preceded by either an an initial *Remember Home* task or an initial *Define* task (the latter two initial tasks yielded target task response latencies that were longer by 478 milliseconds and 530 milliseconds, respectively, than that yielded by an initial *Remember School* task).

Thus, when amount of behavioral experience is manipulated, judgments about the self appear to correspond to the mixed judgment model that described judgments about mother in Experiment 5. When amount of experience is high, subjects can access abstract trait knowledge to judge traits for self-descriptiveness. When amount of experience is low, subjects are more likely to refer to autobiographical evidence in making their judgments.

Accepting this conclusion, of course, requires that one accept our assumption the critical difference between the self-at-home and self-at-school was a temporal

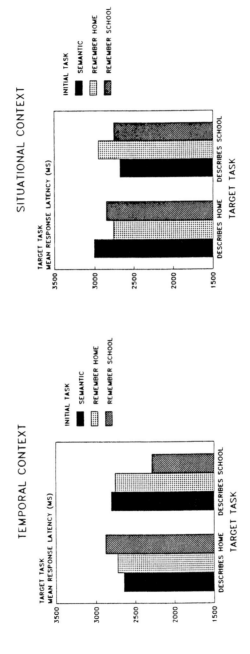

FIG. 1.7. Target task mean response latencies as a function of initial task performed and context (Experiments 6 and 7).

one. Clearly, having been at college for only a few months, our subjects had far less experience at school than they had at home. But there are many other differences between these two social contexts, and it is by no means clear that the temporal difference alone accounts for our findings in Experiment 6. A recent study by McGuire, McGuire, and Cheever (1986), for example, found that high school students had very different perceptions of the social environments at home and at school and that they had corresponding differences in their views of themselves in the two contexts, even though their experience of home and school was occurring simultaneously. Thus, it is possible that our findings in Experiment 6 were due to qualitative, rather than quantitative, differences in subjects' experience of home and school.

Experiment 7: Unconfounding Type and Amount of Experience Associated With a Context

To explore this possibility, we conducted a study identical to Experiment 6, except that we equated the time period referenced by the *Home* and *School* context cues (Klein, Loftus, Trafton & Fuhrman, 1992, Experiment 4). Specifically, the context cue *School* asked subjects to refer to their experience at school during their 4 years of high school, and the context cue *Home* asked them to refer to their experience at home during the 4 years prior to entering college. By specifying the same 4-year time period for both cues, we equalized the amount of experience associated with *Home* and *School*.

If, in Experiment 6, the difference in facilitation between the *Describes Home* and *Describes School* tasks was due to a difference in the *amount* of experience associated with the two contexts, then equating the amount of experience should eliminate the difference in facilitation. Specifically, by defining both home and school as 4-year periods, we should increase the likelihood that subjects will have a considerable body of abstract trait knowledge about the self in each context. Hence, no facilitation should be expected for either the *Describes Home* or *Describes School* target tasks. However, if the results obtained in Experiment 6 were the result of different *types* of experience associated with home and school, then we should still see a difference in facilitation between *Describes Home* and *Describes School* target tasks even when the amount of experience is equated. We again should see facilitation for the *Describes School* target task, but not for the *Describes Home* target task.

The results are shown in the right panel of Fig. 1.7. Neither target task shows evidence of autobiographical facilitation. This strongly suggests that the facilitation found for the descriptive-school task in Experiment 6 is due to subjects' relatively low level of self-relevant experience in this context. It appears then, that when conditions are adjusted to take into account the comparatively large amount of information we have about our own behavior, self-judgments can be seen to operate under the same rules that apply to judgments about familiar others—those specified by the mixed model.

DISCUSSION OF OUR FINDINGS

Implications for Current Models of the Self

Exemplar Models of the Self. Exemplar models of the self assert that trait self-knowledge is represented at the level of behavioral exemplars, and that trait self-descriptiveness judgments require accessing relevant behavioral exemplars. Our findings converge on the conclusion that although trait self-descriptiveness judgments can be exemplar-based under highly constrained circumstances (e.g., judgments of the self in a novel context), they typically are made *without* accessing behavioral exemplars. If this conclusion is correct, then trait knowledge cannot be represented only at the level of exemplars; otherwise, self-descriptiveness judgments would not be possible. We believe that long-term trait knowledge about the self is represented primarily in abstract, summary form, and that summary representations, not exemplars, are the basis of trait self-descriptiveness judgments.

Associative Network Models of Self. Our data also have implications for another class of self-models—those that attempt to specify the structural relation in memory between trait knowledge and trait-relevant behaviors. These models, based on the general concepts of associative network models of memory, propose that trait knowledge about the self consists of summary trait representations that are linked in memory to the behavioral exemplars from which they have been abstracted (e.g., Bower & Gilligan, 1979; Chew, 1983; Greene & Geddes, 1988; Kihlstrom & Cantor, 1974; Kihlstrom et al., 1988; Mancuso & Ceely, 1980). Specifically, they describe the representation of trait knowledge as a graph structure with nodes representing traits linked to nodes representing behaviors (see Fig. 1.8).

An important feature of many associative network models is a process called *spreading activation* (e.g., J. Anderson, 1976, 1983a; Collins & Loftus, 1975). A node in an associative network becomes activated when a person sees, hears, or thinks about the information the node represents. Activation then spreads from that node to adjacent nodes in the network, along the associative links. For example, in the network shown in Fig. 1.8, activating the node for "friendly" would cause activation to spread to the behavioral exemplars to which "friendly" is linked. The hypothesized effect of spreading activation is the enhanced availability of activated nodes, relative to those at resting state, for subsequent processing or retrieval. Therefore, activation spreading from the node for "friendly" to the nodes representing friendly behaviors should enable those behaviors to be retrieved more quickly than would be possible if they had not been activated.

Thus, associative network models of trait self-knowledge may be seen as making predictions similar to those of exemplar models regarding the outcome of the task-facilitation paradigm. Specifically, a trait self-descriptiveness judgment should result in the spread of activation from the node for the trait being judged

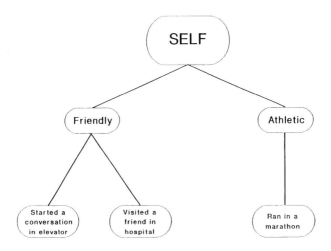

FIG. 1.8.   An associative network representation of self-knowledge.

to nodes for trait-relevant behaviors, thereby facilitating the retrieval of those behaviors from memory. A definition task, by contrast, should not activate trait-relevant behaviors, as the information it requires (word meanings) is not included in the self-knowledge network. Therefore, compared to a definition task, a self-descriptiveness judgment should lead to a greater reduction in the time required to then retrieve a trait-relevant behavior.

Our failure to find this kind of facilitation (Experiments 1 and 2) suggests that, like exemplar models, these associative network models cannot adequately describe the representation of trait and autobiographical knowledge about the self in memory.[6]

Why Do Exemplar and Associative Network Models of Self Fail?   It may seem surprising that exemplar and associative network models run into trouble

---

[6]An alternate interpretation of our failures to find the type of facilitation predicted by associative network models is based on the "fan" effect described by Anderson (e.g., J. Anderson, 1983b). A fan-effect interpretation of our results would argue that the greater the number of trait-relevant behaviors in memory, the less excitation available to activate any one behavior. Thus, the failure of a descriptive task to facilitate the retrieval of a specific behavior may reflect the fact that we have so many behaviors linked in memory to any given trait that the spread of excitation among them would mean that no one behavior would receive significant activation. However, the arguments presented in this chapter suggest that this interpretation is limited to traits judged to be highly self-descriptive. As we have suggested, the number of trait-relevant behaviors in memory is positively correlated with trait self-descriptiveness (see also Bruch, Kaflowitz, & Berger, 1988; Markus, 1977). Consequently, although a fan-effect explanation may seem plausible for our failure to find facilitation for highly descriptive traits, it is considerably less compelling for our failure to find facilitation effects with traits rated as medium and low in self-descriptiveness (see Experiment 2).

when they are tested on self-knowledge. They have been quite successful in other areas of social cognitive research. Exemplar models do well in explaining group categorization judgments (e.g., Judd & Park, 1988; Smith & Zarate, 1990), the inferences people make about the traits of others (e.g., Kahneman & Miller, 1986; Smith, 1990b), and social stereotyping (e.g., Lewicki, 1986; Rothbart & John, 1985; Zarate & Smith, 1990). Similarly, associative network models have worked well in describing the representation of others that results from impression formation (e.g., Carlston & Skowronski, 1986; Hamilton, 1989; Srull, 1981; Wyer & Srull, 1989), the cognitive structure of social stereotypes (e.g., Andersen & Klatzky, 1987) and the effects of mood on social judgments (e.g., Bower, 1981; Bower, Gilligan, & Montiero, 1981).

Why, then, do these models fail when it comes to describing the representation of self-knowledge? We believe it is because they have been developed to account for the representation of information that differs from knowledge about the self in important ways. Most of the research supporting these models examines the representation of information that is small in amount, recently learned, and devoid of context: Typically, a list of statements composed by the experimenter about a supposed person. Subjects are presented with this information and then tested shortly thereafter (often within minutes) to determine how the information is represented in memory. Knowledge of self, by contrast, includes a vast amount of information that has been acquired across a variety of meaningful contexts over the course of a lifetime.

These features of self-knowledge—extensive information, acquisition across contexts, and long retention intervals—have known implications for the way it is represented in memory. First, as researchers studying autobiographical memory have noted, repeated exposure to related experiences leads to the formation of abstract self-knowledge (e.g., Barsalou, 1987, 1988; Brewer, 1986; Butters & Cermak, 1986; Neisser, 1988). Second, over time, abstractions tend to remain accessible in memory, whereas the specific experiences that gave rise to them become increasingly difficult to remember (e.g., Barsalou, 1988; Linton, 1982; Neisser, 1988; Watkins & Kerkar, 1985).

It would be difficult to capture these dynamics using a small amount of stimulus information and immediately examining its representation. The potential for abstraction is minimized under these conditions, and the accessibility of exemplars should be high.[7] Thus, it is not surprising that most social cognitive studies find evidence that exemplars play a role in social judgments (a similar perspective is offered in N. Anderson, 1989). Exemplar and associative network models work well under these conditions, but for long-term knowledge about the self a different sort of model is needed.

---

[7]A similar suggestion has been made in the nonsocial category judgment literature by Nosofsky (1987).

The Mental Representation of Trait and Behavioral Self-Knowledge.   If neither exemplar nor associative network models successfully capture the mental representation of long-term trait knowledge about the self, what sort of model might do better? We propose a model of self-knowledge that incorporates the following two features: First, long-term trait knowledge is represented in abstract, summary form; and second, this representation is functionally independent of the representation of behavioral exemplars. In previous sections of this chapter, we have discussed summary representation of trait-knowledge. In this section, we take up the issue of independent representation of trait and behavioral self-knowledge.

Our data offer three arguments in favor of independence. First, we find that accessing either of these representations does not affect subsequent performance on a task assumed to access the other: Judging traits for self-descriptiveness does not affect latency to retrieve trait-relevant behaviors, and retrieving trait-relevant behaviors does not affect latency to judge traits for self-descriptiveness.

Second, tasks that access these representations show different effects of the same variable—trait self-descriptiveness. As shown in Fig. 1.2, self-descriptiveness judgments yield an inverted "U" response latency pattern when plotted against trait self-descriptiveness. Response latencies for retrieval of behaviors, by contrast, form a monotonically increasing function.

Third, the independence we observe appears to reflect a difference in the information retrieved for descriptive and autobiographical tasks, rather than a lack of sensitivity of the paradigm, because these tasks *can* have facilitating effects on each other. However, in accord with the logic of the task-facilitation paradigm, this occurs only when they make available the *same* type of information. For example, when trait-relevant behavioral experience is low, autobiographical retrieval does facilitate trait judgments. This is because with low experience, a trait judgment requires the same type of information (i.e., exemplars) that an autobiographical retrieval makes available (e.g., the "self-in-context" study).

Of course, none of these findings, taken alone, constitutes definitive evidence for a functional distinction between these two types of self-knowledge. As Neely (1988) carefully argued, there are interpretive problems inherent in trying to infer the functional independence of cognitive systems from performance on a single set of experimental tasks. However, we believe that when considered as a whole, the evidence we have presented compels one to seriously entertain the possibility of functional independence. Furthermore, in addition to our data, there also is evidence in the clinical literature on amnesia that is consistent with a functional independence of abstract self-knowledge and behavioral exemplars. And although there are no guarantees that results obtained studying "abnormal" brains can be generalized to the operation of normal memory, we think this evidence, too, is worth considering.

The first piece of evidence comes from the literature on functional retrograde amnesia. The onset of this amnesia is marked by the victim's loss of personal identity, which results from a loss of the ability to remember almost anything from his or her personal past (e.g., Schacter & Kihlstrom, 1989). In this state, called a *fugue state,* the victim is unaware of a memory loss and may wander long distances from home, taking up residence in a new community and adopting a new identity (e.g., Fisher 1945; Fisher & Joseph, 1949; James, 1890). The amnesic episode ends with the victim regaining awareness of his or her original identity and memory for his or her past life, but becoming amnesic for the events of the fugue stage.

The question of interest regarding this amnesia is whether a person in a fugue state, despite having lost the ability to recall any personal experiences, could still have knowledge of his or her traits. If trait knowledge is dependent on knowledge of one's behaviors, then it should be affected by the loss of autobiographical memory. There is little data relevant to this question, but there is one case, reported by Schacter, Wang, Tulving, and Freedman (1982) that suggests that an individual in a fugue state can access trait self-knowledge. These investigators administered a Minnesota Multiphasic Personality Inventory (MMPI) to a patient both during and after his fugue state, and the patient's profile largely was unchanged for the majority of subscales across testings. Because his responses when he could access autobiographical memory were consistent with his responses when he could not, it appears that the loss of autobiographical memory did not greatly affect the availability of trait knowledge. This result suggests that trait knowledge and behavioral knowledge are not dependent.

A second source of amnesia evidence is the case of K.C., who, as a result of a severe brain injury, can no longer consciously bring to mind a single personal experience or event from any point in his life (e.g., Tulving, 1989a; Tulving, Schachter, McLachlan, & Moscovitch, 1988). Although there are many reports of patients who have lost portions of their personal pasts (for a review see Parkin, 1987), K.C. is the only reported case of complete amnesia for specific past occurrences (Tulving, 1989a). Despite his total loss of autobiographical self-knowledge, however, K.C. still has a variety of knowledge about himself. For example, although he is unable to recall his brother's death or any circumstances surrounding it, K.C. reports that this event was the saddest moment of his life. He cannot describe his former workplace, nor can he recall a single event that occurred there, but he knows the name of the company and the nature of its business.

To explain this dissociation, Tulving distinguished between two types of self-knowledge (e.g., Tulving, 1989a; Tulving et al., 1988). Episodic self-knowledge enables people to become consciously aware of specific past events from their lives (e.g., one's recollection of having a hamburger for lunch yesterday). Semantic self-knowledge, by contrast, is personal knowledge that has been abstracted from memories of the self in specific events, and that does not entail recollection of the events themselves (e.g., one's recollection of often having hamburgers for lunch. A similar distinction can be found in Cermak, 1984). Thus, episodic self-knowledge includes what we have referred to as *behavioral exemplars*, whereas semantic self-knowledge includes what we have referred to as *summary trait knowledge*. The fact that K.C. can remember semantic self-knowledge without being able to remember the episodes on which this knowledge is based thus can be interpreted as evidence against a dependence between the two types of representations.

Tulving, in fact, went even further in explaining the dissociation between episodic and semantic self-knowledge, to suggest that the two representations may be structurally as well as functionally independent. He reasoned that if a lesion produces a dissociation between performance on episodic and semantic memory tasks, it is permissable to conclude that these two types of memory are served by different brain mechanisms, one of which has become dysfunctional as a result of the lesion, whereas the other remains unimpaired (Tulving, 1989a). The case of K.C. suggests that the memory system that underlies the utilization of semantic self-knowledge is not affected by damage to the episodic self-knowledge system.

Finally, Tulving reported data from normal subjects suggesting a structural separation between episodic and semantic knowledge (reported in Tulving, 1989a, 1989b). In this study, Tulving monitored the cerebral blood flow of subjects instructed to think either about episodic topics (e.g., personally experienced events), or semantic topics (e.g., abstract knowledge). The experimental monitoring involved injecting a small dose of radioactive tracer into the blood streams of fully conscious subjects. The tracer was carried intravascularly into the subject's brain, where its accumulation could be measured by extracranial detectors. Thus, a record of blood flow to different cortical regions was obtained, from which the level of neural activity in those regions could be determined. Monitoring revealed that the cortical regions to which blood flow increased differed, depending on whether subjects were thinking about episodic or semantic topics.

Although these findings were obtained from a small number of subjects, a few of whom provided inconsistent data, the results are highly suggestive that episodic and semantic knowledge are stored and processed in different areas of the brain. And, although none of the data we have discussed are conclusive, we believe that taken together they are very suggestive. Certainly, they are consistent with our view that within the realm of long-term self-knowledge, knowledge of one's traits is represented and accessed independent of knowledge of one's behaviors.

A General Model of Social Knowledge

We have focused thus far on the implications of our findings for understanding the mental representation of self-knowledge. However, the issues we have discussed regarding self-knowledge are relevant to the representation of knowledge about others as well. If the self is viewed as occupying one end of a continuum defined by the amount of experience one has with a social entity, our data suggest a general model of the representation of trait and behavioral information in memory. According to our model, one's mental representation of a person's traits should vary with the amount of trait-relevant experience one has had with that person. If the amount of experience is not sufficient to support abstraction, then trait knowledge will be represented only at the level of exemplars. But as the amount of experience becomes sufficiently large, trait knowledge is increasingly likely to be abstracted and represented in summary form.

For trait judgments, then, the type of knowledge retrieved should depend on the amount of trait-relevant experience in memory. Exemplars should be retrieved only when experience is low and therefore an appropriate summary representation is not available. However, if summary trait knowledge is available, our research suggests that it will be retrieved in favor of exemplars (see also N. Anderson, 1989; Fiske & Taylor, 1991). In fact, once a summary representation has been formed, it would not even matter for a trait judgment if the episodic information that led to that representation could no longer be recalled (cf. Watkins & Kerkar, 1985).

There is evidence consistent with our proposal in our two studies that examined judgments based on varying amounts of information. In these studies (the "mother" study and the "self-in-context" study), trait judgments appeared to be exemplar-based when behavioral experience was limited, but they were unaffected by exemplars as the amount of experience increased.

There are not many other studies that have examined the representation of information about others beyond that which is formed in a single experimental session. There is one study, however, by Park (1986), that examined the representations subjects formed of acquaintances, starting with the beginning of their acquaintance and continuing until seven weeks later. Park found that as subjects gained more experience with target persons, their use of abstract trait terms to describe targets increased, whereas their use of specific behaviors decreased. Thus, consistent with the general model we propose, Park's results suggest that with increasing experience, our representations of others become increasingly abstract.

Implications for Other Issues in Social and Personality Psychology

Beyond its implications for research on the representation of traits and behaviors, the model we propose may also shed light on various other aspects of social information processing. In this section we consider the implications of this model for several important topics in social and personality psychology.

Self-Perception Theory. Counter to our findings, self-perception research consistently has demonstrated that retrieving trait-relevant autobiographical memories can affect subsequent judgments of a trait's self-descriptiveness (e.g., Chaiken & Baldwin, 1981; Fazio et al., 1981; Salancik & Conway, 1975). For example, Salancik and Conway showed that when subjects' recall of auto-biographical information was manipulated to make salient either proreligious or antireligious behaviors, subjects who recalled proreligious behaviors subsequently judged themselves to be more religious than did subjects who recalled antireligious behaviors. Similarly, Fazio et al. (1981) found that when subjects retrieved autobiographical memories reflecting either introversion or extroversion, those recalling introversion-related memories subsequently rated themselves as more introverted than did those who recalled extroversion-related memories.

If autobiographical memories can influence self-descriptiveness judgments, then why don't we find evidence of this in our studies? We think it is because subjects in our studies retrieved memories of specific events, whereas those in the studies described earlier retrieved memories that summarized their behavior across multiple events. We asked subjects to recall specific incidents in which their behavior exemplified a particular trait. By contrast, Salancik and Conway (1975) asked subjects to endorse statements concerning the *frequency* with which they engaged in various behaviors relating to religion (e.g., "I frequently attend a church or synagogue," "I occasionally donate money to religious organiza-tions"; see also Chaiken & Baldwin, 1981). And Fazio et al. (1981) had subjects answer questions about behaviors and situations that typify their experience of introversion or extroversion (e.g., "What kinds of events make you feel like being alone?" or "What would you do if you wanted to liven things up at a party?").

In contrast to behavioral exemplars, behavioral summaries are representations abstracted from multiple events; and, as such, they are part of semantic self-knowledge (e.g., Brewer, 1986; Cermak & O'Connor, 1983; Conway, 1987). We have proposed that the independence we find between retrieval of behavioral exemplars and performance of self-descriptiveness judgments results from the fact that exemplars and abstract trait knowledge are represented independently in memory: Exemplars are part of episodic self-knowledge, whereas abstract trait representations are part of semantic self-knowledge. However, because behav-ioral summaries and abstract trait representations both are part of semantic self-knowledge, one would not necessarily predict independence between retrieval of behavioral summaries and trait self-descriptiveness judgments.

We recently tested the hypothesis that summary behavioral memories can influence trait self-judgments, by changing the autobiographical memory manip-ulation in the task-facilitation paradigm to elicit summary behavioral memories (Klein, Loftus, & Sherman, in press). Instead of asking subjects to recall a specific incident in which they exemplified a trait, we asked them to recall what they "typically do" when exemplifying a particular trait (e.g., "What do you typically do when you are sociable?"). Our findings were consistent with our suggestion that the self-judgment effects reported by Salancik, Fazio, and others may have resulted from the retrieval of summary rather than specific behavioral memories. Specifically, we found that in contrast to our earlier studies (Experiments 1 and 2), retrieving a behavioral summary (e.g., "I often go to parties with my friends on the weekend") did produce a reliable reduction in the time required for subjects to judge a trait's self-descriptiveness.[8,9]

Thus, the instructions given by an experimenter can influence whether subjects will retrieve specific exemplars or behavioral summaries (e.g., Eder, 1988, 1989; Eder, Gerlach, & Perlmutter, 1987; Hudson, 1986; Klein et al., 1989; Robinson, 1976). It is important to be clear about which of these two types of knowledge subjects are asked to retrieve, as their effects on self-judgment can be very different.

The Actor–Observer Difference.   A well-documented finding in the social psychological literature is the difference between actors and observers in the attributions they make about the causes of behavior. The actor–observer difference first was identified by Heider (1944), and popularized by Jones and Nisbett (1972), who argued that people show a pervasive tendency to attribute their own behavior to external or situational causes, while attributing the behavior of others to internal, dispositional factors. For example, a person who performs poorly on a test may be likely to claim that the test was unfair or that he or she was unable to prepare adequately. However, the person is likely to attribute a classmates' poor performance to lack of ability.

Although early evidence on the actor–observer difference was somewhat conflicting (e.g., Jones, 1976; Monson & Snyder, 1977), the phenomenon now

---

[8]However, although it is apparent from these data that if behavioral summaries are made available, subjects can use them in making trait judgments about themselves, it also remains clear that subjects do not *need* behavioral summaries to make those judgments. If self-descriptiveness judgments require consideration of behavioral summaries, then performing a descriptive task should facilitate retrieval of behavioral summary information. However, just as we found in our earlier studies, subjects in the present study were no faster to retrieve behavioral summaries following performance of a descriptive task than they were following a semantic task. Thus, although behavioral summaries are treated as diagnostic with respect to self-judgments, self-judgments *typically* are made without reference to these memories.

[9]This finding has parallels with the work of Buss and Craik (1983, 1984), who proposed that a reliable trait attribution requires information about the frequency with which behaviors exemplifying a given trait are exhibited. According to these authors, a trait can be attributed to a person to the extent that, over time and across situations, the person has exhibited a relatively high frequency of behaviors exemplifying that trait. They stress that information about the frequency of behaviors is critical, and that a single behavioral exemplar cannot provide a reliable basis for making a trait attribution (see also Epstein, 1979).

appears to be well established (for reviews see Ross & Nisbett, 1991; Watson, 1982). Debate persists, however, concerning the mechanisms responsible for the effect. Jones and Nisbett offered two main explanations. According to their *perceptual* hypothesis, the actor–observer difference reflects differences in attentional focus: The perceptual field of the actor is dominated by the situation, whereas the perceptual field of the observer has the actor as a salient object. Consequently, in interpreting behavior, actors are likely to focus attention on situational causes, whereas observers are likely to focus on personal characteristics of the actor (i.e., traits).

According to Jones and Nisbett's *informational* hypothesis, the actor–observer difference reflects the fact that actors experience their own behavior in a greater variety of situations than they do the behavior of others. As a result, actors recognize that their own behavior varies in response to situational factors, whereas observers are less likely to appreciate this variability in the behavior of others. Therefore, in explaining behavior, actors are sensitive to situational determinants of their actions, whereas observers tend to perceive others as behaving consistently in accord with underlying dispositions.

Of these two hypotheses, the perceptual account has received considerable support (e.g., Arkin & Duval, 1975; McArthur & Post, 1977; Nisbett, Caputo, Legant, & Maracek, 1973; Nisbett & Ross, 1980; Regan & Totten, 1975; Storms, 1973; Taylor & Fiske, 1975), but data regarding the informational hypothesis have been inconsistent (see the review by Watson, 1982).

The model of social knowledge presented in this chapter is consistent with an informational view, albeit one quite different from that of Jones and Nisbett (1972). Ironically, Jones and Nisbett viewed the actor as someone who does not think he or she has dispositions. Our view, by contrast, is that actors have such stable views of their own dispositions that they perceive specific behaviors as undiagnostic (i.e., behavioral exemplars do not influence trait self-descriptiveness judgments), and opt for situational attributions. By contrast, observers, lacking well-developed trait knowledge about the actor, are likely to see individual behaviors as diagnostic of the actor's dispositions, and thus draw correspondent inferences (e.g., Jones & Gerard, 1967).

Regardless of which perspective one takes, an informational explanation of the actor–observer difference implies that as familiarity with an actor increases, an observer's attributions should become increasingly similar to those of the actor him or herself (i.e., more situational). Unfortunately, the literature offers only inconsistent support for this prediction (for a review, see Watson, 1982). Our data, however, help clarify a point that may have contributed to this inconsistency. Actor–observer studies typically have varied only observer familiarity with the actor. Our findings suggest that the more important factor is the observer's familiarity with the actor's behaviors pertaining to the trait dimension being judged. In our "mother" study, for example, even though overall familiarity with mother was constant, familiarity with the trait dimension being judged was the key to determining whether exemplars or abstractions were the basis for making a trait judgment. Thus, it is possible that if investigators defined familiarity on the basis of the trait dimension being judged, rather than simply on the basis of referent familiarity, greater support for the informational hypothesis would emerge.

Self-Deception. A model of self that assumes the independent storage and retrieval of trait and behavioral information offers a new perspective from which to understand what has been termed *the paradox of self-deception* (e.g., Fingarette, 1969; Haight, 1980; Martin, 1985). The paradox emerges from the fact that, in the words of Sartre (1958), "The one to whom the lie is told and the one who lies are the same person, which means that I must know in my capacity as deceiver the truth which is hidden from me in my capacity as the one deceived" (p. 49). Thus, to maintain that a person is engaging in self-deception is to assert that the person both knows and does not know the same thing at the same time.

Most psychological explanations for this paradox view self-deception as a motivated attempt to avoid information by use of cognitive processes such as repression, denial, rationalization, and transformation (e.g., Eagle, 1988; Gur & Sackeim, 1979; Murphy, 1975; Paulhus & Suedfeld, 1988; Sackeim & Gur, 1978). According to this view, maintaining a judgment about oneself that is at odds with one's behavior (e.g., a person who cheats on his or her tax returns, yet considers him or herself honest) requires effortful avoidance of the conflicting behavioral knowledge. Our data, however, suggest that a judgment of self that is at odds with one's behavior need not be seen as purposeful avoidance of information that is painful to acknowledge. Rather, our model of self allows a contradiction between trait and behavioral self-knowledge as a natural consequence of a system in which behavioral episodes normally are not activated when judging one's personal characteristics.

CONCLUSIONS

We began this research project with a simple question: Do trait judgments about the self require retrieval of behavioral exemplars? We discovered that, although conditions can be created under which they do (Experiment 6), typically these judgments do not require autobiographical retrieval. Exemplars are far less important than has typically been assumed by researchers interested in the self.

A related finding is that autobiographical and abstract self-knowledge appear to be accessed independently, and more important, they also may be stored separately in memory. As we have discussed, the independence of autobiographical knowledge and abstract trait knowledge is consistent with several sources of evidence from the clinical amnesia literature. We would like to suggest, in fact, that the domain of clinical amnesia holds considerable untapped potential for formulating and testing models within personality and social psychology. Researchers in cognitive psychology already have taken this approach. Progress has been made in cognitive theorizing on the basis of observations of clinical amnesias, and a number of important cognitive concepts have been tested with amnesic individuals: short- and long-term memory (e.g., Baddeley & Warrington, 1971), the episodic-semantic distinction (e.g., Cermak, 1984), and the implicit-explicit distinction (e.g., Graf & Schacter, 1985) are a few examples. We believe that theories in social and personality psychology also could benefit from consideration and testing of their implications in the clinical amnesia domain.

For example, consider our proposal that general trait knowledge is represented in memory independent of specific trait-relevant behavioral knowledge. This implies the very interesting prediction that a person unable to recall a single trait-relevant personal behavior still could have detailed knowledge of his or her trait characteristics. The availability of an individual such as K.C., who cannot recall the occurrence of any personal episodes, represents a unique opportunity to explore the proposition that knowledge of one's traits is stored and retrieved independent of memories for behaviors in which those traits were manifested. If this idea is correct, then K.C., despite his inability to recall his behaviors, should be able to reliably judge a list of trait adjectives for self-descriptiveness.

As a final comment, our research has reinforced in us the belief that the factors that contribute to the quality and quantity of our knowledge of self—continual input of rich information over time—are the same factors that tend to characterize social experience in general. Thus, we feel it may be wise to shift the focus of research on the representation of social knowledge to pay more attention to these factors. This does not mean abandoning laboratory research in favor of field studies. But what it does mean is that we should start testing within the laboratory the type of knowledge representation we want our lab research to be modeling—real knowledge about real people. This can be done in the lab in either of two ways. First, one can attempt to create a knowledge structure that more closely mimics real social knowledge, by presenting a large amount of information about a person over a long retention interval. Second, as we did in our studies, one can use standard lab techniques to examine the representation of preexperimental long-term knowledge about real people in memory.

ACKNOWLEDGMENTS

Preparation of this chapter was supported by an Academic Senate Research Grant to the first author from the University of California, Santa Barbara.

We wish to thank Greg Trafton, Amy Plog, Jennifer Gentil, Joan Byer, and Chris Carmouche for their assistance in running the experiments reported in this chapter. We also would like to thank Jeff Sherman, Karen Kenworthy, Arlene Asuncion, Steve Stroessner, Matt Chin, and Holly Schroth for their very helpful comments on an earlier version of this chapter.

Correspondence concerning this chapter should be addressed to Stanley B. Klein, Department of Psychology, University of California, Santa Barbara, California, 93106.

REFERENCES

Andersen, S. M., & Klatzky, R. L. (1987). Traits and social stereotypes: Levels of categorization in person perception. *Journal of Personality and Social Psychology, 53,* 235–246.

Anderson, J. R. (1976). *Language, memory, and thought.* Hillsdale, NJ: Lawrence Erlbaum Associates.

Anderson, J. R. (1983a). A spreading activation theory of memory. *Journal of Verbal Learning and Verbal Behavior, 22,* 261–295.

Anderson, J. R. (1983b). Retrieval of information from long-term memory. *Science, 220,* 25–30.

Anderson, N. H. (1989). Functional memory and on-line attribution. In J. N. Bassili (Ed.), *On-line cognition in person perception* (pp. 175–220). Hillsdale, NJ: Lawrence Erlbaum Associates.

Arkin, R. M. (1986). Self-presentation strategies and sequelae. In S. L. Zelen (Ed.), *Self-representation: The second attribution-personality theory conference* (pp. 5–29). New York: Springer-Verlag.

Arkin, R. M., & Duval, S. (1975). Focus of attention and causal attributions of actors and observers. *Journal of Experimental Social Psychology, 11,* 427–438.

Baddeley, A. D., & Warrington, E. K. (1971). Amnesia and the distinction between long-term and short-term memory. *Journal of Verbal Learning and Verbal Behavior, 9,* 176–189.

Barsalou, L. W. (1987). The instability of graded structure: Implications for the nature of concepts. In U. Neisser (Ed.), *Concepts and conceptual development: Ecological and intellectual factors in categorization* (pp. 101–140). New York: Cambridge University Press.

Barsalou, L. W. (1988). The content and organization of autobiographical memories. In U. Neisser & E. Winograd (Eds.), *Remembering reconsidered: Ecological and traditional approaches to the study of memory* (pp. 193–243). New York: Cambridge University Press.

Barsalou, L. W. (1990). On the indistinguisability of exemplar memory and abstraction in category representation. In T. K. Srull & R. S. Wyer (Eds.), *Advances in social cognition* (Vol. 3, pp. 61–88). Hillsdale, NJ: Lawrence Erlbaum Associates.

Baxter, T. L., & Goldberg, L. R. (1987). Perceived behavioral consistency underlying trait attributions to oneself and another: An extension of the actor-observer effect. *Personality and Social Psychology Bulletin, 13,* 437–447.

Bellezza, F. S. (1984). The self as a mnemonic device: The role of internal cues. *Journal of Personality and Social Psychology, 47,* 506–516.

Bem, D. J. (1967). Self-perception: An alternative interpretation of cognitive dissonance phenomena. *Psychological Review, 74,* 183–200.

Bem, D. J. (1972). Self-perception theory. In L. Berkowitz (Ed.), *Advances in experimental social psychology* (Vol. 6, pp. 1–62). New York: Academic Press.

Bower, G. H. (1981). Mood and memory. *American Psychologist, 36,* 129–148.

Bower, G. H., & Gilligan, S. G. (1979). Remembering information related to one's self. *Journal of Research in Personality, 13,* 420–432.

Bower, G. H., Gilligan, S. G., & Montiero, K. P. (1981). Selectivity of learning caused by affective states. *Journal of Experimental Psychology: General, 110,* 451–473.

Brewer, W. F. (1986). What is autobiographical memory? In D. C. Rubin (Ed.), *Autobiographical memory* (pp. 25–49). New York: Cambridge University Press.

Brooks, L. R. (1978). Nonanalytic concept formation and memory for instances. In E. Rosch & B. B. Lloyd (Eds.), *Cognition and categorization* (pp. 169–216). Hillsdale, NJ: Lawrence Erlbaum Associates.

Bruch, M. A., Kaflowitz, N. G., & Berger, P. (1988). Self-schema for assertiveness: Extending the validity of the self-schema construct. *Journal of Research in Personality, 22,* 424–444.

Busemeyer, J. R., & Dewey, G. I., & Medin, D. L. (1984). Evaluation of exemplar-based generalization and the abstraction of categorical information. *Journal of Experimental Psychology: Learning, Memory, and Cognition, 10,* 638–648.

Buss, D. M., & Craik, K. H. (1983). The act frequency approach to personality. *Psychological Review, 90,* 105–126.

Buss, D. M., & Craik, K. H. (1984). Acts, dispositions, and personality. In B. A. Maher & W. B. Maher (Eds.), *Progress in Experimental Personality Research* (Vol. 13, pp. 241–301). New York: Academic Press.

Butters, N., & Cermak, L. S. (1986). A case study of forgetting of autobiographical knowledge: Implications for the study of retrograde amnesia. In D. Rubin (Ed.), *Autobiographical memory* (pp. 253–272). New York: Cambridge University Press.

Cantor, N., & Kihlstrom, J. F. (1987). *Personality and social intelligence.* Englewood Cliffs NJ: Prentice-Hall.

Carlston, D. E., & Skowronski, J. J. (1986). Trait memory and behavior memory: The effects of alternative pathways on impression judgment response times. *Journal of Personality and Social Psychology, 50,* 5–13.

Cermak, L. S. (1984). The episodic-semantic distinction in amnesia. In L. R. Squire & N. Butters (Eds.), *Neuropsychology of memory* (pp. 45–54). New York: Guilford Press.

Cermak, L. S., & O'Connor, M. (1983). The retrieval capacity of a patient with amnesia due to encephalitis. *Neuropsychologia, 21,* 213–234.

Chaiken, S., & Baldwin, M. W. (1981). Affective-cognitive consistency and the effect of salient behavioral information on the self-perception of attitudes. *Journal of Personality and Social Psychology, 41,* 1–12.

Chew, B. R. (1983). *Selective recall of self- and other-referenced information.* Unpublished doctoral dissertation, Harvard University, Cambridge, MA.

Clark, M. S., & Fiske, S. T. (1982). *Affect and cognition.* Hillsdale, NJ: Lawrence Erlbaum Associates.

Collins, A. M., & Loftus, E. F. (1975). A spreading-activation theory of semantic processing. *Psychological Review, 82,* 407–428.

Collins, A. M., & Quillian, M. R. (1970). Facilitating retrieval from semantic memory: The effect of repeating part of an inference. *Acta Psychologica, 33,* 304–314.

Conway, M. A. (1987). Verifying autobiographical facts. *Cognition, 26,* 39–58.

Cornoldi, C., DeBeni, R., & PraBaldi, A. (1989). Generation and retrieval of general, specific and autobiographical images representing concrete nouns. *Acta Psychologica, 72,* 25–39.

Eagle, M. (1988). Psychoanalysis and self-deception. In J. S. Lockard & D. L. Paulhus (Eds.), *Self-deception: An adaptive mechanism?* (pp. 78–98). Englewood Cliffs, NJ: Prentice-Hall.

Eder, R. A. (1988). The self conceived in memory. *Early Child Development and Care, 40,* 25–51.

Eder, R. A. (1989). The emergent personologist: The structure and content of 3½-, 5½-, and 7½-year olds' concepts of themselves and other persons. *Child Development, 60,* 1218–1228.

Eder, R. A., Gerlach, S. G., & Perlmutter, M. (1987). In search of children's selves: Development of the specific and general components of the self-concept. *Child Development, 58,* 1044–1050.

Edwards, A. L. (1957). *The social desirability variable in personality assessment and research.* New York: The Dryden Press.

Edwards, A. L. (1970). *The measurement of personality traits by scales and inventories.* New York: Holt, Rinehart & Winston.

Elio, R., & Anderson, J. R. (1981). The effects of category generalizations and instance similarity on schema abstraction. *Journal of Experimental Psychology: Human Learning and Memory, 7*, 397–417.

Epstein, S. (1979). The stability of Behavior: I. On predicting most of the people much of the time. *Journal of Personality and Social Psychology, 37*, 1097–1126.

Estes, W. K. (1989). Early and late memory processing in models for category learning. In C. Izawa (Ed.), *Current issues in cognitive processes: The Tulane Flowerree symposium on cognition* (pp. 11–24). Hillsdale, NJ: Lawrence Erlbaum Associates.

Fazio, R. H., Effrein, E. A., & Falender, V. J. (1981). Self-perceptions following social interactions. *Journal of Personality and Social Psychology, 41*, 232–242.

Fingarette, H. (1969). *Self-deception*. London: Routledge & Kegan Paul.

Fisher, C. (1945). Amnesic states in war neuroses: The psychogenesis of fugues. *Psychoanalytic Quarterly, 14*, 437–468.

Fisher, C., & Joseph, E. (1949). Fugue with awareness of loss of personal identity. *Psychoanalytic Quarterly, 18*, 480–493.

Fiske, S. T., & Taylor, S. E. (1991). *Social cognition* (2nd ed.). New York: McGraw-Hill.

Ganellen, R. J., & Carver, C. S. (1985). Why does self-reference promote incidental encoding? *Journal of Experimental Social Psychology, 21*, 284–300.

Garner, W. R., Hake, H. W., & Eriksen, C. W. (1956). Operationism and the concept of perception. *Psychological Review, 63*, 149–159.

Graf, P., & Schacter, D. L. (1985). Implicit and explicit memory for new associations in normal and amnesic subjects. *Journal of Experimental Psychology: Learning, Memory, and Cognition, 11*, 501–518.

Graesser, A. C. (1981). *Prose comprehension beyond the word*. New York: Springer-Verlag.

Greene, J. O., & Geddes, D. (1988). Representation and processing in the self-system: An action oriented approach to self and self-relevant phenomena. *Communication Monographs, 55*, 287–314.

Greenwald, A. G., & Banaji, M. R. (1989). The self as a memory system: Powerful, but ordinary. *Journal of Personality and Social Psychology, 57*, 41–54.

Groninger, L. D., & Groninger, L. K. (1984). Autobiographical memories: Their relation to images, definitions, and word recognition. *Journal of Experimental Psychology: Learning, Memory, and Cognition, 10*, 745–755.

Gur, R. C., & Sackeim, H. A. (1979). Self-deception: A concept in search of a phenomenon. *Journal of Personality and Social Psychology, 37*, 147–169.

Haight, M. R. (1980). *A study of self-deception*. Atlantic Highlands, NJ: Humanities Press.

Hamilton, D. L. (1989). Understanding impression formation: What has memory research contributed? In P. R. Solomon, G. R. Goethals, C. M. Kelley, & B. R. Stephens (Eds.), *Memory: Interdisciplinary approaches* (pp. 221–242). New York: Springer-Verlag.

Hampson, S. E. (1982a). *The construction of personality*. Boston: Routledge & Kegan Paul.

Hampson, S. E. (1982b). Person memory: A semantic category model of personality traits. *British Journal of Psychology, 73*, 1–11.

Heider, F. (1944). Social perception and phenomenal causality. *Psychological Review, 51*, 358–374.

Higgins, E. T., & Bargh, J. A. (1987). Social cognition and social perception. *Annual Review of Psychology, 38*, 369–425.

Hintzman, D. L. (1984). MINERVA 2: A simulation model of human memory. *Behavioral Research Methods and Instrumentation, 16*, 96–101.

Hintzman, D. L. (1986). "Schema abstraction" in a multiple-trace memory model. *Psychological Review, 93*, 411–428.

Hintzman, D. L. (1988). Judgments of frequency and recognition memory in a multiple-trace model. *Psychological Review, 93* 411–428.

Hintzman, D. L., & Ludlam, G. (1980). Differential forgetting of prototypes and old instances: Simulation by an exemplar-based classification model. *Memory & Cognition, 8*, 378–382.

Homa, D., & Chambliss, D. (1975). The relative contributions of of common and distinctive information on the abstraction from ill-defined categories. *Journal of Experimental Psychology: Human Learning and Memory, 1*, 351–359.

Homa, D., Dunbar, S., & Nohre, L. (1991). Instance frequency, categorization, and the modulating effect of experience. *Journal of Experimental Psychology: Learning, Memory, and Cognition, 17*, 444–458.

Homa, D., Sterling, S., & Trepel, L. (1981). Limitation of exemplar-based generalization and the abstraction of categorical information. *Journal of Experimental Psychology: Human Learning and Memory, 7*, 418–439.

Hudson, J. A. (1986). Memories are made of this: General event knowledge and the development of autobiographical memory. In K. Nelson (Ed.), *Event knowledge: Structure and function in development* (pp. 97–118). Hillsdale, NJ: Lawrence Erlbaum Associates.

Hunt, R. R., & Einstein, G. O. (1981). Relational and item-specific information in memory. *Journal of Verbal Learning and Verbal Behavior, 20*, 497–514.

James, W. (1890). *The principles of psychology.* New York: Henry Holt.

Jones, E. E. (1976). How do people perceive the causes of their behavior? *American Scientist, 34*, 300–305.

Jones, E. E., & Gerard, H. B. (1967). *Foundations of social psychology.* New York: Wiley.

Jones, E. E., & Nisbett, R. E. (1972). The actor and the observer: Divergent perceptions of the causes of behavior. In E. E. Jones, D. E. Kanouse, H. H. Kelley, R. E. Nisbett, S. Valins, & B. Weiner (Eds.), *Attribution: Perceiving the causes of behavior* (pp. 79–94). Morristown, NJ: General Learning Press.

Judd, C. M., & Park, B. (1988). Outgroup homogeneity: Judgments of variability at the individual and group levels. *Journal of Personality and Social Psychology, 54*, 778–788.

Kahneman, D., & Miller, D. T. (1986). Norm theory: Comparing reality to its alternatives. *Psychological Review, 93*, 136–153.

Keenan, J. M., & Baillet, S. D. (1980). Memory for personally and socially significant events. In R. S. Nickerson (Ed.), *Attention and performance* (Vol. 8, pp. 651–669). Hillsdale, NJ: Lawrence Erlbaum Associates.

Kendzierski, D. (1980). Self-schemata and scripts: The recall of self-referent and scriptal information. *Personality and Social Psychology Bulletin, 6*, 23–29.

Kihlstrom, J. F., & Cantor, N. (1984). Mental representations of the self. In L. Berkowitz (Ed.), *Advances in experimental social psychology* (Vol. 17, pp. 1–47). New York: Academic Press.

Kihlstrom, J. F., Cantor, N., Albright, J. S., Chew, B. R., Klein, S. B., & Niedenthal, P. M. (1988). Information processing and the study of the self. In L. Berkowitz (Ed.), *Advances in experimental social psychology* (Vol. 21, pp. 145–177). New York: Academic Press.

Kirby, D. M., & Gardner, R. C. (1972). Ethnic stereotypes: Norms on 208 words typically used in their assessment. *Canadian Journal of Psychology, 26*, 140–154.

Klein, K., & Saltz, E. (1976). Specifying the mechanisms in a levels-of-processing approach to memory. *Journal of Experimental Psychology: Human Learning and Memory, 2*, 671–679.

Klein, S. B., & Kihlstrom, J. F. (1986). Elaboration, organization, and the self-reference effect in memory. *Journal of Experimental Psychology: General, 115*, 26–38.

Klein, S. B., & Loftus, J. (1987). [The effects of redundant and nonredundant processing on recall]. Unpublished raw data.

Klein, S. B., & Loftus, J. (1988). The nature of self-referent encoding: The contributions of elaborative and organizational process. *Journal of Personality and Social Psychology, 55*, 5–11.

Klein, S. B., & Loftus, J. (1990a). Rethinking the role of organization in person memory: An independent trace storage model. *Journal of Personality and Social Psychology, 59*, 400–410.

Klein, S. B., & Loftus, J. (1990b). The role of abstract and exemplar-based knowledge in self-judgments: Implications for a cognitive model of the self. In T. K. Srull & R. S. Wyer (Eds.), *Advances in social cognition* (Vol. 3, pp. 131–139). Hillsdale, NJ: Lawrence Erlbaum Associates.

Klein, S. B., Loftus, J., & Burton, H. A. (1989). Two self-reference effects: The importance of distinguishing between self-descriptiveness judgments and autobiographical retrieval in self-referent encoding. *Journal of Personality and Social Psychology, 56*, 853–865.

Klein, S. B., Loftus, J., & Plog, A. E. (1992). Trait judgments about the self: Evidence from the encoding specificity paradigm. *Personality and Social Psychology Bulletin, 18*, 730–735.

Klein, S. B., Loftus, J., & Sherman, J. W. (in press). The role of summary and specific behavioral memories in trait judgments about the self. *Personality and Social Psychology Bulletin.*

Klein, S. B., & Loftus, J. (1991). [Latencies to retrieve trait abstractions and behavioral exemplars about the self and other]. Unpublished raw data.

Klein, S. B., Loftus, J., Trafton, J. G., & Fuhrman, R. W. (1992). Use of exemplars and abstractions in trait judgments: A model of trait knowledge about the self and others. *Journal of Personality and Social Psychology, 63*, 739–753.

Kolodner, J. L. (1984). *Retrieval and organizational strategies in conceptual memory: A computer model.* Hillsdale, NJ: Lawrence Erlbaum Associates.

Kuiper, N. A. (1981). Convergent evidence for the self as prototype: The "inverted-U RT" effect for self and other judgments. *Personality and Social Psychology Bulletin, 35*, 63–78.

Kuiper, N. A., & Rogers, T. B. (1979). Encoding of personal information: Self-other differences. *Journal of Personality and Social Psychology, 37*, 499–514.

Lewicki, P. (1986). *Nonconscious social information processing.* Orlando, FL: Academic Press.

Light, L. L., & Carter-Sobell, L. (1970). Effects of changed semantic context on recognition memory. *Journal of Verbal Learning and Verbal Behavior, 9*, 1–11.

Linton, M. (1982). Transformations of memory in everyday life. In U. Neisser (Ed.), *Memory observed: Remembering in natural contexts* (pp. 77–91). San Francisco: Freeman.

Locksley, A., & Lenauer, M. (1981). Considerations for a theory of self-inference processes. In N. Cantor & J. F. Kihlstrom (Eds.), *Personality, cognition, and social interaction* (pp. 263–277). Hillsdale, NJ: Lawrence Erlbaum Associates.

Lord, C. G. (1980). Schemas and images as memory aids: Two modes of processing social information. *Journal of Personality and Social Psychology, 38*, 257–269.

Lord, C. G., Gilbert, D. T., & Stanley, M. A. (1982, August). *Individual self-schemas and processing information about the self.* Paper presented at the meeting of the American Psychological Association, Washington, DC.

Malt, B. C. (1989). An on-line investigation of prototype and exemplar strategies in classification. *Journal of Experimental Psychology: Learning, Memory, and Cognition, 15*, 539–555.

Macht, M. L., & O'Brien, E. J. (1980). Familiarity-based responding in item recognition: Evidence for the role of spreading activation. *Journal of Experimental Psychology: Human Learning and Memory, 6*, 301–318.

Mancuso, J. C., & Ceely, S. G. (1980). The self as memory processing. *Cognitive Therapy and Research, 4*, 1–25.

Markus, H. (1977). Self-schemata and processing information about the self. *Journal of Personality and Social Psychology, 35*, 63–78.

Markus, H. (1980). The self in thought and memory. In D. M. Wegner & R. R. Vallacher (Eds.), *The self in social psychology* (pp. 102–130). New York: Oxford Press.

Markus, H., & Sentis, K. (1982). The self in social information processing. In J. Suls (Ed.), *Psychological perspectives on the self* (Vol. 1, pp. 41–70). Hillsdale, NJ: Lawrence Erlbaum Associates.

Martin, E. (1968). Stimulus meaningfulness and paired-associate transfer: An encoding variability hypothesis. *Psychological Review, 75*, 421–441.

Martin, E. (1971). Verbal learning theory and independent retrieval phenomena. *Psychological Review*, *78*, 314–332.

Martin, E. (1972). Stimulus encoding in learning and transfer. In A. W. Melton & E. Martin (Eds.), *Coding processes in human memory* (pp. 59–84). New York: Wiley.

Martin, M. W. (1985). *Self-deception and self-understanding*. Lawrence, KS: University of Kansas Press.

Matlin, M. W. (1989). *Cognition* (2nd ed.). New York: Holt, Rinehart & Winston.

McArthur, L. Z., & Post, D. L. (1977). Figural emphasis and person perception. *Journal of Experimental Social Psychology*, *13*, 520–535.

McGuire, W. J., McGuire, C. V., & Cheever, J. (1986). The self in society: Effects of social contexts on the sense of self. *British Journal of Social Psychology*, *25*, 259–270.

Medin, D. L., Altom, M. W., & Murphy, T. D. (1984). Given versus induced category representations: Use of prototype and exemplar information in classification. *Journal of Experimental Psychology: Learning, Memory, and Cognition*, *10*, 333–352.

Medin, D. L., & Shaeffer, M. M. (1978). Context theory of classification learning. *Psychological Review*, *85*, 207–238.

Medin, D. L., & Smith, E. E. (1984). Concepts and concept formation. *Annual Review of Psychology*, *35*, 113–138.

Monson, T. C., & Snyder, M. (1977). Actors, observers, and the attribution process: Toward a reconceptualization. *Journal of Experimental Social Psychology*, *13*, 89–111.

Monson, T., Tanke, E., & Lund, J. (1980). Determinants of social perception in a naturalistic setting. *Journal of Research in Personality*, *14*, 104–120.

Morton, J. (1969). The interaction of information in word recognition. *Psychological Review*, *76*, 165–178.

Mueller, J. H., Thompson, W. B., & Dugan, K. (1986). Trait distinctiveness and accessibility in the self-schema. *Personality and Social Psychology Bulletin*, *12*, 81–89.

Murphy, G. (1975). *Outgrowing self-deception*. New York: Basic Books.

Neely, J. H. (1988). Experimental dissociations and the episodic/semantic memory distinction. In H. L. Roediger & F. I. M. Craik (Eds.), *Varieties of memory and consciousness: Essays in honor of Endel Tulving* (pp. 229–270). Hillsdale, NJ: Lawrence Erlbaum Associates.

Neisser, U. (1988). What is ordinary memory the memory of? In U. Neisser & E. Winograd (Eds.), *Remembering reconsidered: Ecological and traditional approaches to the study of memory* (pp. 356–373). New York: Cambridge University Press.

Nisbett, R., Caputo, C., Legant, P., & Marecek, J. (1973). Behavior as seen by the actor and as seen by the observer. *Journal of Personality and Social Psychology*, *27*, 154–165.

Nisbett, R., & Ross, L. (1980). *Human inference: Strategies and shortcomings of social judgment*. Englewood Cliffs, NJ: Prentice-Hall.

Nosofsky, R. M. (1987). Attention and learning processes in the identification and categorization of integral stimuli. *Journal of Experimental Psychology: Learning, Memory, and Cognition*, *13*, 87–108.

Park, B. (1986). A method for studying the development of impressions of real people. *Journal of Personality and Social Psychology*, *51*, 907–917.

Park, B., & Hastie, R. (1987). Perception of variability in category development: Instance versus abstraction-based stereotypes. *Journal of Personality and Social Psychology*, *53*, 621–635.

Parkin, A. J. (1987). *Memory and amnesia: An introduction*. New York: Basil Blackwell.

Paulhus, D. L., & Suedfeld, P. (1988). A dynamic complexity model of self-deception. In J. S. Lockard & D. L. Paulhus (Eds.), *Self-deception: An adaptive mechanism?* (pp. 132–145). Englewood Cliffs, NJ: Prentice-Hall.

Posner, M. I., & Keele, S. W. (1968). On the genesis of abstract ideas. *Journal of Experimental Psychology*, *77*, 353–363.

Pratkanis, A. R., Breckler, S. J., & Greenwald, A. G. (1989). *Attitude structure and function.* Hillsdale, NJ: Lawrence Erlbaum Associates.

Pryor, J. B., & Ostrom, T. M. (1981). The cognitive organization of social information: A converging operations approach. *Journal of Personality and Social Psychology, 41,* 628–641.

Regan, D. T., & Totten, J. (1975). Empathy and Attribution: Turning observers into actors. *Journal of Personality and Social Psychology, 32,* 850–856.

Robinson, J. A. (1976). Sampling autobiographical memory. *Cognitive Psychology, 8,* 578–595.

Rogers, T. B., Kuiper, N. A., & Kirker, W. S. (1977). Self-reference and the encoding of personal information. *Journal of Personality and Social Psychology, 35,* 677–688.

Rosch, E. H. (1975). Cognitive representations of semantic categories. *Journal of Experimental Psychology: General, 104,* 192–233.

Rosch, E. R., Mervis, C. B., Gray, W. D., Johnson, D. M., & Boyes-Braem, P. (1976). Basic objects in natural categories. *Cognitive Psychology, 8,* 382–439.

Ross, B. H., Perkins, S. J., & Tenpenny, P. L. (1990). Reminding-based category learning. *Cognitive Psychology, 22,* 460–492.

Ross, L., & Nisbett, R. E. (1991). *The person and the situation: Perspectives of social psychology.* New York: McGraw-Hill.

Rothbart, M., & John, O. P. (1985). Social categorization and behavioral episodes: A cognitive analysis of the effects of intergroup contact. *Journal of Social Issues, 41*(3), 81–104.

Sackeim, H. A., & Gur, R. C. (1978). Self-deception, self-confrontation, and consciousness. In G. E. Schwartz & D. Shapiro (Eds.), *Consciousness and self-regulation: Advances in research* (Vol. 2, pp. 139–197). New York: Plenum.

Salancik, G. R., & Conway, M. (1975). Attitude inferences from salient and relevant cognitive content about behavior. *Journal of Personality and Social Psychology, 32,* 829–840.

Sande, G. N. (1990). The multifaceted self. In J. M. Olson & M. P. Zanna (Eds.), *Self-inference processes: The Ontario symposium* (Vol. 6, pp. 1–16). Hillsdale, NJ: Lawrence Erlbaum Associates.

Sande, G. N., Goethals, G. R., & Radloff, C. E. (1988). Perceiving one's own traits and others': The multifaceted self. *Journal of Personality and Social Psychology, 54,* 13–20.

Sartre, J. P. (1958). *Being and nothingness.* (H. Barnes, Trans.). London: Metheun.

Schacter, D. L., & Kihlstrom, J. F. (1989). Functional amnesia. In F. Boller & J. Grafman (Eds.), *Handbook of neuropsychology* (Vol. 3, pp. 209–231). Amsterdam: Elsevier Science.

Schacter, D. L., Wang, P. L., Tulving, E., & Freedman, M. (1982). Functional retrograde amnesia: A quantitative case study. *Neuropsychologia, 20,* 523–532.

Schank, R. C. (1982). *Dynamic memory: A theory of reminding and learning in computers and people.* New York: Cambridge University Press.

Schank, R. C., & Abelson, R. P. (1977). *Scripts, plans, goals, and understanding.* Hillsdale, NJ: Lawrence Erlbaum Associates.

Schlenker, B. R., & Trudeau, J. V. (1990). Impact of self-presentations on private self-beliefs: Effects of prior self-beliefs and misattribution. *Journal of Personality and Social Psychology, 58,* 22–32.

Smith, E. R. (1990a). Reply to commentaries. In T. K. Srull & R. S. Wyer (Eds.), *Advances in social cognition* (Vol. 3, pp. 181–202). Hillsdale, NJ: Lawrence Erlbaum Associates.

Smith, E. R. (1990b). Content and Process specificity in the effects of prior experiences. In T. K. Srull & R. S. Wyer (Eds.), *Advances in social cognition* (Vol. 3, pp. 1–59). Hillsdale, NJ: Lawrence Erlbaum Associates.

Smith, E. R., & Zarate, M. A. (1990). Exemplar and prototype use in social categorization. *Social Cognition, 8,* 243–262.

Smith, E. R., & Zarate, M. A. (in press). Exemplar-based models of social judgment. *Psychological Review.*

Srull, T. K. (1981). Person memory: Some tests of associative storage and retrieval models. *Journal of Experimental Psychology: Human Learning and Memory, 7,* 440–463.

Srull, T. K. (1984). Methodological techniques for the study of person memory and social cognition. In R. S. Wyer & T. K. Srull (Eds.), *Handbook of social cognition* (Vol. 2, pp. 2–72). Hillsdale, NJ: Lawrence Erlbaum Associates.

Storms, M. D. (1973). Videotape and the attribution process: Reversing actors' and observers' points of view. *Journal of Personality and Social Psychology, 27,* 165–175.

Taylor, S. E., & Fiske, S. T. (1975). Point of view and the perception of causality. *Journal of Personality and Social Psychology, 32,* 439–445.

Tulving, E. (1979). Relation between encoding specificity and levels of processing. In L. S. Cermak & F. I. M. Craik (Eds.), *Levels of processing in human memory* (pp. 405–428). Hillsdale, NJ: Lawrence Erlbaum Associates.

Tulving, E. (1983). *Elements of episodic memory.* New York: Oxford University Press.

Tulving, E. (1989a). Remembering and knowing. *American Scientist, 77,* 361–367.

Tulving, E. (1989b). Memory: Performance, knowledge, and Experience. *European Journal of Cognitive Psychology, 1,* 3–26.

Tulving, E., Schacter, D. L., McLachlan, D. R., & Moscovitch, M. (1988). Priming of semantic autobiographical knowledge: A case study of retrograde amnesia. *Brain & Cognition, 8,* 3–20.

Tulving, E., & Thompson, D. M. (1973). Encoding specificity and retrieval processes in episodic memory. *Psychological Review, 80,* 352–373.

Turner, J. C. (1987). *Rediscovering the social group: A self-categorization theory.* New York: Basil Blackwell.

Van Dijk, T. A., & Kintsch, W. (1983). *Strategies of discourse comprehension.* New York: Academic Press.

Warren, M. W., Chattin, D., Thompson, D. D., & Tomsky, M. T. (1983). The effects of autobiographical elaboration on noun recall. *Memory & Cognition, 11,* 445–455.

Watkins, M. J., & Kerkar, S. P. (1985). Recall of a twice-presented item without recall of either presentation Generic memory for events. *Journal of Memory and Language, 24,* 666–678.

Watson, D. (1982). The actor and the observer: How are their perceptions of causality divergent? *Psychological Bulletin, 92,* 701–725.

Wiggins, J. S. (1968). Personality structure. *Annual Review of Psychology, 19,* 293–350.

Wiggins, J. S. (1973). *Personality and prediction: Principles of personality assessment.* Reading, MA: Addison-Wesley.

Wyer, R. S., & Gordon, S. E. (1984). The cognitive representation of social information. In R. S. Wyer & T. K. Srull (Eds.), *Handbook of social cognition* (Vol. 2, pp. 73–150). Hillsdale, NJ: Lawrence Erlbaum Associates.

Wyer, R. S., & Srull, T. K. (1986). Human cognition in its social context. *Psychological Review, 93,* 322–359.

Wyer, R. S., & Srull, T. K. (1989). *Memory and cognition in its social context.* Hillsdale, NJ: Lawrence Erlbaum Associates.

Zarate, M. A., & Smith, E. R. (1990). Person categorization and stereotyping. *Social Cognition, 8,* 161–185.

2 Does "Perplexing" Describe the Self-Reference Effect? Yes!

Francis S. Bellezza
Ohio University

Some researchers, myself included (Bellezza, 1984), have assumed that during the self-reference task people search their memories for autobiographical events that confirm or deny as self-descriptive trait terms such as *friendly, loyal, dishonest,* and so on. In a persuasive series of experiments Klein, Loftus, and their associates demonstrated that deciding whether a trait term is self-descriptive has little to do with remembering a specific occasion in which one behaved in a manner related to the trait term. It is most certainly wrong to explain the self-reference effect by using an exemplar model based on accessing autobiographical information in memory. Klein and Loftus (Chapter 1) have used a variety of experimental paradigms to demonstrate this. For example, they showed that recalling a trait-related autobiographical event from memory does not shorten the time it takes for a person to decide (a few seconds later) whether the trait term is self-descriptive. Similarly, making a decision as to whether a trait term is self-descriptive does not shorten the time to recall a trait-related autobiographical memory. These two self-reference tasks, the descriptive and the auto-biographical, do not seem to represent the same process, access the same information, nor facilitate each other more than tasks unrelated to the self, such as defining the trait word. As described by Klein and Loftus, this failure in task facilitation also occurs using a recognition paradigm (Experiment 3) and using a free-recall paradigm (Experiment 4). The various self-reference tasks appear to affect different parts of the memory system and to access different information regarding self-descriptive traits.

Part of my motivation (Bellezza, 1984) for using an exemplar explanation of self-knowledge was to avoid to the use of the levels-of-processing approach of Rogers, Kuiper, and Kirker (1977). I have tried to explain the self-reference effect and related phenomena using a mental cuing framework in which the retrieved personal experiences function as mental cues for the recall of the judged trait terms (Bellezza, 1984, 1986, 1987; Bellezza & Hoyt, 1992). This approach has much in common with explanations of the self-reference effect that empha-size the importance of associative networks (Bower & Gilligan, 1979; Kihlstrom & Cantor, 1984) and the importance of organizational factors in remembering (Klein & Kihlstrom, 1986). Although an associative explanation of the self-reference effect remains, I believe, a defensible position, it now seems implausi-ble that recall of memories of autobiographical events are necessary to decide if trait adjectives are self-descriptive. Exemplar models that use memory represen-tations of events as category exemplars are problematic for a number of reasons, which I explore here.

EXEMPLAR MODELS AND THE REPRESENTATION OF EVENTS IN MEMORY

Exemplar Models and Infinite Regress

In a classic formulation of an exemplar model of categorization Medin and Schaffer (1978) proposed that during classification, learning category instances are stored in memory each associated with its appropriate category label but with no information abstracted from these instances and stored in summary form. According to this model, when a test item is to be categorized, a computation is made to determine which category contains an instance or instances most similar to the test item. Some measure of similarity based on the features of the catego-rized and test items determines into which category the test item is classified. In exemplar models, no abstracted information in the form of prototypes or stereo-types exist in memory. Only representations of particular category instances exist, and these are labeled only as category members. That is, after categoriza-tion the representation of the test item in memory possesses a feature represent-ing category membership.[1] Only category instances are used as sources of infor-mation in classifying test items or in any other use of category information.

Categorization can occur on many levels. Categories of objects exist on the superordinate level (furniture), on the basic level (chair), and on the subordinate level (kitchen chair; Rosch, Mervis, Gray, Johnson, & Boyes-Braem, 1976). But additional levels also exist. Furniture is part of the category of artifacts and is a subordinate of it. On the other end of the scale, kitchen chairs are comprised of

---

[1]In a pure exemplar model the only mental constructs allowed are exemplars. Categories are not allowed as separate mental constructs abstracting information from the exemplars. Therefore, the exemplars themselves contain the information regarding category membership, and category mem-bership is defined implicitly. Hence, the cognitive economy obtained by inheritance of properties found in hierarchical models such as that of Quillian (1968) is not found in exemplar models.

even smaller subcategories. This would be especially true for someone who is an expert in the design, manufacture, or sale of kitchen chairs. There are Early American kitchen chairs, Danish Modern kitchen chairs, Shaker kitchen chairs, and so on. According to an exemplar model, all of these categories are made up of sets of feature-based memory representations of objects, where some of these representations of chairs belong to the categories chairs, furniture, artifacts, but do not belong to other categories such as kitchen chairs, tables, fish, or vehicles.

But something is missing in this classification scheme. Assumptions must be added to the formulation of exemplar models of categorization to deal with the identification of individual objects. The category, kitchen chair, must include memory representations of individual kitchen chairs. There are the four kitchen chairs that belong to me, the six kitchen chairs that belong to my friend, and so on. In an exemplar model, these kitchen chairs cannot be abstracted or summarized into a prototypical kitchen chair. So, there must be additional subcategories representing sets made up of individual kitchen chairs that may be identical except for features such as spatial location and possession.

The time dimension, as well as the dimension of space, must also be taken into account as a feature. The representation of each individual kitchen chair in memory may be made up of a set of representations of a number of individual episodes involving interactions with that particular kitchen chair. Just as we cannot summarize across enduring perceptual features of objects in an exemplar model, we cannot summarize over features representing time and place. Hence, under the category label, "my kitchen chair near the door," must be representations of the times that I sat in it, the times I tripped over it, the times I stood on it, and so on. No abstraction is possible in an exemplar model. If I must decide if some test object is my kitchen chair, then these individual events in memory must be accessed.

This argument can be extended indefinitely. Within a particular episode a person may interact with a particular kitchen chair in a sequence of distinct behavioral units. For example, yesterday I wanted to sit down in the kitchen, so first I looked for my kitchen chair near the door. I found it, I moved it to an appropriate place near the table, I sat on it, and I pulled it forward toward the kitchen table. With an exemplar model I cannot summarize the information in these separate memory representations of episodes into an abstracted form. All I can do is to create a new category label for a subset of memory representations. This label would approximate "Using my kitchen chair at breakfast on October 31, 1991." Whenever I make a decision regarding this particular kitchen chair of mine, any kitchen chair, any chair, any article of furniture, or any artifact, I will have to use information from memory representing miniepisodes from events using my kitchen chair. Exemplar models do not allow abstraction or summarization of information.

Let's consider categories of people. Some features are observable and enduring, such as gender, eye color, and other physical features. These features are possessed by a person independent of time and place. However, differences among people are not based completely on observable and enduring features. Other features are based on events; that is, on features of time and place. Let us forget for the moment that in the exemplar model particular events cannot be abstracted into summary representations but themselves are categories of subevents. Let's assume events form those basic memory representations that contain features. Buss and Craik (1983) suggested that a personality trait such as dominance is based on information regarding acts dispersed over time. For example, dominance in a person may be evidenced by events such as giving orders to other people, not responding to other's suggestions, and so on. However, because acts occur in a particular time and place and are not enduring features, a person may act at times that suggests dominance as a trait and act at other times act suggesting that dominance is not a trait. Whether a person is characterized as dominant depends on the relative frequency with which these dominant acts occur. Hence, there is a set of specific behavioral events that are in the category labeled *dominant,* and a label such as *gives orders* may identify a subclass of these behaviors. However, using an exemplar model, all the individual instances of acting dominant or not acting dominant would be stored in memory. The representations of all these relevant events would have to be accessed to make a decision as to whether a trait term such as dominant describes a person.

Representations of individual events would also be part of person categories (Cantor & Mischel, 1979). For example, at some particular time not only did an act of domination occur, but John was the dominating actor. If one were asked "Is John a dominant person?", how could an exemplar model provide an answer to this question? It seems that one would search all the behavioral acts in the dominance category in memory and all of the behavioral acts in the John category and determine how many of these acts there were. Also in memory would be behavioral events in categories with labels like submissive that could provide evidence against dominance, and these would include acts representing John as one of the participants. Because no summary information is assumed, all of the representations behavior in memory would be accessed, but only those of John acting dominant and non-dominant would be retrieved and counted. The frequencies would them be used to come up with a "yes" or "no" response. In summary, a count would be made of events in the intersection of the John and dominance categories and a count would be made of the events in the intersection of the John and nondominance categories, and these frequencies would be somehow compared. A similar process would occur if one were asked "Does dominant describe you?" As mentioned earlier, this explanation assumes that the pure exemplar model has been relaxed to allow events to be abstracted from subevents so that events can be represented in memory as the irreducible category exemplars.

The Exemplar Model and the Association
of Events in Memory

The exemplar model assumes that representations of individual objects or events exist in memory and each representation belongs to a hierarchy of categories, but the representations are not associated with one another. That is, hierarchical relations exist between category and category exemplars but not coordinate associations among the category exemplars (Mandler, 1979; Wickelgren, 1979). This means that if a novel object, person, or event is encountered which results in the retrieval of a similar object, person, or event belonging to Category X, then the novel instance will be classified into Category X (see Medin & Schaffer, 1978, for examples of this process). Yet, according to the exemplar model, no direct association is formed between between the representation of the novel instance and the exemplar retrieved from memory that is similar to it. If we assume that both the novel instance and the similar exemplar retrieved from Category X each have a representation in memory, then the failure to form an association between the two is at odds with the classical associationist principle stating that similarity is a basis for the association of mental constructs. According to the exemplar model, the novel instance and the retrieved exemplar simply remain part of Category X and share the property of belonging to the same category, but no association exists between category members themselves. Considering that the novel instance reminded one of a category exemplar and that it may have been exceedingly similar to it, the two representations should thereby become associated in memory, and this association should be strengthened with repeated presentations independent of decisions regarding category membership. If this process does not occur, then it is difficult to understand how the small, discrete behavioral sequences comprising an event can be represented as a unit in memory. The classical principles of association, contiguity and similarity, provide an explanation for the integration of these subevents into a represented event in memory. As a result of this process of association, each integrated event becomes represented in memory in an integral manner, and the subevents making it up may no longer have independent representations in memory.

If, contrary to exemplar models, this integration occurs, then what are the features of these events? One can speculate that they must be features abstracted from the subevents during the process of integration. Furthermore, there is no reason to believe that this integration and abstraction of features cannot occur at all levels of representation (McClelland & Rumelhart, 1985).

The arguments that can be made against pure exemplar models suggest that some sort of summarization or abstraction can occur in the memory system, perhaps at a number of different levels of specificity. At the same time it is apparent that information specific to individual objects, events, and people also exists in memory. Abstraction doesn't always occur. This postulation of mixed memory models is the position taken by many investigators (e.g., Smith & Zarate, 1990), and is a position that seems to correspond to the conclusions of Klein and Loftus.

MULTIPLE MEMORY MODES

As I just discussed, I do not believe that a pure exemplar model is a plausible model for the self-reference effect nor is a plausible model of event representation. Even if the exemplar model is an implausible one, however, in some respects the Klein and Loftus results that are used to argue against it seem too good to be true. They have convincingly demonstrated that a self-reference judgment can be made without retrieval of a specific autobiographical experience from memory. That is, a self-descriptive judgment regarding a trait does not facilitate, a few seconds later, retrieval from memory of an autobiographical event relevant to the judgment. This seems a reasonable result according to their argument. Somewhat less understandable is the result that retrieval of an autobiographical experience relevant to a trait does not facilitate a later self-descriptive judgment. For example, as shown in Fig. 1.1 of Klein and Loftus, making a descriptive self-judgment following the retrieval of an trait-relevant autobiographical event is no faster than making a descriptive self-judgment following the retrieval of a definition of the trait word. One could argue that information regarding the self-descriptiveness of the trait should be automatically (or unintentionally) be retrieved or, at least, be primed to some extent during the search for the autobiographical experience. After all, the two cues for the search of relevant autobiographical experience are the self concept and the trait label. If these two cues do not result in some activation of the information relevant to a self-descriptive judgment, then it is difficult to think of any information that will. Memory priming occurs for a variety of different kinds of information (Matlin, 1989). Of course, Klein and Loftus report just the kind of facilitation described here when judgments are made about traits of one's mother if these traits are low or medium in descriptiveness.

How can one explain why facilitation occurs when judging traits about one's mother but no facilitation occurs when judging traits about oneself? It may be that many of the self-descriptive statements regarding self and mother are stored simply as facts (Collins & Loftus, 1975) requiring little memory search or inference. These "facts" may or may not be true and may or may not be based on information abstracted from behavior (Greenwald, 1980). Because the autobiographical response times reported by Klein and Loftus are long and on the order of 5 to 10 seconds, it is difficult to know what cognitive processes are being engaged or what criteria for terminating memory search are being used by the subjects. Perhaps, an experimental paradigm requiring faster responses would find some priming even for high-descriptiveness judgments.

Another concern I have about the Klein and Loftus facilitation paradigm is that not only the content but also the format of each question remains constant. Would facilitation occur if the descriptive question "I am honest" is followed by the descriptive question "Honest is a term that describes me." The degree of facilitation may not be as great when the format is changed because (a) rewording of the statement will required additional time for encoding, (b) the meaning of the statement may change because rewording may produce some subtle change in how the statement is interpreted. There are lexical and semantic processing times involved here that may be negligible, but we don't know this for sure.

Klein and Loftus suggest that different memory systems may mediate their autobiographical, descriptive, and semantic tasks. Not only is the distinction between episodic and semantic memory relevant here but also Tulving's (1989) distinction between episodic self-knowledge and semantic self-knowledge. If the memory system is partitioned in this manner, might we not expect within-mode facilitation for the various tasks? A descriptive statement "I am honest" should have a greater facilitating effect on a subsequent descriptive statement such as "I am loyal" than on a subsequent autobiographical request "Think of an experience in which you were loyal." If intermediate amounts of facilitation are found when the contents of the tasks are changed but the memory subsystem is held constant, then this result would, I believe, support the notion that different memory systems are involved in the three tasks.

THE STATUS OF THE SELF-REFERENCE EFFECT

My interest in the self-reference effect (Bellezza, 1984; Bellezza & Hoyt, 1992) resulted from the demonstration by Rogers et al. (1977) of the mnemonic properties of the self. Is the self important in learning, or does the self-reference effect reflect the operation of memory processes and the activation of memory structures unrelated to the self-concept? Other researchers also have been interested in the mnemonic processes underlying the self-reference effect, and a large literature has accumulated that tries to describe these processes. Understanding the self-reference effect may enable us to develop better mnemonic devices for the classroom and for other learning situations (e.g., Reeder, McCormick, & Esselman, 1987).

Why does self-reference result in better recall than other ways of processing information? Klein and Loftus do not address this issue and, of course, never intend to. Their concern is the mental representation of the self. However, some of their results bear on issues concerning the mnemonic properties of the self. For example, they show in Experiment 4 (Table 1.2), that autobiographical and descriptive tasks used alone result in approximately the same levels of recall. There is reason to believe, however, that recall following the autobiographical task should be superior to recall following the descriptive task (Bellezza, 1986; Warren, Chattin, Thompson, & Tomsky, 1983). The reason for this is that the autobiographical task results in deeper semantic processing and elaboration of the trait words than does the descriptive task (Anderson & Reder, 1979; Craik & Tulving, 1975). Similarly, the recognition results from Experiment 3 (Table 1.1) do not seem to replicate the self-reference effect (Groninger & Groninger, 1984; Rogers et al., 1977). Adjusted recognition performance for the semantic task (46%) appears to be higher than performance for the autobiographical task (38%) and the self-description task (35%). Because no tests of statistical inference comparing these performance levels are reported, however, it is difficult to interpret these data.

In spite of these concerns regarding their recall and recognition data, the Klein and Loftus results suggest new lines of research in which the mnemonic effects of various types of self-reference tasks, reflecting different memory systems, may not only be compared (Bellezza & Hoyt, 1992) but may also be combined to explore ways to optimize memory performance. For example, in Experiment 4 they show that the use of two different self-reference tasks results in better recall than the use of only one.

REFERENCES

Anderson, J. R., & Reder, L. M. (1979). An elaborative processing explanation of depth of processing. In L. S. Cermak & F. I. M. Craik (Eds.), *Levels of processing and human memory* (pp. 385–403). Hilldale, NJ: Lawrence Erlbaum Associates.

Bellezza, F. S. (1984). The self as a mnemonic device: The role of internal cues. *Journal of Personality and Social Psychology, 47,* 506–516.

Bellezza, F. S. (1986). Mental cues and verbal reports in learning. In G. H. Bower (Ed.), *The psychology of learning and motivation* (Vol. 20, pp. 237–273). New York: Academic Press.

Bellezza, F. S. (1987). Mnemonic devices and memory schemas. In M. McDaniel & M. Pressley (Ed.), *Imagery and related mnemonic processes* (pp. 34–55). New York: Springer-Verlag.

Bellezza, F. S., & Hoyt, S. K. (1992). The self-reference effect and mental cuing. *Social Cognition, 10,* 51–78.

Bower, G. H., & Gilligan, S. G. (1979). Remembering information related to one's self. *Journal of Research in Personality, 13,* 420–432.

Buss, D. M., & Craik, K. H. (1983). The act frequency approach to personality. *Psychological Review, 90,* 105–126.

Cantor, N., & Mischel, W. (1979). Prototypes in person perception. In L. Berkowitz (Ed.), *Advances in experimental social psychology* (Vol. 12, pp. 3–52). New York: Academic Press.

Collins, A. M., & Loftus, E. F. (1975). A spreading activation theory of semantic processing. *Psychological Review, 82,* 407–428.

Craik, F. I. M., & Tulving, E. (1975). Depth of processing and the retention of words in episodic memory. *Journal of Experimental Psychology: General, 104,* 268–294.

Greenwald, A. G. (1980). The totalitarian ego: Fabrication and revision of personal history. *American Psychologist, 35,* 603–618.

Groninger, L. D., & Groninger, L. K. 1984). Autobiographical memories: Their relation to images, definitions, and word recognition. *Journal of Experimental Psychology: Learning, Memory, and Cognition, 10,* 745–755.

Kihlstrom, J. F., & Cantor, N. (1984). Mental representations of the self. In L. Berkowitz (Ed.), *Advances in experimental social psychology* (Vol. 17, pp. 1–47). New York: Academic Press.

Klein, S. B., & Kihlstrom, J. F. (1986). Elaboration, organization, and the self-reference effect in memory. *Journal of Experimental Psychology: General, 115*, 26–38.

Mandler, G. (1979). Organization, memory, and mental structure. In C. R. Puff (Ed.), *Memory organization and structure* (pp. 303–319). New York: Academic Press.

Matlin, M. W. (1989). *Cognition* (2nd ed.). New York: Holt, Rinehart and Winston.

McClelland, J. L., & Rumelhart, D. E. (1985). Distributed memory and the representation of general and specific information. *Journal of Experimental Psychology: General, 114*, 159–188.

Medin, D. L., & Schaffer, M. M. (1978). Context theory of classification learning. *Psychological Review, 85*, 207–238.

Quillian, M. R. (1968). Semantic memory. In M. Minsky (Ed.), *Semantic information processing* (pp. 216–260). Cambridge, MA: MIT Press.

Reeder, G. D., McCormick, C. B., & Esselman, E. D. (1987). Self-referent processing and recall of prose. *Journal of Educational Psychology, 79*, 243–248.

Rogers, T. B., Kuiper, N. A., & Kirker, W. S. (1977). Self-reference effect and the encoding of personal information. *Journal of Personality and Social Psychology, 35*, 677–688.

Rosch, E. H., Mervis, C. B., Gray, W. E., Johnson, D. M., & Boyes-Braem, P. (1976). Basic objects in natural categories. *Cognitive Psychology, 8*, 382–439.

Smith, E. R., & Zarate, M. A. (1990). Exemplar and prototype use in social categorization. *Social Cognition, 8*, 243–262.

Tulving, E. (1989). Remembering and knowing. *American Scientist, 77*, 361–367.

Warren, M. W., Chattin, D., Thompson, D. D., & Tomsky, M. T. (1983). The effects of autobiographical elaboration on noun recall. *Memory & Cognition, 11*, 445–555.

Wickelgren, W. A. (1979). *Cognitive psychology.* Englewood Cliffs, NJ: Prentice-Hall.

3

Response Times, Retrieval Strategies, and the Investigation of Autobiographical Memory

Norman R. Brown
Carnegie Mellon University

Memorable personal events have many aspects. Inevitably these events involve some sort of action or activity performed at a specific location and time, during some more general life period. Such events are often carried out in pursuit of some goal and/or in response to some prior event, and are often accompanied by thoughts and emotions. In addition, these events may involve a variety of actors and objects, and they may be evaluated on a number of dimensions, both as they take place and in retrospect. In principle, any of these aspects (i.e., activity, location, period, participants, causes, effects, affects, goals, objects, reactions, evaluations) may be encoded in memory as part of one's knowledge of events, and any of them may serve to index events for retrieval. In practice, however, some aspects will typically be encoded, and others will not. Determining which aspects do play an important role in autobiographical memory is an empirical issue.

When psychologists study autobiographical memory, they tend to focus on one or two of aspects of the event and to neglect the others. The aspect that Klein and Loftus focus on in their target chapter, "The Mental Representation of Trait and Autobiographical Knowledge About the Self," is "self-trait knowledge." This is the knowledge one uses to judge whether trait terms such as *selfish*, *honest*, and *athletic* can be applied to one's own behavior. The authors contend that "long-term trait knowledge about the self is represented primarily in abstract, summary form, and that summary representations, not exemplars, are the basis of trait self-descriptiveness judgments" (p. 30). In addition, they argue against what might be called a *trait-centered* organization of autobiographical memory. As portrayed in their Fig. 1.8, a trait-centered organization is a simple hierarchy with "the summary trait representations . . . linked in memory to the behavioral exemplars from which they have been abstracted" (p. 30). In other words, it is assumed that memories for specific autobiographical events are generally associated with and indexed by knowledge of the personal trait(s) they exemplify.

In this chapter, I first review Klein and Loftus' reasons for rejecting a trait-centered organization and conclude that the evidence they present does not warrant the conclusion they reach. Having rejected Klein and Loftus' approach, I propose that absolute cuéd-retrieval times (as opposed to differential task-facilitation effects) and strategy-use data can be used to determine whether self-trait knowledge (or any other class of event-relevant information) typically serves to index personal events. In support of this proposal, I consider the processes people use to retrieve autobiographical memories and review a number of cued-retrieval studies. I conclude by describing an extended and modified version of the cued-retrieval task that has the potential of providing an empirically based ordering of event-relevant categories in terms of their organizational importance.

DIFFERENTIAL TASK FACILITATION AND THE REJECTION OF TRAIT-CENTERED EVENT MEMORY

Klein and Loftus' argument against a trait-centered organization is based on their failure to obtain differential task facilitation in the cued retrieval of trait-relevant autobiographical memories. In the cued-retrieval task, subjects were presented with a trait term and were required to "retrieve from memory a specific incident in which they manifested the stimulus trait" (p. 6). The authors found that the nature of task that preceded the cued-retrieval task did not influence the ease with which subjects recalled trait-relevant personal events; subjects retrieved events no faster after they had judged the self-descriptiveness of a trait term than after they sought a definition for it.

A very specific set of processing and representational assumptions were required to view this null result as a critical test of the hypothesis that personal events are organized in a trait-centered manner. The rejected organization is one in which (a) personal events are directly associated with self-trait knowledge, and (b) general knowledge of traits is associated with neither self-trait knowledge nor knowledge of trait-relevant personal events. Given this particular configuration of general and personal knowledge, trait-relevant autobiographical events should be "activated" when subjects make self-descriptiveness judgments, but not when they perform a purely semantic task. Hence, if personal events are represented in a trait-centered manner (and general trait knowledge "is not included in the self-knowledge network," p. 13), then trait-relevant personal events should be retrieved more rapidly following the descriptiveness task than following the semantic task. Because performance in Experiments 1 and 2 was inconsistent with this prediction, the authors argue that trait self-knowledge and knowledge of personal events are necessarily independent.

A crucial, but unmotivated, aspect of the preceding argument is the assumption that there are no links between knowledge of the meaning of a trait term and knowledge of the applicability of that trait to one's self. Indeed, this assumption seems rather implausible given that people must have access to the meaning of a trait term when they decide whether an action is representative of that trait. The development of summary trait knowledge would seem to require such a process, and the existence of such a process should foster associations between the general trait concept, trait self-knowledge, and trait-relevant exemplars. In contrast to Klein and Loftus' distinct-knowledge structures position, a position that recognizes the possibility of associations between all forms of trait-relevant information does not predict differential task facilitation. Rather, it predicts facilitation in cued retrieval regardless of whether this task is preceded by a semantic task or a descriptiveness task. Likewise, it predicts that prior completion of either the semantic task or the autobiographical task should facilitate performance on descriptiveness task, and that prior completion of either the descriptiveness task or the autobiographical task should facilitate performance on the semantic task.

Data relevant to two of these three predictions are available for Experiment 1 in a previous report (see Klein, Loftus, & Burton, 1989, Experiment 2). Both the cued-retrieval of autobiographical events and judgments of the self-descriptiveness of trait terms were performed most rapidly when they were preceded by other tasks. For the autobiographical task, mean response time was 5,486 ms when it was the initial task; 5,356 ms when it was preceded by the descriptiveness task; and 5,092 ms when it was preceded by the semantic task. Similarly, for the self-descriptiveness task, mean response time was 2,875 ms when it was the initial task; 2,303 ms when its was preceded by a semantic task; and 2,237 ms when it was preceded by an autobiographical task.

Of course, these data are not conclusive; the authors do not report whether the "primed" responses were significantly faster than the "unprimed" responses. More importantly, these comparisons confound task order with priming condition (i.e., the unprimed data always came from the initial task, and the primed data from the target task). A more appropriate design would include some form of "neutral" initial task; this would allow for a direct comparison between primed and unprimed performance on the target task. Despite these problems, this pattern of results suggests that it may be too soon to conclude that self-trait knowledge, general trait knowledge, and knowledge of trait-relevant events are necessarily independent.

CUED RETRIEVAL OF AUTOBIOGRAPHICAL EVENTS

In the rest of this chapter, I argue that absolute response times in conjunction with an assessment of subjects' retrieval strategies can be used to determine, at least roughly, whether concepts from a particular category play an important role in organizing of autobiographical events in memory. In order to make this argument two things are required: first, a way of specifying what it means for a category to be organizationally important; second, an understanding of the temporal and strategic character of the cued-retrieval task. In response to the first requirement, I assume that a category plays an important organizational role when the concepts in that category are typically associated with personal events. This definition leaves open the possibility that many categories may play a role in organizing autobiographical memory. It also acknowledges that organizational importance is a matter of degree.

In response to the second requirement, it is necessary to distinguish between the *direct* retrieval of personal events and retrieval requiring some form of *mediation*. This distinction has long been recognized in the mainstream memory literature (e.g., Brown & McNeill, 1966; Camp, Lachman, & Lachman, 1980) and among psychologists interested in real-world memory phenomena (e.g., Norman & Bobrow, 1979; Williams & Hollan, 1981). Direct retrieval is just what it says; a cue directly evokes a memory, and this memory is evaluated and found to meet the task requirements. When a cue fails to evoke a specific memory or evokes a memory that does not satisfy the task demands, the retrieval process must either terminate or reformulate the initial cue. Reformulating a cue may involve refining it, redefining it, and/or augmenting it. When the task is to retrieve an autobiographical memory possessing specific features, reformulation can take on a problem-solving flavor, with people drawing on general knowledge and knowledge of their lives and habits to generate a new cue or set of cues (Reiser, Black, & Kalamarides, 1986). Moreover, when the features of the sought after event are uncommon or obscure, a successful search may require subjects to reformulate and test the cue(s) many times before an acceptable memory is retrieved (Norman & Bobrow, 1979; Williams & Hollan, 1981).

The important point here is that responses based on direct retrieval should be faster than those requiring mediation. Although this conclusion seems quite straightforward, there is as yet no direct support for it. There is, however, evidence indicating that conditions that produce the most rapid response times also yield the smallest percentage of mediated responses. Reiser has reported two experiments that speak to this issue. In one (Reiser, Black, & Abelson, 1985, Experiment 2), response times were collected from subjects as they attempted to retrieve personal events matching "event descriptions." In another (Reiser et al., 1986), verbal protocols were collected as a different set of subjects performed the same task. The protocols were examined for the presence of "retrieval strategies," which, in the current context, can be taken as evidence for mediated retrieval. Consistent with the preceding analysis, the condition that led to the fastest response times in one experiment was the one that produced the fewest mediated responses in the other. Specifically, in both experiments subjects were most facile with cues describing common "activities" (e.g., "had a hair cut," "went to a museum"). In the protocol study, only 38% of the responses to these cues required subjects to resort to some sort of retrieval strategy; in the response time study, the average time to retrieve an event given an activity cue was only 2.1 seconds (excluding reading time).

In order to make the connection between response times, retrieval strategies, and the organizational importance of categories, it is necessary to assume that direct retrieval occurs when there is a direct link between a personal event and the concept specified by a cue, and that, otherwise, some form of mediated retrieval is required. It follows from this that both average retrieval times and the percentage of direct retrievals should provide indices of a category's organizational importance. When a category plays an important role in organizing autobiographical events, many of its concepts will be directly linked to personal events. Hence, cuing memory with words or concepts drawn from such a category will frequently result in the rapid direct retrieval of personal memories and will only occasionally require subjects to make use of slower mediated retrieval strategies. This implies that response times averaged over this set of cues should be quite fast. In contrast, when a category plays little or no role in organizing autobiographical events, its subordinate concepts will rarely be directly linked to personal events. Responses to cues drawn from such categories will frequently require mediation. As a result, average response time should be quite slow, reflecting a mixture of many slow mediated retrievals and, at most, a few fast direct ones.

USING CUED RETRIEVAL TO EXPLORE
AUTOBIOGRAPHICAL MEMORY

The preceding analysis implies that response time data reported in previously published cued-retrieval studies might yield an ordering of categories in terms of their organizational importance, or at least a starting point for such an ordering. Unfortunately, it turns out to be very difficult to compare retrieval times obtained in one laboratory with those obtained in others. For example, Robinson (1976), Larsen and Plunkett (1987), and Conway and Bekerian (1987) all used object terms (e.g., *letter, book, flower*) and emotion terms (e.g., *happy, surprised, lonely*) as stimulus items in cued-retrieval studies. In all three studies, subjects responded more rapidly to the object terms than to the emotion terms. Despite the replicability of this "category effect," there were large between-experiment differences in overall retrieval times. In the Conway and Bekerian study (1987, Experiment 1), the mean response time for object terms was 2.8 seconds and the mean response time for emotion terms was 3.6 seconds. The equivalent means were 6.1 seconds and 8.3 seconds in the Larsen and Plunkett (1987) study, and 10.5 seconds and 14.0 seconds in the Robinson (1976) study.

Note, Conway and Bekerian's subjects responded faster to emotion terms than

Larsen and Plunkett's subjects responded to object terms, and Larsen and Plunkett's subjects responded faster to emotion terms than Robinson's subjects responded to object terms. Given such results, what can one conclude from Klein and Loftus' finding that subjects required about 5.5 seconds to retrieve a personal event in response to a trait term? One might conclude that trait concepts are less important than emotions in organizing autobiographical memory. This would follow if one were to compare the Klein and Loftus data to the data reported by Conway and Bekerian. Or, if one used the results published by Robinson (1976) or Larsen and Plunkett (1987) as the standard of comparison, one might conclude that trait concepts are organizationally more important than object conceptions.

Regardless of their origins, these large between-experiment differences make it unlikely that a coherent understanding of the organization of autobiographical memory will emerge simply by collating results from many unrelated cued-retrieval studies. This is not to say that the cued-retrieval methodology could not be extended and applied more systematically to address organizational issues. Indeed, I believe that this method, appropriately modified, may provide a platform for the development of an empirical model of autobiographical memory.

The modifications I have in mind concern both the way in which cued-retrieval experiments are designed and the way in which they are conducted. In the typical cued-retrieval experiment, subjects are presented with cues that have been selected from a small number of categories in a rather haphazard manner. Limiting the number of categories used and leaving cue selection to chance constrains both the type of between-category comparisons that can be made and the validity of the generalizations based on the comparisons that are made. These problems can be overcome by designing experiments that included stimuli from all (or a large subset) potentially relevant categories (e.g., activities, friends and family, locations, time periods, emotions, traits, important events, etc.), and by adopting a sensible and consistent criterion for cue selection. For example, one might select only those cues that refer to concepts that subjects have a good deal of direct experience with. For some categories (e.g., activities), norms may be useful in identifying appropriate cues; for others (e.g., friends and family), cue selection may have to be tailored for the individual subject.

In addition to widening the range of stimuli subjects are exposed to, I believe that both response times and strategy-use data should be collected on all trials. In order to do this, the standard cued-retrieval method could be modified so that subjects report their retrieval strategies immediately after they indicate that they have recalled an appropriate memory. Specifically, on each trial, subjects would be presented with a cue and would press a button as soon as they recall a personal event related to it. Following the button press, subject would be required to report (verbally or through select of an option listed on a computer display) the strategy or strategies used to retrieve the recalled event. (See Siegler, 1987, for a demonstration of the way that response times and retrospective strategy-use reports can be coordinated.)

Data collected in an appropriately extended cued-retrieval study can be used to order the stimulus categories in terms of their organizational importance: For organizationally important categories, response times should be fast and percent direct retrievals high; for organizationally unimportant categories, response times should be slow and percent direct retrievals low. These data also will allow researchers to analyze response times conditional on strategy use. In particular, it will be interesting to determine whether mediated responses take the same amount of time regardless of category, or whether mediated responses are typically longer for cues drawn from some categories than from others. If mediated responses are equally fast across categories, then response times and percent of direct retrieval can be treated as equivalent measures of organizational importance. However, if they are not, the interpretation of average response time becomes an issue. The problem here is that identical average response times may be produced by different mixtures of direct and mediated retrievals. For example, a given response time may reflect a combination of many fast direct responses and a few very slow mediated responses, or it may reflect a combination of a few fast direct responses and many not-so-slow mediated responses. Given a situation of this sort, it would make sense to treat percent direct retrievals as the dependent measure of primary interest.

To summarize, I believe that the cued-retrieval task can be used to explore the organization of autobiographical memory in a systematic manner. To this end, a large set of potentially relevant categories will have to be identified and methods for cue selection devised. In the experiment itself, subjects should be exposed to cues from all of the potentially relevant categories, and both response times and strategy reports should be collected. Depending on the between-category analysis of mediated response times, either percent direct retrievals alone or percent direct retrievals and average response time can be used to order the categories in terms of their relative organizational importance.

The ordering of stimulus categories should provide the empirical basis for concluding that concepts such as trait terms either do or do not play an important role in organizing autobiographical events. My intuition is that such an analysis would provide evidence that both supports and refutes conclusions reached by Klein and Loftus. On the positive side, I suspect that responses to trait terms will frequently be mediated. This would imply that traits terms are not typically associated personal events and would be consistent with the conclusion that autobiographical memory is not trait-centered. I also suspect that trait cues will occasionally directly evoke a personal memory. This would imply that trait concepts are occasionally associated personal events and would be inconsistent with the conclusion that self-trait knowledge and knowledge of trait-relevant events are necessarily independent. As I said, these are intuitions; they await an empirical test.

ACKNOWLEDGMENTS

This work was supported by a grant from the A. W. Mellon Foundation. I thank Fred Conrad for his comments.

REFERENCES

Brown, R., & McNeill, D. (1966). The "tip-of-the-tongue" phenomenon. *Journal of Verbal Learning and Verbal Behavior, 5,* 325–337.

Camp, C. J., Lachman, J. L., & Lachman, R. (1980). Evidence for direct-access and inferential retrieval in question-answering. *Journal of Verbal Learning and Verbal Behavior, 19,* 583–596.

Conway, M. A., & Bekerian, D. A. (1987). Organization in autobiographical memory. *Memory & Cognition, 15,* 119–132.

Klein, S. B., Loftus, J., & Burton, H. A. (1989). Two self-reference effects: The importance of distinguishing between self-descriptiveness judgments and autobiographical retrieval in self-referent encoding. *Journal of Personality and Social Psychology, 56,* 853–865.

Larsen, S. F., & Plunkett, K. (1987). Remembering experienced and reported events. *Applied Cognitive Psychology, 1,* 15–26.

Norman, D. A., & Bobrow, D. G. (1979). Descriptions: An intermediate stage in memory retrieval. *Cognitive Psychology, 11,* 107–123.

Reiser, B. J., Black, J. B., & Abelson, R. P. (1985). Knowledge structures in the organization and retrieval of autobiographical memory. *Cognitive Psychology, 17,* 89–137.

Reiser, B. J., Black, J. B., & Kalamarides, P. (1986). Strategic memory search processes. In D. Rubin (Ed.), *Autobiographical memory* (pp. 100–121). New York: Cambridge University Press.

Robinson, J. A. (1976). Sampling autobiographical memory. *Cognitive Psychology, 8,* 578–595.

Siegler, R. S. (1987). The perils of averaging data over strategies: An example from children's addition. *Journal of Experimental Psychology: General, 116,* 250–264.

Williams, M. D., & Hollan, J. D. (1981). The process of retrieval from very-long term memory. *Cognitive Science, 5,* 87–119.

4

An Exemplar Model Can Explain Klein and Loftus' Results

Janice M. Keenan
University of Denver

Not too long ago, many of us could feel comfortable discussing a range of paradigms and theories within broad domains such as social psychology or cognitive psychology. But with the explosion of scientific research in recent years, we now feel lucky if we can keep up with all the theories and paradigms in fairly narrow areas of specialization, like word identification or hindsight. Thus, it is impressive to see people like Klein and Loftus who not only have a broad knowledge of social psychology, but who are equally conversant with the literature on cognitive psychology. Their breadth of knowledge has served them well for it has allowed them to take some of the most promising paradigms and models from cognitive psychology and apply them to social phenomena that are often more relevant than the verbal learning phenomena (such as paired associate learning) for which these paradigms and models were initially developed. The result is that Klein and Loftus have produced some of the most interesting findings in recent years concerning how information about the self is represented and processed.

The findings presented in the target chapter are some of their most intriguing because they run counter to the common assumptions about how trait descriptiveness judgments are made. As Klein and Loftus note, it is commonly assumed that specific behavioral exemplars play at least some role in decisions about whether traits are self-descriptive, if they are not also the primary basis for these decisions. Thus, we would expect that having just recalled an event in which you displayed "intelligence" would allow you to respond to the question "Are you intelligent" faster than if you had just generated a definition of "intelligence." But Klein and Loftus showed in Experiments 1 and 2 that this is not the case. Recalling a behavioral incident related to your own intelligence does not speed your judgment of the self-descriptiveness of intelligence; and judging the self-descriptiveness of intelligence does not speed the retrieval of an incident from autobiographical memory. On the basis of these data, Klein and Loftus conclude that judgments about the self-descriptiveness of trait adjectives are made without reference to behavioral evidence; in other words, traits and behaviors are functionally independent.

Klein and Loftus interpret their data as evidence against an exemplar model of self-descriptiveness judgments and as support for what they call the "mixed model." This model states that the more trait-relevant experience one has for a person, the more likely one is to create a trait representation for that person; and if a trait is available, a trait judgment will be based on the trait, not the trait-relevant experiences.

One of my goals in writing this chapter is to question the plausibility of this mixed model and its central assumption—the functional independence of behaviors and traits. Although it provides an intuitively appealing account of the present data, it is difficult to reconcile with certain findings in the literature. In particular, the assumption of independence between behaviors and traits is completely contrary to the assumptions required to account for one of the most well-established findings involving self-descriptive trait judgments, namely the self-reference effect in memory. As I show here, the mixed model actually predicts a pattern of results that is quite different than what is observed in self-reference studies.

Another goal of this chapter is to show that Klein and Loftus' model is not the only account of their data. In fact, I show that the exemplar model, which they dismissed on the basis of their data, can easily account for their data. Furthermore, the exemplar model is more parsimonious because it uses the same single process to account for all the data.

Before discussing the self-reference data and explaining how an exemplar model can account for Klein and Loftus' data, I wish to first raise a more minor question of interpretation. Is it legitimate to assume, as Klein and Loftus do, that the definitions task did not involve autobiographical information? This question is important because the finding of lack of facilitation from autobiographical retrieval to self-descriptiveness judgments and vice versa is always defined relative to the amount of facilitation obtained from the definitions task.

DOES GENERATING DEFINITIONS INVOLVE AUTOBIOGRAPHICAL INFORMATION?

Klein and Loftus always define the absence of facilitation from descriptiveness to autobiographical tasks relative to the semantic task of generating definitions of trait terms. Thus, their conclusion that "descriptiveness judgments neither require nor are influenced by autobiographical information" (p. 15) is going beyond the data. The appropriate conclusion is that descriptiveness judgments do not include any more autobiographical information than providing a definition.

Klein and Loftus assume that generating definitions does not involve autobiographical information. However, it is quite plausible that in generating definitions subjects do look to their own behaviors. For example, they may think, "*kind* is like when I take care of the neighbor's cat, so *kind* means helping out your neighbors when they need it." If subjects indeed generated definitions in such a self-referring way, then definitions could involve behavioral incidents just like autobiographical retrieval. In that case, the finding that autobiographical retrieval does not lead to any more facilitation on self-descriptiveness judgments than generating a definition would not be at all surprising. Furthermore, it would not imply anything about the functional independence of traits and behaviors. It would simply mean that both the definition task and the recall task involved retrieving information that overlapped about equally with the information retrieved in the self-descriptiveness judgments.

Klein and Loftus argue that subjects are not using their own behaviors in generating definitions because there was no effect of self-descriptiveness of the traits on the time it took to define them. This is a reasonable argument, but not fully convincing. The reason is that it depends on accepting the null hypothesis.

What is needed is to show that the same results can be obtained with another control task, especially one that would not so easily lend itself to the criticism that autobiographical information could have been involved. For the remainder of this chapter we assume that Klein and Loftus are correct that the definitions did not involve autobiographical information. However, we should not forget that this is still a debatable issue.

PROBLEMS THAT THE SELF-REFERENCE EFFECT PRESENTS FOR KLEIN AND LOFTUS' MODEL

The self-reference effect (SRE) refers to the fact that information and events tend to be remembered best when they are encoded with respect to the self. There are two types of self-reference memory studies. There are those that compare self-reference to other types of encoding tasks. For example, a self-reference task like judging the self-descriptiveness of traits might be compared to an encoding task that does not involve the self, such as judging whether the trait means the same thing as some other word. Such studies often find that the self-reference task leads to better performance on an incidental memory test for the traits (e.g., Rogers, Kuiper, & Kirker 1977). Self-reference has also been studied in comparison to encodings involving other people. These studies also show that traits are remembered better when the encoding involves self-reference (e.g., Keenan & Baillet, 1980). We focus our discussion here on the self-reference versus other-reference studies, because only in these studies can the memory results be unambiguously interpreted as due to the involvement of the self (cf. Keenan, Golding, & Brown, 1992).

One of the most common explanations of the SRE is in terms of the amount of elaboration target words receive during encoding. It is well-known that the more elaborate an encoding, the more easily it can be retrieved (Anderson & Reder, 1979; Craik & Tulving, 1975). The better retrieval of self-reference items is thus attributed to the fact that they get elaborated more during encoding than other-reference items. Why do they get elaborated more? It is assumed that when a trait word, such as "kind," is judged with respect to the self, there is more information available in memory to bear on the judgment than when it is judged with respect to another person. It is further assumed that this difference in the amount of available information in memory is reflected in the information used to make the judgment. So, more information gets used in the judgment of "kind" with respect to the self than with respect to another person. The result is that "kind" is more elaborated and thus more memorable following a self-reference judgment than an other-reference judgment.

If amount of elaboration is responsible for the SRE, and if amount of elaboration depends on the amount of information available, then you would expect that the less you know about a person, the less elaborate the encoding of a trait judged with respect to that person would be and thus the less memorable it would be. That is exactly what happens. Keenan and Baillet (1980) had subjects judge traits with respect to either themselves or six other people; the people represented a range of how much the subject was expected to know about them, with best friend at the high end and Jimmy Carter (who was president at the time of the study) representing the low end. Keenan and Baillet found that memory was a monotonically increasing function of the amount known about the person.

To further support the view that elaboration is the critical factor underlying the memory results, Keenan and Baillet showed that the same memory function occurred for another type of judgment—judgments about whether certain objects, like a museum, could be found in various cities. Subjects made these judgments with regard to four cities that varied in how much each subject knew about them. Again, memory was a monotonically increasing function of the amount known about the city. So, *museum* was remembered best when it was judged with respect to the city that the subject was most familiar with. But as knowledge about a city declined, and hence the potential for elaboration declined, *museum* was less well remembered.

The mixed model that Klein and Loftus propose for how trait judgments are made cannot readily accommodate these data. In fact, it seems to make predictions that are quite different from the data. The problem is that they assume that behaviors are not involved in trait judgments of the self (except under unusual circumstances, like Experiments 5 and 6). But by eliminating the role of behaviors in trait judgments, they eliminate the basis for claiming that self encodings are more elaborate than other-reference encodings.

According to Klein and Loftus, judging whether a trait is self-descriptive involves comparing the target trait to a trait representation of the self. Consequently, the target word gets elaborated only by the trait. The rich set of behaviors that support the trait description do not get activated, and hence cannot elaborate the memory representation of the trait term.

On the other hand, when judging a trait with respect to some other person, such as when judging a medium mother-descriptiveness trait, behaviors would be evaluated because trait information is not available. This leads to a more elaborate representation of the trait for mother than for self. And this would result in a reversal of the SRE (i.e., poorer memory of the trait following self-reference than other-reference). A prediction that runs counter to the data; self-reference always leads to better memory than other-reference in the trait judgment task.

In fact, the mixed model seems to predict an inverted U-shaped function relating amount known to elaboration and hence memory. For high levels of knowledge (the self and for well-known others on highly descriptive traits), traits would be available for the judgment, so the target would get very little elaboration, only that provided by the trait. For medium levels of knowledge, there would be no trait, so behaviors would be used; and because this is a medium level of knowledge, there would be plenty behaviors with which to elaborate the target. Hence, medium levels of knowledge would lead to more elaboration than high levels of knowledge because the set of behaviors used to make the judgment represent more information than the trait used to make the judgment for high levels of knowledge. For low levels of knowledge, there would again be no trait, but there would also be very few behaviors; consequently, targets encoded with respect to low-knowledge people would get very little elaboration, much like the high level. Thus, we have an inverted U-shaped function.

As we have seen, the data relating amount known to memory do not give any evidence of an inverted U-shaped function. Instead, they show a monotonically increasing function. Given that Keenan and Baillet (1980) examined the function over as many as seven levels of knowledge, it would seem that if there was an inverted U-shaped function there, they would have detected it.

In summary, Klein and Loftus' model, in which trait judgments about the self are made without activating any behaviors, is difficult to reconcile with the self-versus other-reference memory effect and the fact that memory for a trait is a monotonically increasing function of the amount known about the person referenced by the trait judgment. By eliminating the role of behaviors in self-descriptiveness judgments, the model eliminates the basis for self-encodings being more elaborate and hence more memorable. Furthermore, it predicts an inverted U-shaped function relating memory and knowledge that is not at all supported by the data. Of course, Klein and Loftus could dispute the U-shaped function prediction. Perhaps they would want to claim that traits are more memorable when they have been encoded with respect to traits (as in self-reference judgments) than with respect to behaviors. But that would not really constitute an explanation; it would simply be restating the data.

AN EXEMPLAR MODEL EXPLANATION OF KLEIN AND LOFTUS' RESULTS

The basic findings that Klein and Loftus' mixed model is trying to account for are: (a) when judgments involve the self (or mother on highly descriptive traits), there is no facilitation between autobiographical retrieval and trait judgments, and (b) when judgments involve others, there is facilitation. In order to produce these two different patterns of facilitation, they assume that there are two different processes underlying the trait judgment task. One process, the use of traits, produces no facilitation; the other process, the use of behaviors, does produce facilitation.

What I wish to point out is that it is not necessary to assume that if you have two different patterns of facilitation, then there must be two different types of processing underlying them. In fact, the same process can produce facilitation or no facilitation depending on other factors.

What I propose as the critical factor determining the occurrence of facilitation between trait judgments and behavior retrieval is the number of behaviors activated by the trait judgment. This factor is important because it determines the proportion of overlap between the retrieval task and the trait judgment task. It is this amount of overlap that determines the amount of facilitation between the two tasks.

The model I propose is an exemplar model. In other words, it assumes that trait judgments (no matter if they are about the self or others) always involve activating behaviors, even when trait information is available. It assumes that trait judgments involve activating all or most of the behaviors available, whereas the behavior retrieval task involves activating only one or some small number of them (because the instructions request that the subject recall just one incident). Finally, it assumes that the extent to which the retrieval task will facilitate trait judgment is a function of the proportion of overlap in activated behaviors between the two tasks.

To see how this behavior overlap model can account for Klein and Loftus' results, let us first examine the case where the behavior retrieval task precedes the trait judgment task. Why does behavior retrieval produce no facilitation on trait judgment when there is high familiarity (self or mother with high-descriptive traits)? The reason is that there is very little overlap in the activated behaviors between the two tasks. The proportion of overlap is the ratio of number of behaviors activated in retrieval to number of behaviors activated in the trait judgment task; in other words, "1/huge N." In contrast, when the task involves a less familiar other, the proportion of overlap between activated behaviors is much greater, "1/smaller N," so there will be more facilitation.

Now consider the case where trait judgment precedes the behavior retrieval task. Trait judgments activate the set of available behaviors. When many behaviors are available, as for the self or significant others on familiar traits, then the amount of activation received by any particular behavior is too small to raise it above the threshold needed for the conscious retrieval required by the behavior retrieval task. The result is no facilitation between the tasks. When only a small number of behaviors are available, however, as would be the case for less familiar others, then it is more likely that one of these behaviors would get sufficiently activated to exceed the threshold. Thus, there would be facilitation from the trait judgment task on the retrieval task.

The exemplar model I propose can also account for Klein and Loftus' findings in Experiments 5 and 6. In these experiments, subjects were asked to base their trait judgments and behavior retrievals on either the time since they were in college or the time when they were in high school. Klein and Loftus found that when the tasks referred to the high school years, there was again no facilitation between retrieval and trait judgment. However, when the task referred to the couple of months of college, there was significant facilitation. Frankly, I was quite surprised to see that trait judgments would be influenced by this manipulation, because I think of traits as more enduring than such context effects would suggest. Nonetheless, this finding is easily explained by the amount of overlap in the exemplar model.

According to the model, the high school versus college manipulation is affecting the size of the database activated in the trait judgment task. In other words, it is affecting the size of the denominator in the proportion of overlap. The high school years involves a much larger set of behaviors than the couple of months of college. Consequently, the proportion of overlap between retrieval and trait judgment is "1/large N" for high school, whereas it is only "1/small N" for the college time.

COMPARING THE MIXED MODEL AND THE EXEMPLAR MODEL

The exemplar model I have described can account for all the same data as Klein and Loftus' model can explain. So, are there any grounds on which to prefer one model over the other?

As I see it, the principle reason to prefer the exemplar model over Klein and Loftus' mixed model is that it uses just one process for trait judgments to account for the different patterns of facilitation. This means it is more parsimonious. All other things being equal, the more parsimonious model is to be preferred.

More important than parsimony, however, is the fact that by using one process, the exemplar model predicts a continuum of facilitation depending on the proportion of overlap, whereas Klein and Loftus' model predicts a dichotomy—either facilitation or no facilitation. It is my impression that the data are far more amenable to a continuum of facilitation than a dichotomous split of all or none facilitation. To illustrate, look at the data in Klein and Loftus' Fig. 1.6. These are the latencies for the Describes Mother and Remember Mother tasks. For both tasks, there is the same pattern of facilitation across high-, medium-, and low-descriptive traits; however, the difference is smaller, and presumably not significant, for high-descriptive traits. Although such gradations in facilitation are to be expected with the exemplar model, they are hard to handle in the mixed model. So, Klein and Loftus are forced to choose whether the nonsignificant facilitation for the high-descriptive mother traits should be called facilitation or no facilitation. They decide to consider it no facilitation and thus lump it with the self-data. They state: "we found no evidence of facilitation for judgments about traits rated 'high' in mother-descriptiveness, which suggests that these judgments were accomplished by accessing abstract trait knowledge about mother in memory. For judgments about traits rated 'medium' or 'low' in mother-descriptiveness, however, we found considerable facilitation, from which we infer that these judgments were computed from a consideration of trait-relevant behavioral memories about mother" (p. 22). But as Fig. 1.6 shows, the data do not exhibit the dichotomy that Klein and Loftus impose on them.

Another reason for preferring the exemplar model is that it can handle the self-versus other-reference effect in memory. Because it assumes that behaviors are activated in trait judgments, traits judged with respect to the self get more elaborated than traits judged with respect to other people and thus are more memorable.

In conclusion, Klein and Loftus' mixed model presents an intuitively appealing account of their data. However, it's assumption that behaviors are not used in trait judgments about the self means that the model cannot account for one of the most robust findings in trait judgment research, the self-reference versus other-reference effect. Furthermore, the mixed model predicts that facilitation is all or none, whereas Klein and Loftus' data suggest that there is a continuum of facilitation. Fortunately, Klein and Loftus' model is not the only possible explanation of their data. The exemplar model I described can account for all the same data, is more parsimonious, and is compatible with the continuum of facilitation suggested by their data.

ACKNOWLEDGMENTS

I thank George Potts and the other members of the Cognitive Research Group at the University of Denver for lending me their ears and their comments regarding the ideas expressed in this chapter.

REFERENCES

Anderson, J. R., & Reder, L. M. (1979). An elaborative processing explanation of depth of processing. In L. S. Cermak & F. I. M. Craik (Eds.), *Levels of processing in human memory* (pp. 385–404). Hillsdale, NJ: Lawrence Erlbaum Associates.

Craik, F. I. M., & Tulving, E. (1975). Depth of processing and the retention of words in episodic memory. *Journal of Experimental Psychology: General, 104,* 268–294.

Keenan, J. M., & Baillet, S. D. (1980). Memory for personally and socially significant events. In R. S. Nickerson (Ed.), *Attention and performance* (Vol. 8, pp. 651–669). Hillsdale, NJ: Lawrence Erlbaum Associates.

Keenan, J. M., Golding, J. M., & Brown, P. (1992). Factors controlling the advantage of self-reference over other-reference. *Social Cognition, 10,* 79–94.

Rogers, T. B., Kuiper, N. A., & Kirker, W. S. (1977). Self-reference and the encoding of personal information. *Journal of Personality and Social Psychology, 35,* 677–688.

5 What Does the Self Look Like?

John F. Kihlstrom
University of Arizona

Cogitive psychology asks questions about how information is acquired, stored, and used to guide adaptive behavior: Primarily, it studies the representation and processing of knowledge. Social cognition asks these questions about social objects and events: ourselves, other people, the situations in which we encounter them, and the behavior that transpires between us. In their chapter, Klein and Loftus are especially concerned with the mental representation of a social entity that is particularly close to us: ourselves.

In a pair of papers, Cantor and I defined the self as the mental representation of one's own personality (Kihlstrom & Cantor, 1984; Kihlstrom et al., 1988; see also Cantor & Kihlstrom, 1987). From a structural point of view, we construed the self as either a feature list or a propositional network. That is, the self consisted of a summary of the personality features and attributes characteristic of oneself; or, alternatively, the self was a node linked to a web of factual statements about one's characteristics, behaviors, and experiences. However, consideration of the various forms that mental representation can take suggests that our definition, although in the right ballpark, was perhaps too narrow. From a cognitive point of view, it now appears that the self is nothing less than one's mental representation of *one's self,* including one's personality but going far beyond. Let me explain.

ALTERNATIVE MODES OF MENTAL REPRESENTATION

In an influential discussion, Anderson (1983, 1990) described two different major types of representation, perception-based and meaning-based, each with two subtypes. Perception-based representations store one's knowledge of the perceptual structure of objects and events, and come in two forms: spatial images and linear orderings. Spatial images encode information about the configuration, or relative position of an array of features or objects: up/down, left/right, front/back, and the like. But they are not *visual* images, although neuropsychological evidence suggests that knowledge can be represented in this form as well (Farah, Hammond, Levine, & Calvanio, 1988). This finding, in turn, suggests that there may be other forms of analog representation, corresponding to other sensory/perceptual modalities—for example, olfactory, gustatory, tactile, and kinesthetic images. Linear orderings, by contrast, encode information about the progression, sequential order, or temporal succession, of events: first/last, before/after/inbetween, and the like.

Meaning-based representations are more abstract than perception-based representations, and encode information about the semantic relations among objects and events. They too come in two forms: verbal propositions stating the relation between two arguments, such as *subject–verb–object* relations; and schemata, organized knowledge structures that contain slots for various attributes of a category, and typical values for these attributes. Propositions represent specific objects and events (e.g., *John's house was made of wood and stucco*), whereas schemata represent general categories of objects and events (e.g., *Houses are types of buildings, sometimes made of wood and stucco but sometimes made of brick, and rarely made of straw*).

For the most part, Cantor and I had meaning-based propositions in mind when we discussed the self. We had the idea that the self, as a memory structure, consists of declarative statements such as *SELF likes Stravinsky* and *SELF is kind* and *SELF helped an old man across the street on Monday* (Kihlstrom & Cantor, 1984, Figure 4). A good example of this point of view is the associative network model of person memory proposed by Hastie (1980, 1981, 1988) and Srull (1981), which in turn is based on a forerunner of Anderson's (1983) ACT* model of memory known as HAM (Anderson & Hastie, 1974). Hastie proposed that social memory is organized by persons who are represented as single nodes in a larger associative network (see also Kihlstrom & Hastie, in press). These nodes are then linked to other nodes that represent behaviors that the person has displayed, events in which the person has participated, and attributes that the person possesses. The self, then, is one of these nodes—perhaps richer than the others, because of the sheer amount of knowledge we possess about ourselves, compared to even our most intimate acquaintances; but not qualitatively different from a representation of knowledge about other people.

THE WORK AT HAND

This general point of view also appears to guide the work of Klein and Loftus, and in fact their specific proposal—a dual exemplar/summary view that includes both abstract knowledge about general attributes and concrete knowledge about specific behaviors and experiences—closely resembles the Hastie–Srull proposal. One important difference is that models of person memory are usually tested by having the subject memorize facts, or form impressions, concerning artificial people—synthetic concoctions of the experimenter designed to satisfy the requirements of careful experimental control, but not resembling anybody the subject knows. In such a task, the subjects must rely on a small set of resources: the architecture of cognition, and of memory in particular; and their abstract knowledge about people in general, of trait-behavior relationships, and the relationships among traits.

The experimenter's situation is quite different when it comes to the self, because subjects do not come into the experiment cold. They appear at the laboratory door with a substantial fund of knowledge (or, at least, beliefs) about the self—information that is not, in principle, amenable to rigorous experimental control. Thus, it is not possible to present subjects with a set of items, and have them accept them as self-descriptive, just as they would accept them as descriptive of some other person. Moreover, subjects do not possess only a single memory structure representing their self-concept. They also own an ideal self, representing their goals and aspirations for themselves, and an "ought" self, representing others' hopes and ambitions for them (Higgins, 1987). Given the pressures to maintain self-esteem and a positive self-presentation, it is never completely clear which self is serving as the basis for the subject's response to the experimental task. And finally, subjects have an investment in themselves that is lacking in the artificial targets of the typical person-memory experiment. Thus, emotional and motivational factors come into play, and may muddy the picture considerably. In short, the instant one turns to the self, one loses a great deal of precious experimental control.

Klein and Loftus attempt to get around these problems by employing an alternative set of experimental procedures. Instead of asking subjects to form impressions and remember behaviors, the canonical tasks of the person-memory literature, they ask subjects to make judgments about themselves. In principle, this sort of task (e.g., *Are you EXTRAVERTED?*) is no different from that involved in studies of lexical access (e.g., *Is PLAUDIT a word?*) or category verification (e.g., *Is a CHICKEN a bird?*). In all three cases, the experimental task is designed to get at the structure of preexisting knowledge. Moreover, Klein and Loftus make good use of priming techniques (Meyer & Schvaneveldt, 1971; Ratcliff & McKoon, 1981), to see whether knowledge activated in one task influences performance on a subsequent task. In their basic experiment, subjects are presented with a trait word, and asked to perform one of three tasks: to indicate whether the word is self-descriptive (Describe), to retrieve and auto-biographical memory related to the word (Remember), or to supply the semantic, denotative meaning of the word (Define). Then they are asked to perform another task on the same word: This task is either the same or different from the first one. In general, they found that the autobiographical memory task did not prime performance on the self-descriptive task, nor did the self-descriptive task prime performance on the autobiographical memory task.

These results indicate that subjects do not search through autobiographical memory in the course of making judgments about themselves; nor do they access abstract self-knowledge in the course of retrieving autobiographical memories. These results, in turn, support the conclusion that autobiographical and trait information is encoded, and retrieved, independently in memory—an inference that is bolstered by a wealth of collateral evidence involving encoding specificity and encoding variability. Klein and Loftus consider their results to be inconsistent with conventional associative network models of self-structure, but this is so only for that subclass of models that assumes that nodes representing traits are interposed between nodes representing the people who possess them and others representing the behaviors exemplifying them. In fact, their conclusions are quite congruent with the associative network models of person memory offered by Hastie (1981, 1988) and Srull (1981), in which trait and behavioral information are encoded independently.

THE ROLE OF ORGANIZATION

Still, the memory structure representing the self is a very rich one, containing a vast amount of information, and it would be strange if there weren't some organization to the structure. One of the earliest discoveries leading to the development of cognitive psychology was of organization in free recall: associative clustering, category clustering, and subjective organization. This shows that perceivers have imposed some structure on their experiences, so that the mental representation of a set of events does not simply mirror the way those events occurred in the world. Items that have some preexisting associative or conceptual relationship tend to be recalled together, regardless of whether they appeared in adjacent positions during presentation; and even if the experimenter goes to great lengths to create lists of ostensibly unrelated items, subjects will impose some narrative or imagistic structure on the list.

Obviously, organizational recoding of this sort is an adaptive feature of large knowledge structures, because it permits easy access to information. And just as the sorts of items that appear in word lists may be organized by conceptual category, it makes sense that social information be organized as well. If so, traits would seem to be a prime candidate for an appropriate organizational rubric: Neurotic behaviors would fan out from a node representing neuroticism, whereas conscientious behaviors would fan out from another node representing conscientiousness. In the same fashion, traits themselves would be organized by higher order traits: Qualities like talkative and frank would fan out from a node representing extraversion, whereas qualities like gentle and cooperative would fan out from another node representing agreeableness. It is a rational way to build a memory.

The paradox is that this sort of organization is hard to detect (Smith & Kihlstrom, 1987). Klein and Loftus show clearly that memory search does not pass through subjects' traits on its way to their behaviors. And unpublished research in my laboratory by Jeanne Sumi Albright (for a brief description see Kihlstrom et al., 1988) and by Shelagh Mulvaney failed to reveal priming in the recall of interpersonal or emotional events. That is, recalling one ambitious-dominant behavior facilitate recall of another ambitious-dominant behavior on the very next trial; nor did recall of one pleasant event did not facilitate recall of the next. Similar findings have been obtained in more conventional person-memory paradigms (e.g., Hamilton, 1981; Hamilton, Katz, & Leirer, 1980; Hoffman, Mischel, & Mazze, 1981; Jeffrey & Mischel, 1979; Ostrom, Lingle, Pryor, & Geva, 1980; Ostrom, Pryor, & Simpson, 1981). And Smith and Kihlstrom (1987) found little evidence that recall of primary traits (e.g., talkative and adventurous, tidy and persevering) was organized by superordinate trait categories (e.g., extraversion, conscientiousness)—although they did find evidence for illusory correlations between related traits created by subjects' implicit theories of personality.

On the other hand, there is good reason to believe that behavioral information does come into contact with trait information as it is processed in memory. One of the most well-established results in the person memory literature is the schematic processing effect (Hastie, 1980, 1981): Given that a subject has formed a personality impression (or schema) of a target person, behaviors congruent with that impression are remembered better than those that are wholly irrelevant, whereas behaviors that are incongruent with the impression are remembered best of all. The theory is that subjects are surprised by schema-incongruous behaviors, attempt to explain them, and this extra processing at the time of encoding yields a more memorable trace; and that the subject can draw on the personality impression to generate cues that facilitate access to schema-congruent behaviors. Given this experimental outcome, and the obvious advantages of an organized memory system, the problem is to determine how trait and behavioral information are related. Apparently, this problem remains unsolved by Klein and Loftus.

SELF-SCHEMATA

The question of organization is central to the question of the self as a schema, a mental structure that preserves information about the interrelationships among objects, events, and their features. Social cognition is full of such schemata. Some of these are reflected in what has come to be known as implicit personality theory (Bruner & Tagiuri, 1954; Schneider, 1970): The halo effect, or the assumption that socially desirable traits are positively correlated (Rosenberg &

Sedlak, 1972); and the "Big Five" notion that extraversion, agreeableness, conscientiousness, emotional stability, and intelligence (or openness; see Glisky, Tataryn, Tobias, Kihlstrom, & McConkey, 1991) are the basic dimensions of personality. Natural language contains a number of personality-type terms that label categories of people: On today's college campus, jargon terms such as wonk, nerd, jock, hippie, hood, preppie, and princess abound (Cantor & Mischel, 1979; Cantor, Mischel, & Schwartz, 1982). We carry in our heads an assortment of scripts that describe generic sequences of actions that take place in broadly defined situations such as restaurants (Schank & Abelson, 1977) and sexual encounters (Gagnon, 1974). And, as much as we might try to deny or overcome them, we all hold social stereotypes about outgroups: men about women, Whites about Blacks, Anglos about Hispanics, straights about gays and lesbians, young about old, Israelis about Palestinians, Greeks about Turks (and vice-versa, of course).

These all are schemata, with slot structures that specify characteristic attributes and typical values on these attributes, embedded in a hierarchy of supersets and subsets, wholes and parts. Propositions represent the specific, although schemata represent the shared; they permit us to make inferences about unseen attributes of objects, events, people, and situations. Schemata are important mental structures, and it would be interesting to know whether the self participates in them. Klein and Loftus approach the self as if it were a person like any other. And because we have schemata for other people, it may very well be that we have schemata for ourselves, as well.

In an influential line of research, Markus (1977) described the self as a schema, but she used the term *schema* to refer to those characteristics that were highly descriptive of and very important to one's self-concept. The schema concept as used here, however, refers to something a little different—actually, two things. First, knowledge about the self must somehow cohere into a unified whole: It must be possible to capture the "gist" of oneself, or what one is like in general, just as it is possible to capture the gist of another person, or of a story, or of a category of natural objects; and second, that the self itself (pardon the expression) participates in a larger structure that somehow defines the relationship(s) between self and others. Cognitive psychology has developed a large number of paradigms for establishing the psychological reality of schemata in the domain of natural objects and for exploring the structure of these representations. This was once a hot topic in social cognition as well, and perhaps it is time to return to it.

One difficulty with thinking of the self as a schema is that schemata represent categories, while each self is, almost by definition, unique. However, each individual is a member of a number of different social categories. A person may be a White male, young, and a former hippie; he may also be an Easterner, highly educated, a member of the professional class, and a registered Independent. These groups confer attributes upon their members, and if they do not they are perceived as doing so; in any event, they are a part of that individual's identity, and they make him more like some people, and less like others. Similarly, each individual plays a number of different social roles. She may be a doctor, sit on the zoning board, and coach a soccer team; she may also be a daughter, spouse, sister, aunt, mother. These roles also confer attributes on the individual (or are perceived as doing so); they too are part of that individual's identity, and make her more like some and less like others. An individual may be a typical Easterner, with his intellectual airs and contempt for the provinces; or he may be quite atypical; either way, these relationships must be somehow represented in the self-schema. Klein and Loftus rightly focus their work on the specific knowledge that one has about oneself; but it is also important to locate the self in the broader interpersonal space (Kihlstrom & Cunningham, 1991), and take into account the impact of the person's group memberships and social roles.

Moreover,, the self may not be a monolithic, unitary cognitive structure. Rather, there may well be a whole host of selves. We know that human social behavior is very flexible, and can vary markedly from one situation to the next (Mischel, 1968; Ross & Nisbett, 1991). And because we are usually conscious of what we do, there is no reason to think that this cross-situational flexibility is not given mental representation.[1] Thus, there may well be multiple mental representations of self, corresponding to the broad social categories of social situations (at home alone; at home with family; at work with colleagues; at work with students; at the bowling alley; in the tavern) where the self resides. There are also those moments when we recognize that our thoughts, feelings, desires, and behaviors, are uncharacteristic of the self we (and others) know. Under these circumstances, we are likely to say "That wasn't me" or "I'm just not myself today." Such perceptions imply a hierarchical arrangement of context-specific selves, with some selves more typical than others; this conceptual hierarchy also constitutes a self-schema.

PERCEPTION-BASED REPRESENTATIONS OF THE SELF

Schemata are meaning-based knowledge structures, but they are not comprised wholly of propositions. They can include perception-based knowledge structures as well, including spatial images, visual images (and perhaps images in other modalities as well), and linear orderings (of course, scripts themselves are linear

---

[1]There are exceptions to this proposition, in the case of multiple personality and other dissociative disorders (Kihlstrom, 1992; Kihlstrom, Tataryn, & Hoyt, in press; Spiegel & Cardeña, 1991). In this case, an amnesic barrier appears to prevent normal communication and interaction between subordinate selves—a point that cannot be pursued here.

orderings). This fact raises the question of the role that these forms of mental representation might play in the self, and how we would study them.

That we possess something else besides verbal, meaning-based, propositional knowledge about the self is betrayed by one of our most familiar self-idioms: the self-image. Perhaps it is time to get concrete about this metaphor. There cannot be much doubt that we have analog representations of our bodies, with respect to both their external appearance and their internal sensations. Monkeys and infants recognize when their faces have been painted; adolescents perceive changes in their bodies; amputees experience phantom limbs; the obese are conscious of what their bodies look like, and feel like, as they move about; lovers recognize each others' touch, and smell, and taste; anorectics have views of themselves as fat that depart so radically from objective reality as to be marked as quasi-delusional. Cognitive psychologists have developed a number of ingenious techniques, such as mental scanning, mental rotation, mental comparison, and mental mapping, for studying the structure and processing of spatial images (see, e.g., Kosslyn, 1980; Shepard & Cooper, 1982), but these images have been of nonsocial objects. Perhaps it is time to deploy them in the study of the self.

In their research, Klein and Loftus honored the distinction between two types of declarative knowledge concerning oneself: autobiographical and trait information, or episodic and semantic memory (Tulving, 1972). And episodic memory is a prime candidate for yet another form of representation, linear orderings. Specific episodes in our lives may be represented by single propositions (e.g., *SELF helped an old man across the street on Monday*), but as we unpack these events they often reveal a plot structure, so that the event has a prologue, a beginning, a middle, an end, and an aftermath (Pennington & Hastie, 1986). For example, when subjects remember the events and experiences that transpired during a hypnosis session, they tend to recall them in the order in which they occurred—unless this temporal organization is disrupted by posthypnotic amnesia (Evans & Kihlstrom, 1973; Kihlstrom & Evans, 1979). Similarly, the fact that people can correctly order the personal and public events of their lives (Fuhrman & Wyer, 1988; Wyer, Shoben, Fuhrman, & Bodenhausen, 1985) indicates that the representations of these individual events are also related to each other by a temporal string.

But even allowing for gaps caused by infantile and childhood amnesia, normal forgetting, and the memory failures of old age, the entire life span of an individual, from birth to death, encompasses a lot of events. If a string as short as the alphabet is divided into chunks, yielding the strings-within-strings phrase structure of the "Alphabet Song" we learned as children (Anderson, 1990), this must also be true for autobiographical memory. The question is: Where are the phrase boundaries? What are the natural chunks in a person's life? It seems hardly likely that autobiographical memories are organized like desk calendars, week by week, month by month, year by year. Perhaps, in schooled, literate, industrial, and postindustrial cultures, some of a person's life history may be organized by school and work: preschool, elementary, junior high, high school, college, graduate or professional school, job entry, first promotion, new job, next promotion, retirement. In addition, the natural divisions of the life cycle, similar to Erikson's "eight ages of man," may provide the structure: infancy, toddlerhood (both fairly completely covered by infantile and childhood amnesia; see Kihlstrom & Harackiewicz, 1982), early childhood, preadolescence, adolescence, young adulthood, middle age, and old age. Another plausible scheme is provided by important cultural rituals: first day at school, bar/bat mitzvah or first communion, first sweetheart, first lover, marriage, first house, childbirth, divorce, remarriage, and the like. Obviously, each individual has all these schemes, and others, available to him or her; and the precise location of the divisions varies markedly from person to person. This fact of human complexity and individuality makes nomothetic research difficult, but the problem is an interesting one nonetheless.

THE ROAD NOT TAKEN

Klein and Loftus address few of these issues directly, but the fact that they are raised here should not be construed as any sort of criticism. Rather, they are raised as a sort of tribute to the stimulating nature of their research. Klein and Loftus epitomize that all too small group of personality and social psychologists who try to take cognition seriously, and who seek to work within the framework of concepts, principles, models, and methods provided by cognitive psychology and cognitive science. They have gone far beyond the hand waving that characterizes so much work in the field, and put detailed formal models of mental representation to rigorous empirical test. Their work is a stimulus to the imagination, and it reminds us that, for all the attention paid these days to everyday cognition, interesting questions still can be addressed and answered within the confines of the laboratory.

ACKNOWLEDGMENTS

The point of view represented in this chapter is based on research supported by Grants #MH-35856 and #MH-44739 from the National Institute of Mental Health, and Subcontract #1122SC from Program on Conscious and Unconscious Mental Processes of the John D. and Catherine T. MacArthur Foundation through the University of California, San Francisco. I thank Jeffrey Bowers, Jennifer Dorfman, Elizabeth Glisky, Martha Glisky, Lori Marchese, Shelagh Mulvaney, Robin Pennington, Michael Polster, Barbara Routhieux, Victor Shames, Michael Valdessari and Susan Valdessari for their comments.

REFERENCES

Anderson, J. R. (1983). *The architecture of cognition.* Cambridge, MA: Harvard University Press.

Anderson, J. R. (1990). *Cognitive psychology and its implications* (3rd ed.). San Francisco: Freeman.

Anderson, J. R., & Hastie, R. (1974). Individual and reference in memory: Proper names and definite descriptions. *Cognitive Psychology, 6,* 495–314.

Bruner, J., & Tagiuri, R. (1954). Person perception. In G. Lindzey (Ed.), *Handbook of social psychology* (Vol. 2, pp. 634–654). Reading, MA: Addison-Wesley.

Cantor, N., & Kihlstrom, J. F. (1987). *Personality as social intelligence.* Englewood Cliffs, NJ: Prentice-Hall.

Cantor, N., & Mischel, W. (1979). Prototypes in person perception. In L. Berkowitz (Ed.), *Advances in experimental social psychology* (Vol. 12, pp. 3–52). New York: Academic Press.

Cantor, N., Mischel, W., & Schwartz, J. (1982). A prototype analysis of psychological situations. *Cognitive Psychology, 14,* 45–77.

Evans, F. J., & Kihlstrom, J. F. (1973). Posthypnotic amnesia as disrupted retrieval. *Journal of Abnormal Psychology, 82,* 317–323.

Farah, M. J., Hammond, K. M., Levine, D. N., & Calvanio, R. (1988). Visual and spatial mental imagery: Dissociable systems of representation. *Cognitive Psychology, 20,* 439–462.

Fuhrman, R. W., & Wyer, R. S. (1988). Event memory: Temporal-order judgments of personal life experiences. *Journal of Personality & Social Psychology, 54,* 365–384.

Gagnon, J. H. (1974). Scripts and the coordination of sexual conduct. In J. K. Cole & R. Dienstbier (Eds.), *Nebraska Symposium on Motivation 1973* (pp. 27–59). Lincoln: University of Nebraska Press.

Glisky, M. L., Tataryn, D. J., Tobias, B. A., Kihlstrom, J. F., & McConkey, K. M. (1991). Absorption, openness to experience, and hypnotizability. *Journal of Personality & Social Psychology, 60,* 263–272.

Hamilton, D. L. (1981). Cognitive representations of persons. In E. T. Higgins, C. P. Herman, & M. P. Zanna (Eds.), *Social cognition: The Ontario Symposium* (pp. 135–159). Hillsdale, NJ: Lawrence Erlbaum Associates.

Hamilton, D. L., Katz, L. B., & Leirer, V. O. (1980). Organizational processes in impression formation. In R. Hastie, T. M. Ostrom, E. B. Ebbesen, R. S. Wyer, D. L. Hamilton, & D. E. Carlston (Eds.), *Person memory: The cognitive basis of social perception* (pp. 121–153). Hillsdale, NJ: Lawrence Erlbaum Associates.

Hastie, R. (1980). Memory for behavioral information that confirms or contradicts a personality impression. In R. Hastie, T. M. Ostrom, E. B. Ebbesen, R. S. Wyer, D. L. Hamilton, & D. E. Carlston (Eds.), *Person memory: The cognitive basis of social perception* (pp. 155–177). Hillsdale, NJ: Lawrence Erlbaum Associates.

Hastie, R. (1981).Schematic principles in person memory. In E. T. Higgins, C. P. Herman, & M. P. Zanna (Eds.), *Social cognition: The Ontario Symposium* (pp. 39–88). Hillsdale, NJ: Lawrence Erlbaum Associates.

Hastie, R. (1988). A computer simulation model of person memory. *Journal of Experimental Social Psychology, 24,* 423–447.

Higgins, E. T. (1987). Self-discrepancy: A theory relating self and affect. *Psychological Review, 94,* 319–340.

Hoffman, C., Mischel, W., & Mazze, K. (1981). The role of purpose in the organization of information about behavior: Trait-based versus goal-based categories in person cognition. *Journal of Personality & Social Psychology, 40,* 211–225.

Jeffrey, K., & Mischel, W. (1979). Effects of purpose on the organization and recall of information in person perception. *Journal of Personality, 47,* 397–419.

Kihlstrom, J. F. (1992). Dissociative and conversion disorders. In D. J. Stein & J. Young (Eds.), *Cognitive science and clinical disorders* (pp. 247–270). Orlando, FL: Academic Press.

Kihlstrom, J. F., & Cantor, N. (1984). Mental representations of the self. In L. Berkowitz (Ed.), *Advances in experimental social psychology* (Vol. 17, pp. 1–47). New York: Academic Press.

Kihlstrom, J. F., Cantor, N., Albright, J. S., Chew, B. R., Klein, S., & Niedenthal, P. M. (1988). Information processing and the study of the self. In L. Berkowitz (Ed.), *Advances in experimental social psychology* (Vol. 21, pp. 145–177). New York: Academic Press.

Kihlstrom, J. F., & Cunningham, R. L. (1991). Mapping interpersonal space. In M. J. Horowitz (Ed.), *Person schemas and maladaptive interpersonal patterns* (pp. 311–336). Chicago: University of Chicago Press.

Kihlstrom, J. F., & Evans, F. J. (1979). Memory retrieval processes during posthypnotic amnesia. In J. F. Kihlstrom & F. J. Evans (Eds.), *Functional disorders of memory* (pp. 179–218). Hillsdale, NJ: Lawrence Erlbaum Associates.

Kihlstrom, J. F., & Harackiewicz, J. M. (1982). The earliest recollection: A new survey. *Journal of Personality, 50,* 134–148.

Kihlstrom, J. F., & Hastie, R. (in press). Mental representations of self and others. In S. R. Briggs, R. Hogan, & W. H. Jones (Eds.), *Handbook of personality psychology*. Orlando, FL: Academic Press.

Kihlstrom, J. F., Tataryn, D. J., & Hoyt, I. P. (in press). Dissociative disorders. In P. B. Sutker & H. E. Adams (Eds.), *Comprehensive handbook of psychopathology* (2nd ed.). New York: Plenum.

Kosslyn, S. M. (1980). *Image and mind*. Cambridge: Harvard University Press.

Markus, H. (1977). Self-schemata and processing information about the self. *Journal of Personality & Social Psychology, 35,* 63–78.

Meyer, D. E., & Schvaneveldt, R. W. (1971). Facilitation in recognizing pairs of words: Evidence of a dependence between retrieval operations. *Journal of Experimental Psychology, 90,* 227–234.

Mischel, W. (1968). *Personality and assessment*. New York: Academic Press.

Ostrom, T. M., Lingle, J. H., Pryor, J. B., & Geva, N. (1980). Cognitive organization of person impressions. In R. Hastie, T. M. Ostrom, E. B. Ebbesen, R. S. Wyer, D. L. Hamilton, & D. E. Carlston (Eds.), *Person memory: The cognitive basis of social perception* (pp. 55–88). Hillsdale, NJ: Lawrence Erlbaum Associates.

Ostrom, T. M., Pryor, J. B., & Simpson, D. D. (1981). The organization of social information. In E. T. Higgins, C. P. Herman, & M. P. Zanna (Eds.), *Social cognition: The Ontario Symposium* (pp. 3–38). Hillsdale, NJ: Lawrence Erlbaum Associates.

Pennington, N., & Hastie, R. (1986). Evidence evaluation in complex decision making. *Journal of Personality & Social Psychology, 51,* 242–258.

Ratcliff, R. A., & McKoon, G. (1981). Does activation really spread? *Psychological Review, 88,* 552–572.

Rosenberg, S., & Sedlak, A. (1972). Structural representations of implicit personality theory. In L. Berkowitz (Ed.), *Advances in experimental social psychology* (Vol. 6, pp. 235–297). New York: Academic Press.

Ross, L., & Nisbett, R. E. (1991). *The person and the situation: Perspectives of social psychology*. New York: McGraw-Hill.

Schank, R. C., & Abelson, R. P. (1977). *Scripts, plans, goals, and understanding*. Hillsdale, NJ: Lawrence Erlbaum Associates.

Schneider, D. (1970). Implicit personality theory: A review. *Psychological Bulletin, 79,* 294–309.

Shepard, R. N., & Cooper, L. A. (1982). *Mental images and their transformations*. Cambridge: MIT Press.

Smith, S. S., & Kihlstrom, J. F. (1987). When is a schema not a schema? The "Big Five" traits as cognitive structures. *Social Cognition, 5,* 26–57.

Spiegel, D., & Cardeña, E. (1991). Disintegrated experience: The dissociative disorders revisited. *Journal of Abnormal Psychology, 100,* 366–378.

Srull, T. K. (1981). Person memory: Some tests of associative storage and retrieval models. *Journal of Experimental Psychology: Human Learning & Memory, 7,* 440–463.

Tulving, E. (1972). Episodic and semantic memory. In E. Tulving & W. Donaldson (Eds.), *Organization of memory* (pp. 381–403). New York: Academic Press.

Wyer, R. S., Shoben, E. J., Fuhrman, R. W., & Bodenhausen, G. V. (1985). Event memory: The temporal organization of social action sequences. *Journal of Personality & Social Psychology, 49,* 857–877.

6

The "Social Self" Component of Trait Knowledge About the Self

Charles G. Lord
Texas Christian University

In their thought-provoking chapter, Klein and Loftus (Chapter 1, this volume) address the question of how people go about deciding that they do or do not have various personality traits. This type of decision is not a trivial one. People often make important life choices and commitments about entering a particular career or about forming close interpersonal relationships for example, on the basis of conclusions that they draw about their own personality traits. A student who thinks of herself as extraverted might dismiss a career in chemistry because "I need to be surrounded by people, not by test tubes." A different student who thinks of himself as dependent might look for self-assured women as potential spouses. Almost any analysis of human social behavior would be more complete if we understood exactly how people assign trait labels to themselves.

An "easy" answer to the question of how people "know" their own personality traits is that they cite specific behavioral incidents. The woman "knows" she is extraverted because she told jokes and made many friends at the party last Saturday evening. The man "knows" he is dependent because he is still living at home and lets his mother do his laundry. We can all cite such "evidence" if asked to defend the traits to which we lay claim, so it seems logical that we "must" base our conclusions about our own traits on memories of just such specific behavioral incidents. As with many "common sense" propositions in personality and social psychology however, this "easy" answer turns out to be in error. In study after elegant study, Klein, Loftus, and their associates have provided convergent evidence that "judgments about the self-descriptiveness of trait adjectives are made without reference to behavioral evidence."

In one of Klein and Loftus' studies, students made two consecutive decisions about the same trait. For some traits, the students first decided whether they could define the word and then decided whether it described them. For other traits, the students first decided whether they could remember a specific behavioral episode in which they displayed the trait and then decided whether it described them. We know from previous research that even fairly simple decisions actually consist of several component tasks. In deciding whether a trait is self-descriptive, for example, at least two component tasks are involved: comprehension and application. The decision maker must comprehend the word's meaning and must then judge whether the meaning may be accurately applied to the self. Decisions occur faster when one of the component tasks has been performed in advance (Collins & Quillian, 1970). People are reliably faster to decide whether a trait describes them if they have recently been asked what the word means than if they have not, because one of the component tasks (comprehension) has been performed recently and does not need to be performed again.

Klein and Loftus reason that the application task might itself be divided into two component tasks: recalling relevant behavioral episodes, and drawing conclusions from those behavioral episodes. The complete sequence of deciding on a trait's self-descriptiveness, then, might include three component tasks: comprehending the word's meaning, recalling relevant behavioral episodes, and drawing conclusions from the remembered behavioral evidence. If this were the case, students who were asked to recall specific behavioral episodes before deciding on a trait's self-descriptiveness would make the self-descriptiveness decision faster than would students who were asked about the word's meaning before deciding on its self-descriptiveness, because the former would have performed two component tasks in advance, whereas the latter would have performed only one component task in advance (Macht & O'Brien, 1980).

In reality, however, students who were first asked whether they could remember specific behavioral episodes were no faster to decide on a trait's self-descriptiveness than were students who were first asked about the word's meaning (Klein, Loftus, & Burton, 1989). These reaction time results suggested strongly that recalling specific behavioral episodes is not one of the component tasks that people perform during the process of deciding whether they have or do not have a particular personality trait.

In two other studies, Klein and Loftus used memory measures to provide convergent evidence for the proposition that people do not spontaneously recall specific behavioral episodes when assessing their own personality traits. One of the studies used the "encoding specificity effect" that recognition memory accuracy improves when the cognitive processes employed during encoding overlap with the cognitive processes employed during retrieval (Tulving, 1983). Some students were first asked to recall specific autobiographical incidents relevant to a trait. Two weeks later, they decided whether the trait described them and then tried to remember whether they had previously made a self-descriptiveness judgment about that trait. Other students did the same, except that the first task was to decide on the trait's meaning rather than to recall auto-biographical incidents. If deciding on a trait's self-descriptiveness involved both comprehending the word's meaning and recalling behavioral episodes, then students who initially recalled autobiographical episodes would have had better recognition memory than would students who initially completed only one of those tasks, namely comprehension. In fact, however, recognition memory accuracy was equivalent in the two conditions, exactly as would happen if recalling relevant behavioral episodes played no part in deciding on one's own personality traits.

In the other memory study, Klein and Loftus took advantage of the fact that recall memory is better for decisions that involve two distinct types of encoding than for decisions for which the component processes overlap (Martin, 1971). Students either recalled autobiographical episodes relevant to a trait, decided on the trait's self-descriptiveness, or both. If recalling specific behavioral episodes played a large part in deciding on a trait's self-descriptiveness, then performing both tasks would not increase recall relative to performing either of the tasks twice. In fact, however, students who both recalled autobiographical evidence and decided on the trait's self-descriptiveness displayed enhanced recall relative to students who performed either of the tasks twice. As in Klein and Loftus' other studies, the results of this second memory study suggested strongly that trait-descriptiveness judgments about the self do not involve recalling specific behavioral episodes.

In discussing how people might decide on their own personality traits without reference to specific behavioral episodes, Klein and Loftus refer to considerable research in which subjects made judgments on the basis of an abstract conclusion, without reference to the specific instances on which that conclusion was originally drawn (e.g., Barsalou, 1987, 1988; Neisser, 1988; Watkins & Kerkar, 1985). We have all had the experience of "knowing" that we loved a particular novel or movie without being able to remember much about the plot or about the specific characters. In the same way, we may have decided long ago that we are in general extraverted, so that we do not need to recall any specific behavioral displays of extraversion in order to determine whether or not we have that personality trait (Carlston, 1980). We may not have done anything all that extra-verted within the past month, but that surely does not prevent us from "know-ing" that we are extraverted.

Consistent with the proposition that trait judgments about the self are made by referring to abstractions or general conclusions, Klein and Loftus use their reaction time procedure to show that judgments about a trait's self-descriptiveness within a circumscribed time frame do involve autobiographical memories. When they asked students to recall relevant behavioral episodes that had occurred since they entered college, subsequent judgments about the trait's self-descriptiveness were facilitated relative to performing an initial semantic task. If we are trying to decide whether we have been extraverted this week, we are likely to recall specific relevant episodes as appropriate evidence on which to make such a decision. If we are trying to decide whether we are extraverted in general, specific behavioral episodes do not enter into the judgment.

Klein and Loftus' results and conclusions are, of course, counterintuitive. If we asked people how they decide on their own personality traits, they would no doubt believe that they consider relevant behavioral episodes. It is well known, however, that people are poor judges of which components enter into their cognitive processes. They may be very confident that they are using certain kinds of evidence in making a decision and yet not be doing so, just as they may use a particular type of evidence and not be aware of doing so (Nisbett & Wilson, 1977).

My own research has been concerned with whether, regardless of what they may believe or what accords with "common sense," people consider, as part of the process of deciding whether a trait describes them or not, an aspect of their general (not specific) behavior that William James (1890/1950) described as the "social self." The social self is, in essence, a person's reputation. According to James, a person "has as many social selves as there are individuals who recognize him and carry an image of him in their mind. To wound any one of these images is to wound him" (p. 294). When deciding on a trait's self-descriptiveness, I believe, people may comprehend the word's meaning, recall their abstract conclusions about themselves ("I'm an extravert"), and consider briefly whether their abstract conclusion matches what important other people think of them.

The "reflection on reputation" component does not occur for every trait, but only for traits on which the decision maker realizes that he or she actually has a reputation in the eyes of important others. A college student may "know" that he is extraverted strictly by recalling the abstract conclusion without reference to anyone else's opinion, but decide that he is not dependent only after admitting to himself that his mother, who does his laundry every week, acts as though she considers him very dependent. "Overall, I'm quite an independent person," he might think, "despite the fact that my mother thinks otherwise." As this example illustrates, reflections on reputation sometimes dictate the conclusion, but sometimes they do not. A person might as easily decide that "I've always considered myself a little introverted, but all my friends say I'm a huge extravert, so I guess it must be true" as that "I know I'm not an extravert no matter what they say." In either case, a person who has a reputation on a specific personality trait might have at least some fleeting thought of that reputation during the process of deciding on the trait's self-descriptiveness.

To test whether these propositions have any validity, whether reflections on the social self might enter into private ruminations about one's own personality traits, my associates and I borrowed the Klein and Loftus reaction time procedure (Lord, Desforges, Chacon, Pere, & Clubb, in press, Study 1). We had students make two consecutive decisions about the same trait. For some traits, the students first decided whether they could remember a specific behavioral episode in which they displayed the trait and then decided whether the trait described them. For other traits, they first decided whether one of their parents thought they had the trait and then decided whether the trait described them. For yet other traits, the students first decided whether a friend or an acquaintance thought they had the trait and then decided whether the trait described them. Our reasoning matched that of Klein and Loftus. We believed that decisions about a trait's self-descriptiveness do not involve recalling specific behavioral episodes, but do involve, at least for some traits, (presumably different ones for each individual depending on which traits are salient in his or her reputation), reflections on the social self. Because we believed that reflections on reputation in the eyes of other people would have a higher probability of occurring as the other person became more important in one's life (or perhaps as the other person had a greater number of interactions with self and thus more opportunities to make trait-relevant opinions known), we also predicted that the initial task of deciding what a parent thinks would be more likely than the initial task of deciding what an acquaintance thinks to facilitate subsequent self-descriptiveness judgments.

As can be seen in Table 6.1, our predictions were confirmed. Reaction times for deciding on a trait's self-descriptiveness after recalling autobiographical evidence about the same trait were almost identical to those reported for the same task sequence by Klein and Loftus. We know from their work that the autobiographical task facilitates subsequent self-descriptiveness decisions no more than does a semantic task, so the autobiographical task reaction times ($M = 2,051$ msec) may be taken as a "baseline" indicator of how rapidly people decide on their own traits when only the semantic component has been performed in advance. Preceding decisions about the social self, in contrast, facilitated self-descriptiveness judgments significantly. Students were fastest to decide whether a trait described themselves when they had just finished thinking about their

TABLE 6.1

Mean Response Latencies (in Milliseconds) for Deciding Whether a Positive or Negative Trait Described Self or Not, as a Function of Whether an Immediately Preceding Decision About the Trait Concerned Past Behavior (Autobiographical) or Reputation in the Eyes of Parent, Friend, or Acquaintance

| | | Preceding Decision | | |
	Autobiographical	*Acquaintance*	*Friend*	*Parent*
Positive traits	1,956	1,779	1,714	1,628
	(1,058)	(891)	(701)	(768)
Negative traits	2,146	2,003	1,897	1,718
	(1,060)	(960)	(800)	(689)

Note: Standard deviations are in parentheses.

reputation on that trait in the eyes of their parents ($M = 1, 673$), next when they had just finished thinking about their reputation in the eyes of a friend ($M = 1, 805$), and next when they had just finished thinking about their reputation in the eyes of an acquaintance ($M = 1, 891$). According to planned comparisons, the average of the three reputational questions facilitated trait self-descriptiveness judgments more than did the autobiographical question, and the parent question facilitated trait self-descriptiveness judgments more than did the acquaintance question.

Because the participating students were also asked how much they cared what their parent, friend, and acquaintance thought of them, we were also able to determine that reputational questions facilitate subsequent trait self-descriptiveness decisions as a function of the importance of the particular reputation or "social self" in question. We interpreted these results as support for the hypothesis that reputational reflection is one component in the process of deciding on a trait's self-descriptiveness. An alternative explanation is that our subjects simply turned the reputational questions into self-descriptiveness questions, so that they were answering the self-question twice. One problem with this alternative explanation is that it does not explain the difference between parent and acquaintance questions in facilitating self-descriptiveness judgments. If anything, it is the acquaintance question, not the parent question, on which students might be more likely to lack information and to say to themselves "How would I know what he/she thinks? I'll just go by what I think."

Our reaction time results thus buttress Klein and Loftus' argument that the autobiographical task did not fail to facilitate subsequent decisions about trait self-descriptiveness because the procedure is insensitive. The differences may be measured only in milliseconds, but our results show that other types of initial decisions, unlike reflections on autobiographical incidents, do facilitate subsequent decisions about one's own traits. The procedure is sensitive enough to detect differences when the initial decision actually forms a component of the subsequent decision process, but people do not spontaneously reflect on specific behavioral incidents when they decide whether or not they generally have a personality trait. Instead they consider only a summary conclusion that they have drawn after observing their own behavior and their reputations across a lifetime of related behavioral episodes.

Like Klein and Loftus, we supplemented the reaction time study with a memory study (Lord et al., in press, Study 2) in order to provide convergent evidence for the hypothesis that reflections on reputation, unlike retrieval of autobiographical episodes, occur during the process of deciding whether or not one has a personality trait. In our memory study, we reasoned that recognition memory should be greater for self-descriptiveness decisions that were made about traits on which an individual has a reputation than on traits for which the individual does not have a reputation, because thinking about one's reputation would add cognitive elaboration to the encoding process (Klein & Kihlstrom,

1986). Because the reaction time results indicated that parental opinions are the most likely to form a component of self-descriptiveness judgments, we determined actual reputations by asking parents of second, third, and fourth graders what they thought of their children. Instead of asking the parents about specific personality traits, we assessed each child's parental reputation indirectly by asking the parent how well he or she expected the child to do in future academic pursuits.

Some parents expected their young children to perform brilliantly as adults, achieving all A averages in college and going on to get a PhD or other higher degree. Other parents revealed a relatively negative opinion of their children by predicting that the child would get C grades in high school and would never attend college. We therefore split parental opinions at the mean of predicted academic performance to form two groups of children, those who had relatively positive and those who had relatively negative parental reputations. We reasoned that these children might not be able to verbalize their parents' positive or negative opinions of them and might not agree with their parents, but they would be aware at some level that their parents expected relatively much or little of them, so some of them would have relatively positive "social selves" to consider in deciding on the self-descriptiveness of both positive and negative personality traits, whereas others of the children would have relatively negative "social selves" to consider.

We predicted that knowledge of the social self would be more likely to enter into the process of deciding on a trait's self-descriptiveness for the positive reputation children on positive traits and for the negative reputation children on negative traits. Without mentioning the expectations that their parents had earlier expressed, we asked these second, third, and fourth graders whether or not various personality traits, half of the traits positive and half negative, described themselves. We then gave them an unexpected recognition memory test for the traits. Consistent with our predictions, as shown in Fig. 6.1, positive parental reputation children remembered more of the positive traits about which they had made self-descriptiveness judgments and negative parental reputation children remembered more of the negative traits.[1] In addition, negative parental reputation children remembered significantly more of the negative than of the positive traits to which they answered "No, that trait does not describe me." They might not have agreed with their parents' opinions by endorsing negative traits for themselves, but these memory results suggest that thoughts of their relatively negative reputations entered into the decision process, adding cognitive elaboration and thus memorability, even if the negative reputations were dismissed as undeserved.

---

[1]The figure shows adjusted means, relative to memory for semantic decisions about traits of the same valence. Thus the result cannot be explained by positive parental reputation children simply choosing more of the positive traits from the recognition list and negative parental reputation children doing the opposite.

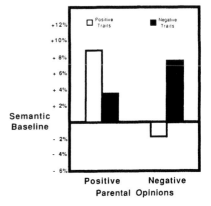

FIG. 6.1. Mean percentage (relative to semantic baseline) of self-referent question traits correctly recognized for positive and negative traits, as a function of parent opinions.

We replicated this memory result using the child's teacher's opinion of classroom conduct instead of the parent's opinion of future academic success. We also replicated the memory result using college roommate's opinion of future academic success (Lord et al., in press, Study 3). In each instance we were able to predict in advance which students would remember more of the positive traits about which they had made self-descriptiveness judgments and which students would remember more of the negative traits. In each case also, memory was especially good for the participants who had relatively negative reputations, on negative traits to which they answered "No, that trait does not describe me." (For other research in which negative reputations matter more than positive reputations, see Gollwitzer & Wicklund, 1985, and Higgins, 1987). Our prediction, of course, was not the symbolic interactionist prediction that people come to agree with their negative reputations in the eyes of important others (Shrauger & Schoeneman, 1979), but rather that people spontaneously consider their reputations on traits for which they have a reputation, even if in the process they conclude that the reputation is unwarranted and reject it. Saying, "I'm not dependent even if my mother thinks I am" is more memorable than simply saying, "I'm not dependent."

Klein and Loftus argue that the "paradox of self-deception" (Fingarette, 1969) occurs not because people find it too painful to admit to unwanted traits, but because specific behavioral episodes are not considered when deciding on a trait's self-descriptiveness. Individuals can draw biased conclusions from selective interpretation of their own specific behaviors and then consider only the summary conclusions in deciding whether a trait describes them or not. An individual can easily cheat on his tax returns and yet call himself generally honest. My memory results support Klein and Loftus' reasoning, adding only that a person who has acquired a reputation as a cheat may genuinely regard himself as honest and consider other people in error, yet he will remember very well being asked the question "Are you dishonest?"

Like Klein and Loftus, I believe that trait knowledge about the self is represented primarily in abstract, summary form. In addition, I believe that knowledge of one's reputation is itself a summary representation. If pressed, an individual might be able to recall specific instances in which his father acted as though he could not be trusted to perform various tasks competently, but he has also abstracted from these incidents the summary representation "My father thinks I'm incompetent." The social self is thus one type of summary representation, and one's own opinion another. For any given trait or set of related traits, the two summary representations may agree or disagree. Because each individual is known to others by only a handful of salient traits (Bem, 1983a, 1983b), most trait self-descriptiveness judgments may involve only one's own opinion. Nonetheless, my reaction time and memory results suggest that self-descriptiveness judgments that involve an individual's salient traits and traits closely related to them include reflections on reputation as one type of summary representation that may enter into the cognitive process of deciding whether or not one has a personality trait. If abstract trait representations are a part of semantic self-knowledge, so is the social self.

REFERENCES

Barsalou, L. W. (1987). The instability of graded structure: Implications for the nature of concepts. In U. Neisser (Ed.), *Concepts and conceptual development: Ecological and intellectual factors in categorization* (pp. 101–140). New York: Cambridge University Press.

Barsalou, L. W. (1988). The content and organization of autobiographical memories. In U. Neisser & E. Winograd (Eds.), *Remembering reconsidered: Ecological and traditional approaches to the study of memory* (pp. 193–243). New York: Cambridge University Press.

Bem, D. J. (1983a). Constructing a theory of the triple typology: Some (second) thoughts on nomothetic and idiographic approaches to personality. *Journal of Personality, 51,* 566–577.

Bem, D. J. (1983b). Toward a response style theory of persons in situations. In R. A. Dienstbier & M. M. Page (Eds.), *Nebraska Symposium on Motivation 1982: Personality—Current theory and research* (Vol. 30, pp. 201–231). Lincoln: University of Nebraska Press.

Carlston, D. E. (1980). Events, inferences, and impression formation. In R. Hastie, T. M. Ostrom, E. B. Ebbesen, R. S. Wyer, Jr., D. L. Hamilton, & D. E. Carlston (Eds.), *Person memory: The cognitive basis of social perception* (pp. 89–119). Hillsdale, NJ: Lawrence Erlbaum Associates.

Collins, A. M., & Quillian, M. R. (1970). Facilitating retrieval from semantic memory: The effect of repeating part of an inference. *Acta Psychologica, 33,* 304–314.

Fingarette, H. (1969). *Self-deception.* London: Routledge & Kegan Paul.

Gollwitzer, P. M., & Wicklund, R. A. (1985). Self-symbolizing and the neglect of others' perspectives. *Journal of Personality and Social Psychology, 48,* 702–715.

Higgins, E. T. (1987). Self-discrepancy: A theory relating self and affect. *Psychological Review, 94,* 319–340.

James, W. (1950). *The principles of psychology* (Vols. 1 and 2). New York: Dover. (Original work published 1890)

Klein, S. B., & Kihlstrom, J. F. (1986). Elaboration, organization, and the self-reference effect in memory. *Journal of Experimental Psychology: General, 115,* 26–38.

Klein, S. B., Loftus, J., & Burton, H. A. (1989). Two self-reference effects: The importance of distinguishing between self-descriptiveness judgments and autobiographical retrieval in self-referent encoding. *Journal of Personality and Social Psychology, 56,* 853–865.

Lord, C. G., Desforges, D. M., Chacon, S., Pere, G., & Clubb, R. (in press). Reflection on reputation in the process of self-evaluation. *Social Cognition.*

Macht, M. L., & O'Brien, E. J. (1980). Familiarity-based responding in item recognition: Evidence for the role of spreading activation. *Journal of Experimental Psychology: Human Learning and Memory, 6,* 301–318.

Martin, E. (1971). Verbal learning theory and independent retrieval phenomena. *Psychological Review, 78,* 314–332.

Neisser, U. (1988). What is ordinary memory the memory of? In U. Neisser & E. Winograd (Eds.), *Remembering reconsidered: Ecological and traditional approaches to the study of memory* (pp. 193–243). New York: Cambridge University Press.

Nisbett, R. E., & Wilson, T. D. (1977). Telling more than we can know: Verbal reports on mental processes. *Psychological Review, 84,* 231–259.

Shrauger, J. S., & Schoeneman, T. J. (1979). Symbolic interactionist view of self-concept: Through the looking glass darkly. *Psychological Bulletin, 86,* 549–573.

Tulving, E. (1983). *Elements of epidosic memory.* New York: Oxford University Press.

Watkins, M. J., & Kerkar, S. P. (1985). Recall of a twice-presented item without recall of either presentation: Generic memory for events. *Journal of Memory and Language, 24,* 666–678.

7 Knowledge of the Self: Is it Special?

Ruth H. Maki
Angela K. Carlson
North Dakota State University

Klein and Loftus' (Chapter 1, this volume) model of self-knowledge has two main features. One is that long-term trait knowledge about the self is represented in an abstract, summary form, and the second is that this summary representation is independent of the representation of behaviors that serve as examples of the traits. One type of evidence that Klein and Loftus offer for this is that remembering an episode in which one exhibited a trait does not facilitate a later decision about whether the trait is self-descriptive. Likewise, deciding whether a trait is self-descriptive does not facilitate the speed with which one can remember an episode involving the trait. A second type of evidence is that the relationship between how well a trait describes oneself and the time to make self-descriptiveness judgments is different from the relationship between how well a trait describes oneself and the time to remember episodes in which the trait was exhibited. When subjects judge self-descriptiveness, they respond faster to traits that are high or low in self-descriptiveness than to traits that are medium in self-descriptiveness. However, behavioral episodes involving highly descriptive traits are remembered faster than episodes involving traits of medium descriptiveness, which in turn are faster than episodes involving low descriptive traits.

Other experiments in the Klein and Loftus chapter show that the independence of judging self-descriptiveness and remembering episodes involving traits does not hold for less well-learned descriptions, such as descriptions of mother and descriptions of the self in a new context, namely college. Traits that were judged to be highly descriptive of mother showed the same pattern as in the self-descriptive task, but traits judged as medium or low in descriptiveness showed a dependence between the descriptive and the episodic tasks. That is, judging whether a medium or low descriptive trait was descriptive of mother sped up remembering an episode in which she exhibited that trait and remembering an episode sped up judgments of mother-descriptiveness. Similarly, descriptive judgments of subjects about themselves in college showed a dependence between the descriptive and episodic tasks. Klein and Loftus suggest that degree of learning about traits in a category may be the key to whether the descriptiveness and episode memory tasks are dependent or independent. The self, which is a highly overlearned category, may be organized with abstract summary descriptions of traits stored separately from behaviors exemplifying those traits. However, for other, less well-learned, categories, trait representations and behavioral episodes may be stored together in memory, or at least they may access the same information.

Separate storage of descriptive and behavioral episodes may occur because the two types of memories are in different memory systems. Klein and Loftus discuss the possibility that self-knowledge is stored both in an episodic memory system and a semantic memory system of the types described by Tulving (1989). These memory systems are thought to be independent and, thus, differential use of them might produce the effects that Klein and Loftus found with the self. Because semantic knowledge only develops with overlearning, such an explanation might also help to explain the mother-descriptiveness and the college-context data. If the episodic-semantic explanation is correct for Klein and Loftus' self-data, then the next question might be "How is the self different from any other category that has episodic and semantic components?" Would any well-known category produce results similar to those of Klein and Loftus if an episodic task were preceded by a semantic task and vice versa? Or, is the self special? Does it produce data that are different from other well-learned categories? Because we could find nothing in the literature that provided a clear answer to this question, we conducted an experiment designed in exactly the same way as Klein and Loftus' first experiment, except that we used the category "animal" and instances of animals rather than the category "self" and trait exemplars.

If the independence of the self-descriptiveness task and the behavioral episodes task occurs because the two tasks tap into semantic and episodic memory (Tulving, 1989), then any well-learned category should produce such independence. We selected "animal" as a well-learned category that is stored in semantic memory in an organized way. Its instances vary in typicality (Rosch, 1975), just as traits vary in self-descriptiveness. In addition, episodes concerning specific animals should be stored in episodic memory. Thus, if the independence observed by Klein and Loftus is due to an independence of semantic and episodic memory, we should observe a similar pattern with animal as the well-learned category. Typicality judgments (our analog to self-descriptiveness judgments) should be independent of remembering episodes involving the animals. Alternatively, if the self is special, then other common categories may not show the same independence because they are not overlearned enough. Klein and Loftus' results with mother and with the self in college suggest that this may be the case.

The self may indeed be special because it is more overlearned than other categories, including animal. If so, then dependence between judging typicality and
remembering episodes may be found.

Our main question was whether remembering an episode involving an animal
would facilitate deciding about the typicality of the animal and vice versa.
Furthermore, we asked whether the perceived typicality of animals would affect
response time in the typicality task and the episodic memory tasks in the same
way, or in different ways as found by Klein and Lotus.

A TEST OF THE GENERALITY OF EPISODIC-SEMANTIC
DISTINCTION

Our design was the same as that of Klein, Loftus, and Burton (1989). There were
nine within-subject conditions as defined by how animal names were processed
on a first and on a second task. Our version of Klein and Loftus' self-descriptive
task was a task in which subjects judged the typicality of instances of the
category "animal." For the episodic task, we instructed subjects to think of an
episode involving either the animal or the animal name. Because some of the
animals were uncommon, subjects were told to remember any incident involving
the animal, including reading about the animal in a book or seeing it in a film.
They were asked, however, to remember a specific incident in which the animal
name was involved. The third task was the same as Klein and Loftus' define task.
Subjects were asked to give a definition of the animal. The define task with a
taxonomic category, such as animals, is conceptually different from the define
task used with traits. In Klein and Loftus' chapter, the define task was assumed to
be a control task because the self-concept should not be involved when subjects
define traits, but it should be involved in both the self-descriptiveness and the
episodic remember tasks. With taxonomic categories, however, the define task
and the task of judging typicality may both involve semantic memory, whereas
remembering an episode may involve episodic memory. Thus, we may not
expect to see differences between the typicality and the define task. In spite of
these potential differences, we used the same define task as Klein and Loftus,
because we wanted our procedures to be as comparable as possible to theirs.
(Furthermore, we could not think of a task involving the meaning of an animal
that would not access the semantic representation of the word.)

When the typicality, remember, and define tasks were factorially combined as
first and second tasks, there were nine first task–second task combinations.
Because we wanted to look at the time to perform these tasks as a function of
typicality (the analog to self-descriptiveness from Klein and Loftus' experiment),
we selected animal names that varied in frequency from the Battig and Montague
(1969) norms because frequency is generally correlated with typicality (Rosch,
Mervis, Gray, Johnson, & Boyes-Braem, 1976). We selected the 27 most fre-

quently given animal names as highly typical animals. Examples of such animal names are dog, donkey, and moose. The 27 medium typicality names were given by 4 to 34 subjects in the sample and the 27 low typicality names were given by one or two subjects in the sample. Examples of medium animal names are jaguar, hamster, and hyena. Low typicality examples are cobra, ant, and platypus.

The 27 animal names at each level of typicality were used with the nine task combinations such that there were three different animals names used for each combination of task and typicality. These were presented in three randomized blocks. The presentation was controlled by IBM PS-2 computers that were controlled by the Micro Experimental Laboratory (Schneider, 1988). The timing was identical to that described by Klein et al. (1989). Each trial began with an instruction TYPICAL, REMEMBER, or DEFINE which indicated what the subject was supposed to do with the animal name. The animal name was then presented and subjects performed the instructed task and pressed the space bar when the task was completed. As in the Klein and Loftus experiments, subjects did not make any verbal or written responses; they simply did the task "in their heads" and indicated when it was completed. The instruction for the second task then appeared, followed by a repetition of the animal name. Subjects were to perform the second task and to press the space bar when that was completed. Our instructions were similar to those of Klein et al. (1989) in that subjects were told that they did not need to think of a new episode in the Remember–Remember condition, but that they could recall the same episode again. After the 81 animal names had been presented in this way, subjects made typicality judgments of the names. Each was presented in a random order along with a 7-point scale that varied from 1 = "not at all typical" to 7 = "very typical." Subjects were instructed to type in the number that corresponded to how typical they thought the instance was of the category "animal." Twenty-seven students who were volunteers from lower level psychology classes at North Dakota State University served in this experiment.

Second Times as a Function of First Task.   Figure 7.1 shows the time to perform the second task as a function of the first task. Overall, there was an interaction between the task performed first and the task performed second. When the typicality task was presented second, times on that task were significantly faster when the first task had been to remember an incident involving the animal than when it had been to define the animal. There was also a trend for faster times on the second typicality task when the first task had been to judge typicality as compared to when it had been to define the animal, but this difference was short of significance. Performing the remember task first facilitated deciding whether an animal was typical as much as performing the typicality task first facilitated performing the typicality task second. This is in contrast to the findings of Klein and Loftus with their self-descriptiveness task. They found that

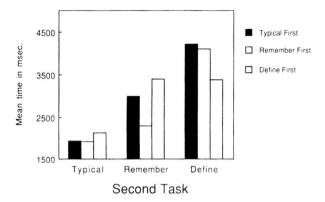

FIG. 7.1. Second task times as a function of initial task.

a first task of remembering an episode in which the trait was displayed did not facilitate the self-descriptiveness task any more than did defining the trait first. With animals, thinking of an episode involving the animal facilitated decisions about the animal's typicality. Thus, our typicality task and our episode memory tasks were dependent, not independent, as were Klein and Loftus' self-descriptiveness and episode memory tasks.

For the remember task second, independence between episodic and semantic memory would be shown by no difference in the time to remember an episode when the initial task had been to judge the animal's typicality and when it had been to define the animal. As can be seen in Fig. 7.1, remembering an episode involving the animal was faster when the subject had just decided whether the animal was typical than when the subject had just defined the animal. Performing the remember task twice was also faster than the other two conditions. Klein and Loftus found that deciding whether or not a trait was self-descriptive did not facilitate retrieval of an episode any more than did defining the trait first. Again, our pattern with animals is different from the pattern that Klein and Loftus found with the self. Typicality judgments facilitated episodic retrieval with animals and vice versa. We found dependence between the typicality tasks and the episode memory tasks when the remembering task was second.

Finally, performance on the define task when it was second was the same whether the typical or remember task was performed first. Both the typical and remember initial tasks produced slower times on the define task second than did the definition initial task. This pattern is similar to that found by Klein et al. (1989) when traits were defined. However, this is somewhat surprising with animals because we had predicted that the typicality and the define tasks would both tap into the same aspect of semantic memory. Evidently, the remember and typicality tasks tapped some aspect of memory that was different from that tapped by the define task.

Typicality Effects Across Tasks.   Animal names were separated into three categories based on individual subjects' typicality ratings. For each subject, names were rank-ordered according to typicality ratings and those in the top third were considered high typicality, those in the middle third were considered medium typicality, and those in the bottom third were considered low typicality. In cases where subjects did not have enough variability in their ratings to produce three categories, the normative frequencies were used to assign instances to typicality levels.

The mean typicality ratings for the high, medium, and low typical names were 6.45, 5.56, and 2.97, respectively. Each mean differed from each other mean. Figure 7.2 shows the time to respond on the first task as a function of the typicality of the animal name. Overall, typicality produced a main effect, but it did not interact with task. Because Klein and Loftus showed different patterns with different tasks, we analyzed each task independently. There was no effect of typicality on the define task, a finding that is similar to that of Klein and Loftus' finding in their Experiment 2. For both the typical and remember tasks, however, typicality produced significant effects. As can be seen in Fig. 7.2, highly typical animal names were responded to significantly faster than low typicality names. For the typical task, the medium names were significantly faster than the low names, but this effect was not significant for the remember task. Overall, however, the typical and remember tasks produced very similar patterns as a function of the subjective typicality of the animal names. This is in contrast to the results of Klein and Lotus who found the same monotonic pattern for the remember task that we found, but who also found an inverted U-shaped pattern on the self-descriptiveness task. There was no evidence for an inverted-U pattern in our typicality task.

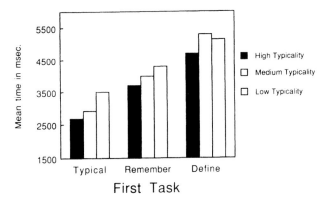

FIG. 7.2.   First task times as a function of subjective instance typicality.

Role of Typicality on Task Dependence. With the self as the target category, Klein and Loftus found that the self-descriptiveness of the traits used in their describe and remember tasks did not affect the independent nature of those two tasks. An initial self-descriptiveness task did not speed up a second remember task and an initial remember task did not speed up a second self-descriptiveness task no matter how high or low the traits were rated in terms of self-descriptiveness. However, with less well-learned categories, such as mother and self at college, they found that an initial remember task facilitated a second describes task and that an initial describes task facilitated a second remember task. It might be that the animal category is more like a less well-learned category, especially because some of the less typical animals, such as impala, are not very familiar. In order to see whether the dependence effects reported here generalized across typicality, we analyzed high- and low-rated animal names separately. Because we had only nine animal names for each first–second task combination, we did not split typicality into thirds but, instead, we used a median split. The median of each subjects' typicality ratings was determined, and animal names that fell at or above the median were considered to be high in typicality and names that fell below the median were considered low in typicality.

Figure 7.3 shows response times when the second task was to judge typicality and when it was to remember an episode. Although there is some suggestion that the facilitation effect was smaller for high typicality than for low typicality animal names, the interaction between the first task and instance typicality was not significant either for the typicality or the remember task second. Thus, there was no evidence that the remember and typicality tasks were independent for typical instances, but dependent for atypical instances. Still, the results look quite similar to Klein and Loftus' results with mother as the target category shown in their Fig. 1.6. It may be that the category "animal" is operating like a

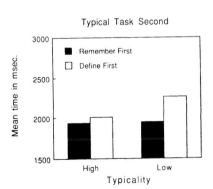 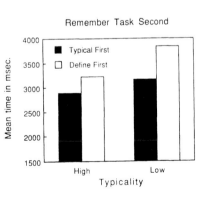

FIG. 7.3. Second task times as a function of instance typicality and initial task.

less well-learned category, such as mother, rather than a well-learned category, such as self.

IS THE SELF JUST ANOTHER
TAXONOMIC CATEGORY?

There are a number of differences between our data with a common taxonomic category and Klein and Loftus' data with the self as the category. First, the typicality task and the remember task were dependent in our data. Performing one of these tasks first facilitated performing the other one second. Following the logic of Klein and Loftus, the conclusion from these data is that the same information was accessed when subjects judged an animal's typicality as when the subject remembered an episode involving the animal. The define task seemed to tap into a different aspect of memory. When it was preceded by itself, times were fairly fast. When the define task was preceded either by the typicality task or the remember task, times to define the animal on the second presentation were slower. Initial typicality and remember tasks produced similar effects on the define task second.

The conclusion that the typicality and the remember tasks tapped into similar aspects of memory, whereas the define task tapped into a different aspect of memory is also supported by the effects of typicality on the three types of processing on the first task. Both the typicality task and the remember tasks showed increasing time with decreasing typicality; the define task was not affected by typicality. Increasing monotonic functions for both the typicality and remember tasks contrasts with the findings of Klein and Loftus. They found the same monotonically increasing function that we found with their remember task, but they found an inverted-U shaped function for their describes task. Their inverted-U shaped function for traits is probably due to traits having polar opposites and our lack of such a function may be due to animal names not having opposites. With traits, subjects could quickly determine that they are not greedy, a low descriptive trait for most people, by thinking that they are generous. However, subjects could not do the same with an atypical animal, such as platypus, because there is no polar opposite. The different patterns for the self-descriptive first task and the typical first task thus may be due to the nature of the stimulus words rather than to different aspects of memory being accessed.

The analysis of second task times as a function of high and low typicality animal names suggested that judging typicality and remembering episodes accessed similar aspects of memory whether the animal names were high or low in typicality. However, we used 81 animal names and, with a median split, some of those that were in the top half were still fairly obscure. Indeed, many of the top 27 animal names that we defined pre-experimentally as high typicality are not encountered very often (e.g., moose, donkey). Thus, the instances of this taxonomic category are probably not as well-learned as traits are for the self. With the self in Klein and Loftus' study, degree of descriptiveness did not affect the independence of the describe and the remember tasks, but with a less familiar category (e.g., one's mother), highly descriptive traits showed independence between the describe and remember tasks, but less descriptive traits showed dependence. In our data, there was evidence for dependence both for high and low typicality instances. It may be that our typical animals are less well-known than the most descriptive traits for mother. Thus, our high typicality animal names may correspond roughly with the medium typicality traits in the mother task. If so, then most of our animal names would involve accessing the same information in order to perform either the remember or the typicality task.

Does the dependence observed in our animal task indicate that subjects use episodes with animals that they remember to decide whether those animals are typical? Conversely, do they use judged typicality to help them to remember specific episodes? Both of these possibilities seem unlikely with this taxonomic category. However, we can argue that the processes involved in memory retrieval for one of these tasks are similar to the processes involved for the other task. Both making typicality judgments and remembering an episode seem to be different from defining an animal. Definitions might involve abstract verbal propositions, whereas making typicality judgments and remembering an episode might involve thinking about a specific exemplar of the category. Subjects may then use how long it took to retrieve an episode as a rough estimate of typicality; thus, the typicality task would be facilitated by first remembering an episode. Subjects may also remember an episode after judging typicality by using the instance of the animal that they accessed for the typicality judgment. Subjects may not normally access specific instances to make typicality judgments, but if they have just done so, they simply use the instance to make the judgment. If specific instances were used in both the remember and typicality tasks, it may be due to the experimental procedures rather than to the usual way of judging typicality. A similar argument might be made for the mother-descriptiveness task and the "describes school" tasks used by Klein and Loftus. Some of the same aspects of the memory representations may be accessed by the successive describes and remember tasks, but that is not solid evidence for the use of behavioral examples to perform the descriptive task and the use of descriptive information to perform the remember task under other situations.

THE SELF IS SPECIAL

The answer to our initial question "Is the self special?" seems to be yes in the sense that it is a category that consists of very well-learned traits. It is probably everyone's best-learned category, so other common categories may never produce data having the same pattern as the self as a category. Of course, only a limited number of other categories have been tested. Klein and Loftus tested mother and "self at school"; we tested animal. There is a large number of other well-learned categories. It may be possible to find some categories that are so well-learned as to produce an independence between judging descriptiveness and remembering episodes. Still, on logical grounds, the self is probably better learned than any other category, so such a search may be futile.

Is it surprising that subjects don't use behavioral examples in deciding whether traits describe themselves? No, it really isn't. It is unlikely that subjects use behavioral episodes to define the typicality of animals either, although the remembering episodes involving an animal and judging the typicality of the animal may access the same representations in memory. In contrast, the self-descriptiveness task may be so automatic as to be independent of information used for the remember task. The self is special in the sense that it is so well-learned. It produces automatic judgments that are based on factors that are different from judgments made with less well-learned categories.

ACKNOWLEDGMENTS

Appreciation is expressed to Dawn Jonas for testing some of the subjects and to Kevin McCaul for his helpful comments on an earlier version of this chapter.

REFERENCES

Battig, W. F., & Montague, W. E. (1969). Category norms for verbal items in 56 categories: A replication and extension of the Connecticut category norms. *Journal of Experimental Psychology Monograph, 80*, 1–44.

Klein, S. B., Loftus, J., & Burton, H. A. (1989). Two self-reference effects: The importance of distinguishing between self-descriptiveness judgments and autobiographical retrieval in self-referent encoding. *Journal of Personality and Social Psychology, 56*, 853–865.

Rosch, E. R. (1975). Cognitive representations of semantic categories. *Journal of Experimental Psychology: General, 104*, 192–233.

Rosch, E. R., Mervis, C. B., Gray, W. D., Johnson, D. M., & Boyes-Braem, P. (1976). Basic objects in natural categories. *Cognitive Psychology, 8*, 382–439.

Schneider, W. (1988). *Micro Experimental Laboratory* (MEL). [Computer program]. Pittsburgh, PA: Psychology Software Tools.

Tulving, E. (1989). Remembering and knowing. *American Scientist, 77*, 361–367.

8 Developing Self-Knowledge From Autobiographical Memory

Katherine Nelson
City University of New York Graduate Center

Developmental psychology can often shed light on issues that arise in the study of adult cognition. Indeed, it is a premise of developmental psychology that mature forms can best be understood through the study of their development. The present issue of the independence of the representation of trait and auto-biographical knowledge about the self is a good case in point. I believe that recent studies of the emergence of autobiographical memory in early childhood, and their implications for memory function and organization, can help to in-terpret the findings from Klein and Loftus' (chapter 1, this volume) elegant series of experiments with adults.

Klein and Loftus found that exemplar models and associative network models of semantic memory cannot account for their data. In explanation, they note that those models have been developed to account for the representation of informa-tion that differs in important ways from knowledge about the self. These models do not seem to be applicable to systems of knowledge that consist of "a vast amount of information that has been acquired across a variety of meaningful contexts over the course of a lifetime" (p. 32). They note further that studies of autobiographical memory have shown (a) "that repeated exposure to related experiences leads to the formation of abstract self-knowledge"; and (b) that abstractions remain accessible in memory while the specific experiences that led to their formation do not. However, with low experience a trait judgment requires the same type of information that an autobiographical retrieval makes possible.

Klein and Loftus support a model of self-knowledge in which (a) long-term trait knowledge is represented in abstract summary form, and (b) this representa-tion is functionally independent of the representation of behavioral exemplars. They cite Tulving's (1989) distinction between episodic self-knowledge and semantic self-knowledge that has been abstracted from specific events. This distinction, of course, is related to Tulving's long-standing differentiation between episodic and semantic memory (Tulving, 1972, 1983). The relation to Klein and Loftus' distinction between behavioral exemplars and trait knowledge is obvious, with semantic self-knowledge equated to summary trait knowledge. I argue here that this distinction is right as far as it goes, but it does not go far enough; finer distinctions must be recognized between different levels of abstraction. Further, trait descriptions (labels) may occur at only one of these levels, and the source of these labels may be the judgments of others, instead of or in addition to self-judgments.

This discussion is based on studies of memory in early childhood. Important questions addressed in these studies are when and why autobiographical memory begins to be established—or in reverse form, when and how infantile amnesia (the inability to recall episodes from the early years of one's life) is overcome. These studies indicate that the relation of the emergence of autobiographical memory to self-knowledge is quite direct.

EMERGENCE OF AUTOBIOGRAPHICAL MEMORY

The developmental problem of the emergence of autobiographical memory attracted little attention until recently, but there has been a surge of research since the late 1980s that has begun to clarify the psychological and social origins of the memory system that constitutes a personal life history for each individual. It is well-established that this life history begins sometime after 3 years of age, and for most people a personal memory record contains very little before the early school years (Rubin, 1986). Two related questions emerge: Is the late development of this system the result of a lack of episodic memories or of some other cause? What enables the development of an autobiographical memory system?

An early approach to this problem was the suggestion, based on research on young children's scripts for familiar events, that in early childhood general event memory was the only available memory system (Nelson & Ross, 1980). The idea was that experiences of novel (unscripted) episodes would not be remembered because they did not fit existing schemas, although we also suggested that one-time events might be schematized and remembered in skeletal script form.

More recent research has shown that even very young children have not only general scripts for familiar events, but often quite extensive and well-organized memories for specific episodes of events that they have experienced (Fivush & Hudson, 1990). If true episodic memories do exist for children younger than 3 years (which is the usual cutoff point for the earliest autobiographical memories) why do some of these memories not persist into adulthood?

To address this question it is necessary to make a principled distinction between episodic and autobiographical memory. The most obvious basis for such a distinction is that autobiographical memories consist of those episodic memories that are long-lasting and that enter into our self-definitional histories, whether or not they are easily accessible to conscious recall. Episodic memories, on the other hand, may include both those that become autobiographical and those that have only an evanescent and nonsignificant existence. For example, what I had for lunch yesterday is today part of my episodic memory of yesterday's events, but it has no other significance to my life history and will not be recallable some weeks hence, except through some process of reconstruction, script knowledge, and guesswork. Selective forgetting is an important component of memory. These considerations suggest that endurance is not the most important dimension along which to distinguish between autobiographical and other episodic memories, but that endurance is itself a function of other dimensions, such as meaningfulness, significance, importance, or novelty. Most basically, what are remembered are episodes that are significant in establishing one's sense of self. From this perspective, self-knowledge and autobiographical memory are but two sides of the same coin. And both emerge late in the early childhood years. Yet as Klein and Loftus demonstrated, they appear to be functionally independent systems in the adult.

This apparent discrepancy may be clarified as we pursue the question as to what lies behind the emergence of a self-history. Research that has established the existence of episodic memories in young children has also demonstrated that (U.S. middle-class) parents and children begin to talk about past experiences when the children are somewhere between 2 and 3 years of age. At first, parents may provide most of the information about what has happened, with children contributing little or nothing, but as experience with such talk accumulates, children take on increasingly active roles and begin to co-construct the memory of a shared experience. In summarizing results from her study of her own daughter's development of memory talk, Hudson (1990) stated:

> over the 7 months of talking about the past, Rachel learned a lot about how to remember, that is, about how to participate and, finally, to initiate conversations about the past rather than rehearsing specific content. . . . Eventually Rachel began to interpret the conversations not as a series of questions to be answered but as an activity of remembering. (p. 183)

In brief, very young children remember specific episodes, and in the course of talking with parents and others about their shared experiences they learn to formulate those memories as narratives that can be shared and compared with others' experiences. They acquire something of the adults' sense of what is valuable in an experience. They may also learn to label actions and emotions with value-laden terms that come to take a place in their self-knowledge system. Thus, *both* semantic and episodic memory contribute to the development of self-knowledge as the autobiographical memory system is established in early childhood.

This aspect of the emergence of self-knowledge can be illustrated with data from the study of a single child between 2 and 3 years, who was taperecorded as her parents put her to bed at night, and after they left the room as she talked to herself before sleep (Nelson, 1989). Emily's pre-sleep monologues contained examples of episodic memories, as well as general scripts. Interestingly, her talk with her father also contained evidence of growing semantic memory in Tulving's sense, for example, in terms of the emergence of a category of breakfast foods from talk about what Emily wanted to eat on the following day (Nelson, in press-a). There is also evidence in these discussions of the emergence of both episodic and semantic knowledge of self.

Consider in this respect, a portion of pre-bed talk from her father when Emily was 23 months:

> What, why are you crying Emily? Cause you're a big girl now, why are you crying? . . . Does Carl [friend] cry when he goes to sleep? . . . Not very much. No . . . cause Carl's a big boy, and you're a big girl . . . and big boys and girls don't cry. Stephen [baby brother] cries when he goes to sleep because he's a little baby, but Emily and Carl . . . Carl's a big boy and Emily's a big girl! They don't cry. . . . You're such a good girl . . . you had such a fun time today . . . Carl came over . . . and did, did we go to Childworld?. . . . We had fun at Childworld? Huh? . . . We had fun at Childworld, didn't we? [. . . indicates a pause; . . . . indicates portions omitted]

In this excerpt the father conveys in specific terms *rules* and *definitions* (big girls and boys don't cry), *labels* distinguishing between self and others (big girls, babies), and *evaluative terms* for self (good girl). These may all be considered potential input to Emily's *semantic memory* system. Her father also summarizes the events of the day, potentially contributing to Emily's organization of *episodic memory*. Such talk was commonly observed in the pre-bed dialogues between parent and child.

Note that even at this early age, Emily was presented with resolving the conflict between the *label* "big girl," the evaluative *label* "good girl," and behavioral *rule* "don't cry" (all inputs to semantic self-knowledge), and her own actual behavior, crying (a characteristic of her episodic self). In a pre-sleep monologue after her father left the room this conflict was specifically addressed as Emily repeated her father's rule about who cries (babies) and who doesn't (big kids). Then she stated: "I big kid but I, I, I, I, I, . . . Ahhh ah ahhh kid . . . I big kid but I do cruu" [very very soft]. Having addressed but not resolved the conflict, she recovered her composure and began to sing. Such conflicts between self-labels and episodic memories may contribute to the dissociation between semantic self-knowledge and autobiographical memory that Klein and Loftus address. Indeed, at the end of the chapter they indicate that their model allows a contradiction between trait and behavioral self-knowledge such as that reflected here.

When Emily was 2½ years old, crying re-emerged as an issue that distinguished Emily from her friend, after they started nursery school:

> See Charlotte, . . . her mommy and dad, Charlotte's mom and dad all leave, and she's going to, then she'll cry and call for [teacher] so?? her daddy or mommy will . . . stay the whole time . . . but my mommy and daddy don't. They just tell me what's happening and then go right to work. Cause I don't cause I don't cause I don't cry.

Here we see that Emily has absorbed her father's rule and brought her behavioral self-knowledge into conformance with her trait self-knowledge so that the conflict no longer exists.

That parental self-descriptive terms may be misunderstood is apparent in the following sequence from 2½ years:

> Mother: Goodnight little dumpling. [exits from room] E [alone]: Well, I'm not a little dumm. You are little dummy . . . Me not. . . .

This misunderstanding in itself probably had no long-term implications for Emily's self-concept, but the potential for conflicting descriptions by self and others is apparent.

Finally, consider the following monologue from when Emily was almost 3 years: "Anyway so then I, then they decided to do with me when I'm cranky because they don't like me to crank. They don't like Em. They don't like me's." Here Emily applies to herself the evaluative term *cranky* and seems to conclude that "they" don't like her. She may be uncertain as to whether this is only when she's cranky or as a general case.

These excerpts from one child's internalization of parental rules and self-descriptions indicate that semantic self-knowledge may be explicitly conveyed to the child from parental or other's talk. This source of trait knowledge is not addressed in the Klein and Loftus model, although it is well-recognized in the social development and childrearing literature. It may seem that talk with a 2-year-old has little bearing on the organization of adult memory, but I suggest that the process of labeling one's own traits begins here in early childhood as the child acquires the labels and concepts that parents and others apply to her. The process continues throughout life, although overt labeling may not always be explicit. Autobiographical memory is not composed simply of a record of one's own behaviors but of the social context in which they occur, and of others' actions and reactions, verbal and nonverbal, to oneself.

LEVELS OF MEMORY FUNCTION AND ABSTRACTION

A premise of the model of memory development that I have been exploring (Nelson, in press-b) is that mammalian memory, including basic human memory is a functional, general, or abstract system for maintaining information about possible happenings. Such information may be retained in general summary script form, and it may be abstracted into more dynamically organized components, as described by Schank (1982). Essentially, this system, composed of event schemas, provides a basis for constructing a model of how the world operates. In this sense it constitutes a general knowledge system abstracted from episodic experience. This general memory system is characteristic of early childhood. Specific episodic memory during this period serves the same function as general event memory of providing information about how things are in the world. Specific episodic memories may be retained for some time if they have some significance in and of themselves for this understanding function. There is nonetheless a dominance of schematic or general knowledge in the young child's event memory system (Hudson & Nelson, 1986). And knowledge of self in early childhood reflects the same reliance on general rather than specific information (Eder, 1989).

This kind of general event memory is apparently similar to what Klein and Loftus describe as Tulving's semantic self-knowledge, abstracted over repeated episodic experiences. Yet Tulving's (1983) description of semantic memory is more conceptual, being organized not according to temporal relations, but categorically, depending to a large extent on verbal principles and input. General event knowledge, although general, is neither semantic—about facts and concepts—nor episodic—specifically located both temporally and spatially. The implication is that dichotomous descriptions like Tulving's are not adequate; contradictions exist within the system, suggesting the need for further distinctions. In fact, implicit in Klein and Loftus' tasks is a system with at least three levels: definitional (semantic), descriptive (conceptual), and autobiographical (episodic), each of which is accessed through a verbal trait label. These levels are more consistent with the system that developmental studies suggest emerges in early to middle childhood from the basic general event memory system just sketched. I turn now to its further development.

Talking about memories with adults or other children provides the basis for establishing a new function for the retention of specific memories, that of socially shared experience. In addition, such talk provides a model of narrative construction of memory that may present the child with a more coherent structure for organizing memories into a system. Further, talk with others about a memory reinstates the experience and thus enables it to persist in memory beyond the time that it otherwise might. Such talk transforms evanescent episodic memories into autobiographical memories. Thus, talking with others about shared experiences is causally connected in multiple ways to the establishment of an auto-biographical system of personal memories in early to middle childhood (Nelson, in press-b).

As outlined here, the first transformation in the memory system is from episodic to general event memory; the second transformation, just described, is from specific episodic to specific autobiographical. Yet another transformation takes place within the system beginning very early, and that is the abstraction from event memory of general concepts and categories (Nelson, 1983, 1985). General categories are evident in the behavior of very young children (Bauer & Mandler, 1989). A basic form of this kind of knowledge is the "slot-filler category" derived from experiences of variations in events over time. For example, children form slot-filler categories of lunch foods, zoo animals, clothes to put on in the morning, on the basis of those items that they have experienced in those contexts on different occasions (Lucariello, Kyratzis, & Nelson, 1992; Nelson, 1988). These kinds of experientially based categories may be similar to experientially based trait summaries or conceptualizations of general behavioral dispositions in the self-knowledge system.

Children may also construct semantic knowledge based on what they are presented with in verbal form from adults. Parents and teachers often engage in teaching specific lessons about the alphabet, the number system, colors, shapes, days of the week, holidays, rules of etiquette, and such abstruse knowledge systems as dinosaurs. These systems are not abstracted from the child's direct experience in the world, but are mediated through the linguistic mode. It is a strong possibility that they are established in the child's representational struc-tures as an independent functional system, as implied in Tulving's original dis-tinction between episodic and semantic memory. The developmental literature suggests that verbally conveyed knowledge may be represented differently from either abstractions across events in the form of summaries or from abstractions in the form of categories. For example, it is possible to have a slot-filler category abstracted from experience consisting of zoo animals, and also recognize on the basis of verbal instruction that humans are animals, but keep the two categories separate in memory.

In summary, the following subsystems emerge in the course of development of the human memory system:

Specific experience → Episodic memory → Summary event
(script) memory
Specific experience → Episodic memory →
Autobiographical memory
Abstraction from scripts and episodes → Concepts,
categories, general knowledge
Verbal knowledge including rules and definitions →
Semantic memory

A further distinction might be entertained in that a behavioral summary based on summary event knowledge might be different in kind from conceptual knowledge organized as abstractions from event components, such as categories of objects or social roles, although both are derived from the first and second order abstractions from specific experience.

SELF-KNOWLEDGE MODEL IN LIGHT OF THE GENERAL MODEL

This model, although more complex, is roughly consistent with Klein and Loftus' claims, and it is suggested here that each of these five (episodic, event schema, autobiographical, conceptual, semantic), or six (behavioral summary) emergent systems may be functionally autonomous, although each may be accessed through verbal labels, and each must have connections with the others. The system is thus an elaboration of Klein and Loftus' two-level system.

Nonetheless, it is important that there is not a simple dichotomy between semantic self-knowledge and episodic memory, but rather that there are at least four *sources* of self-knowledge in memory:

1. short-term episodic memory (e.g., making out a check yesterday to a favorite charity);
2. long-term autobiographical memory (e.g., lending a favorite sweater to a friend in high school who admired it);
3. long-term summary and/or conceptual knowledge derived from episodic/event representations (e.g., more often you give more than others do or expect from you); and
4. semantic memory (e.g., you are called "generous" by self and others).

This last source is neglected in the Klein and Loftus model, but developmental evidence suggests that it is an important source of information about the self and must be taken into account. The semantic system reflects other people's estimations of one's self, together with one's own self-labeling based on the accumulation of evidence in the autobiographical, general event, and conceptual systems.

At this point it is not possible to say how distinct these memory sources are, or whether there are intermediate or continuous connections between them. For example, yesterday's check might have been especially large and have called forth the self-congratulatory "that's certainly very generous," thus connecting the episode directly with semantic memory (just as Emily's father connects his self-labels directly to Emily's behaviors). Episodic memories that are especially significant for self-knowledge enter the autobiographical memory system, but there is no guarantee that one's own evaluation of behavioral evidence is consistent with the evidence from the total flow of life experience, nor with the evaluations expressed by others through their labels of one's behaviors. Thus, there may be conflicts among the functional systems as well as correspondences, as already indicated, and as Klein and Loftus recognize.

Such conflicts in the memory/belief system are likely to be resolved when they involve some objectively decideable fact (e.g., was it 1973 or 1974 when Nixon resigned?) or socially agreed upon concept (e.g., women and men are entitled to equal treatment in the work place, although you may have vivid memories of distinctly unequal treatment 20 years ago). But when the conflicts exist among different *sources* of self-knowledge they may be more difficult to resolve. They may in fact be unresolvable and remain functionally distinct. Recall Emily's bringing forth both her father's appellation of "big kid" and her own (general event) evidence of crying, without discarding either one. Of course a 2-year-old has not moved very far toward a definition of self; and indeed if the developmental story outlined earlier is correct, she has not yet begun to accumulate the most important kinds of evidence for establishing self-knowledge from autobiographical memory. Yet already she is faced with incorporating her father's semantic description into her knowledge system, together with his expectation of what behaviors "big kids" and "good girls" engage in.

The organization of each of these functionally independent systems may be rather different, and this organization may have implications for function and conflict. Summary event knowledge may be organized, as Schank (1982) suggested, in terms of a dynamic memory system in which different components can be recombined in different ways to satisfy the particular circumstances of a present event. Labels may be helpful in calling up and recombining the parts, but are not necessary. Autobiography follows a time line established independently of the particular events remembered, such as school years, first jobs, marriage, and so forth (Barsalou, 1988). Other research has shown that autobiographical episodes may also be cross-referenced and accessed by topic, place, or person. Again, labels might help in accessing but are not essential. For example, thoughts of a sibling may call up a particular episode from childhood that is not specifically attached to any word.

Recent theorizing has suggested that conceptual knowledge is organized in terms of domain-specific theories. In these models, theories consist of causally connected concepts that form a coherent whole, enabling predictions and explanations. In the case of conceptual knowledge of the self one would want to explain and predict one's own behavior. A theory of the self would seek evidence from episodic memory that would be consistent with those concepts that already exist. Thus, to extend the example just given, an episode of nongenerous behavior (perhaps passing by a homeless man on the street) would be justified in terms of some other self-trait (perhaps rationality). The episode might persist in memory, however, for some other reason, perhaps because the person was particularly aggressive, thus frightening, and suggested a reason for considering a move away from the city.

Although according to the present argument the labels for self-traits derive from their use by other people, they attach to the concepts that one has built up from experience. "That's very generous of you" attaches itself to a particular episode of generosity, and eventually to evidence of generous acts in general. Thus, the semantic system may come to reflect the conceptual organization of the conceptual system. However, the semantic system also reflects the culturally constructed system of concepts and word meanings; thus its connections depend on how language is used by the community at large. Applying the term *generous* to oneself may evoke a whole system of culturally embedded knowledge of generous acts.

The autobiographical system, based as it is on actual behavior, can never be as consistent as the conceptual system. The conceptual and semantic systems may be able to maintain two nonconflicting traits (generosity and rationality) simultaneously, but actual behaviors cannot always avoid conflictual motives in real-world experience. Thus, the conceptual (abstract) and autobiographical (experiential) systems must be functionally independent, as indeed Klein and Loftus found.

In summary, Klein and Loftus have gone some way toward taking the development of self-knowledge into account in their differentiation of brief experience and extended experience effects, and have also provided strong evidence for the functional independence of the episodic and conceptual memory systems involved in self-knowledge. The discussion here emphasizes that the memory/knowledge system is more complex than the simple dichotomy implies, and that the social contribution to self-knowledge must be acknowledged, in both its developing and its mature forms.

REFERENCES

Barsalou, L. W. (1988). The content and organization of autobiographical memories. In U. Neisser & E. A. Winograd (Eds.), *Remembering reconsidered: Ecological and traditional approaches to the study of memory* (pp. 193–243). New York: Cambridge University Press.

Bauer, P. J., & Mandler, J. M. (1989). Taxonomies and triads: Conceptual organization in one- to two-year-olds. *Cognitive Psychology, 21*, 156–184.

Eder, R. A. (1989). The Emergent personologist: The structure and content of 3½-, 5½-, and 7½-year-olds' concepts of themselves and other persons. *Child Development, 60*, 1218–1228.

Fivush, R., & Hudson, J. A. (1990). *Knowing and remembering in young children*. New York: Cambridge University Press.

Hudson, J., & Nelson, K. (1986). Repeated encounters of a similar kind: Effects of familiarity on children's autobiographical memory. *Cognitive Development, 1*, 253–271.

Hudson, J. A. (1990). The emergence of autobiographic memory in mother–child conversation. In R. Fivush & J. A. Hudson (Eds.), *Knowing and remembering in young children* (pp. 166–196). New York: Cambridge University Press.

Lucariello, J., Kyratzis, A., & Nelson, K. (1992). Taxonomic knowledge: What kind and when. *Child Development, 63*, 978–998.

Nelson, K. (1983). The derivation of concepts and categories from event representations. In E. Scholnick (Ed.), *New trends in conceptual representation: challenges to Piaget's theory?* (pp. 129–149). Hillsdale, NJ: Lawrence Erlbaum Associates.

Nelson, K. (1985). *Making sense: The acquisition of shared meaning.* New York: Academic Press.

Nelson, K. (1988). Where do taxonomic categories come from? *Human Development, 31,* 3–10.

Nelson, K. (Ed.). (1989). *Narratives from the crib.* Cambridge MA: Harvard University Press.

Nelson, K. (in press-a). Events, narratives, memories: What develops? In C. Nelson (Ed.), *Memory and Affect in Development: Minnesota Symposia on Child Psychology* (Vol. 26). Hillsdale, NJ: Lawrence Erlbaum Associates.

Nelson, K. (in press-b). Explaining the emergence of autobiographical memory in early childhood. In A. Collins, M. Conway, S. Gathercole, & P. Morris (Ed.), *Theories of memory.* Hillsdale, NJ: Lawrence Erlbaum Associates.

Nelson, K., & Ross, G. (1980). The generalities and specifics of long term memory in infants and young children. In M. Perlmutter (Ed.), *Children's memory: New directions for child development* (Vol. 10, pp. 87–101). San Francisco: Jossey-Bass.

Rubin, D. C. (Eds.) (1986). *Autobiographical memory.* New York: Cambridge University Press.

Schank, R. C. (1982). *Dynamic memory: A theory of reminding and learning in computers and people.* New York: Cambridge University Press.

Tulving, E. (1972). Episodic and semantic memory. In E. Tulving & W. Donaldson (Eds.), *Organization of memory* (pp. 382–403). New York: Academic Press.

Tulving, E. (1983). *Elements of episodic memory.* New York: Oxford University Press.

Tulving, E. (1989). Remembering and knowing. *American Scientist, 77,* 361–367.

9 Diverse Ways of Accessing Self-Knowledge: Comment on Klein and Loftus

David J. Schneider
Henry L. Roediger III
Mustaq Khan
Rice University

Klein and Loftus (Chapter 1, this volume) report an important series of experiments that introduce a new paradigm and produce admirably clear results with an interesting theoretical message. The paradigm and chapter are both exciting in our opinion, and represent significant advances in exploring how knowledge about the self may be represented.

We do, however, offer comments suggesting that some of Klein and Loftus' interpretations of their results may be overstated at present. First, we suggest that their results do not provide definitive evidence that no facilitation occurs from prior performance of the tasks related to their target tasks, as they have argued. Second, we argue that the present results may apply to their paradigm but do not necessarily generalize to other ways of accessing self-knowledge.

One of the strong features of this program of research is the use of several methodologies that converge on a common theme. Klein and Loftus are careful to point out that no one set of methods can resolve the issues. Nonetheless, it is clear that the task-facilitation paradigm is central to their thinking, and most of our comments are addressed to issues we see with its use.

THE PRIMING PARADIGM

Klein and Loftus refer to their experimental situation as the task-facilitation paradigm, but it could easily have been referred to as a priming paradigm, a name that would have made clearer the links to existing issues in cognitive psychology. In general, in a priming paradigm cognitive psychologists examine how some target task is facilitated by prior exposure to related information or tasks that are assumed to prime the target task. In the present case, Klein and Loftus gave their subjects trait adjectives and asked them to perform one of three tasks: judging whether the task described them (descriptive), recalling an episode from the past that exemplified the trait (autobiographical), or providing a definition of the trait (semantic). The target task was preceded by one of the three tasks as a priming event. Following Cofer (1967), we may also distinguish between direct and indirect priming. Direct priming refers to facilitation in a task (on the second occasion) when the same task is performed twice. Indirect priming refers to facilitation of a task when it is preceded by a different (but related) task. Both types of priming are typically measured against a neutral baseline or control condition where the target task is performed by itself (i.e., unprimed).

The basic prediction from exemplar views is based on the following logic: If people make an explicit descriptive judgment of whether a trait applies to them by first accessing a specific autobiographical event, then making the descriptive judgment (which includes accessing autobiographical memories) should prime subsequent autobiographical recall. More specifically, greater priming should occur on the autobiographical task from having previously performed the descriptive task than from having previously performed the semantic task. This did not occur: Speed of producing an autobiographical judgment was equivalent after either the semantic or descriptive tasks, but more priming did occur when subjects performed the same autobiographical task both times. Put another way, direct priming from the same task did occur, but the predicted indirect priming from a judgment (assumed to involve the same process of event recall) was not greater than that which occurred from the semantic task (assumed not to involve event recall).

The same pattern of results occurred when the target task was descriptive; speed of judgment was essentially the same when the previous task had been either autobiographical recall or semantic judgment. One would think that if retrieving autobiographical memories is a part of making trait judgments, then these trait judgments should also benefit from previous autobiographical judgments, because a part of the descriptive task had already taken place. In other words, the autobiographical task should prime the descriptive task more than the semantic task should. This also did not occur. So these results argue against the idea that people implicitly retrieve autobiographical memories of deeds when they make trait judgments, at least for one's self. However, when the target person was mother instead of the self (Experiment 5), the predicted pattern of indirect priming did occur, indicating that subjects recalled behavioral episodes in judging mothers' traits (at least for medium and low descriptive traits).

Klein and Loftus drew the following conclusions (among others): Self-knowledge is represented in terms of enduring and abstract representations (such as traits, schemas, or prototypes) that are accessed directly in making self-judgments. However, in assessing knowledge of others we know less well,[1] traits are more likely to be inferred "on the fly" from knowledge of behavioral episodes. Klein and Loftus also suggest that their data are incompatible with representations of self-knowledge in terms of associative network models in which general trait terms are represented as nodes under which are nested specific behaviors exemplifying the traits.

The specific comparisons provided in their experiments permit a test of their ideas, and, in general, the lack of differential priming from, for example, autobiographical or semantic tasks to the self-descriptiveness task supports their conclusions. However, their analysis could be taken further to answer an interesting ancillary question: Does performance of the prior task produce any priming (or facilitation) on this target task? If so, does the same pattern of priming occur across target tasks? Unfortunately, the analyses presented in the target chapter do not permit answers to these questions, because data from an unprimed (or no relevant experience) control condition are not included. The lack of a controlled unprimed baseline is therefore somewhat problematic. For example, when the autobiographical task was the target task, there were three priming conditions, one involving direct priming (the autobiographical task itself) and two involving indirect priming (the descriptive and semantic tasks). There is clearly greater direct than indirect priming, and there was no greater indirect priming from the descriptive than from the semantic task. However, such results do not entitle us to conclude that no indirect priming occurred. For that we would need comparison with an unprimed control. Although such data are not presented in the target chapter, they were presented in Klein, Loftus, and Burton (1989) where latencies are given for each task presented first as a prime. If we use these data as a proxy for the unprimed baseline conditions, then we can examine how much priming occurs in both the direct and indirect priming conditions for the data presented in Fig. 1.1 of chapter 1.

The relevant data showing the amount of priming for the various conditions appear in Table 9.1.[2] The trend that Klein and Loftus point to, of greater direct than indirect priming for each target task, is clearly present, but these data speak to another point on which Klein and Loftus were silent. There seems to be considerable indirect priming on the self-descriptiveness task; that is, compared to the self-descriptiveness baselines, judgments for this task are facilitated when the subjects had made either an autobiographical or a semantic judgment about the same trait previously. Indeed, such indirect priming is more than half that of

---

[1]The comparison between self and other has thus far used only mother as a target other person. We would resist sweeping conclusions about how knowledge of others is organized and differs from self-knowledge based on this one target person who conceivably has special features for many subjects.

[2]We thank Stan Klein for providing these data.

TABLE 9.1
Reaction Times and Amounts of Priming (in Milliseconds) for the Descriptive, Autobiographical, and Semantic Tasks in Experiment 1 as a Function of Priming Task. The Unprimed Baseline Data are from Figure 1a of Klein, Loftus, and Burton (1989) and the Primed Data are from Figure 2. Data in Parentheses Represent the Estimated Amounts of Priming (Unprimed–Primed)

	Target Task		
Priming Task	Descriptive	Autobiographical	Semantic
None	2,875	5,486	4,235
Descriptive	1,780 (1,095)	5,356 (130)	4,108 (127)
Autobiographical	2,237 (638)	2,433 (3,053)	3,867 (368)
Semantic	2,303 (572)	5,092 (394)	2,381 (1,854)

the direct priming (from having previously done the descriptiveness task itself). This indirect priming cannot have been due merely to spreading activation in the lexicon or even facilitation due to practice at reading the trait words, or else similar amounts of facilitation should appear in all indirect priming conditions.

Although there is considerable indirect priming when the descriptive task was the target task, there seems to be little when the other two tasks were target tasks. This statement may seem to be belied by the rather sizeable numbers in parentheses for the other two tasks, because priming is often measured in tens of milliseconds in tasks such as naming and lexical decision. However, the unprimed base rates in these traditional tasks are quite low relative to the ones in Klein and Loftus' experiments; subjects in the semantic and autobiographical tasks take over 4 and 5 seconds, respectively, when they perform the task for the first time. A clearer picture of relative priming effects in the three tasks can be seen from the proportion priming measures given in Table 9.2, where the amount of priming observed in each condition (unprimed–primed) is divided by the unprimed base rate. So, for example, the .38 in the upper left-hand corner is derived by dividing 1,095 (the amount of priming) by the baseline time to perform the task (2,875). This measure may be called the relative proportion of priming.

Table 9.2 shows that the relative proportion of direct priming (the diagonal cells) is quite large (.38, .56, and .44) in the three conditions. However, sizeable indirect priming occurs only when the descriptive task is the target task. Performing the descriptive task first produces almost no priming on either of the other tasks, although the other relevant conditions seem to show a bit more indirect priming (albeit still not close to that seen when the descriptive task was the target). It is not obvious, from Klein and Loftus' theory (or any other we

TABLE 9.2
Relative Proportion of Priming for the Data in Table 9.1

Prime Task	Target Task		
	Descriptive	Autobiographical	Semantic
Descriptive	.38	.02	.03
Autobiographical	.22	.56	.09
Semantic	.20	.07	.44

know), how to explain these differences in indirect priming across tasks (assuming they are real).

If replicable, these data have important consequences for Klein and Loftus' larger claims that lack of indirect priming argues against spreading activation theories of self-judgments. There was in fact some indirect priming in their experiment, which may be interpreted as indicating that some sort of activation spreads throughout the system. However, the fact that indirect priming is less than direct priming still supports their point that self-definitions are facilitated more by direct performance of the task than indirect performance by having to produce a behavioral episode. Note that the autobiographical task did not create more indirect priming than did the semantic task even on the descriptive task (where there was sizeable indirect priming in both cases). The general point is that in the task-facilitation paradigm, one should examine facilitation from a prior task against some relevant baseline, rather than only comparing tasks against one another. A general theory applied to this task should be able to explain the various patterns of indirect priming, as well as the difference between direct and indirect priming that the authors' have examined.

GENERALITY OF THE PARADIGM

Central to Klein and Loftus' argument is the proposition that for self-knowledge there is a functional independence between abstract trait information and behaviors that are somehow tied to those traits. Generally, the Klein and Loftus data suggest that subjects do not seem to use behavioral exemplars to help them make more general trait judgments. But there are two major limitations that we find in this generalization. First, nothing is implied about what subjects might do when they are asked to perform a different sort of task. Second, the fact that subjects do not use behavioral information in this task to inform their trait judgments does not logically imply that these two domains are radically distinct. Subsequently, we agree that behaviors and traits are quite independent domains but our argument is along quite different lines from that of Klein and Loftus.

Method Limitation

Klein and Loftus used a clever methodology with latency measures having pride of place. However, their methods, like all methods, constrain results and limit generality. In this case, latency measures are not the only probe into underlying cognitive processes, nor do they necessarily provide good data on what *can* go on as opposed to what has gone on in a particular laboratory setting. The same, of course, might be said of the other memory measures they employ in their research. Specifically, the research presented by Klein and Loftus may say little or nothing about what people usually do when they are trying to generate trait judgments. It certainly says nothing about what they are capable of doing under differing circumstances.

Perform the following thought experiment. You are asked whether you are hard working. According to Klein and Loftus, you bypass the opportunity to think about the times in your life when you have been hard working and instead reach right into the trait folder you keep for such purposes and pull out a "yes"[3] answer. There clearly are times in everyday life when one would make such a judgment in that way. A job interview is a situation where you might be asked to make a quick, unreflective judgment, for example, and the job interviewer conceivably might even be assessing latency of response as an index of confidence or honesty. Now, however, imagine a different situation. Suppose you have been accused of being insensitive on gender or race issues, and you are now asked if you are sensitive to the concerns of disadvantaged groups. Do you now reach for the "sensitivity folder" as rapidly as you previously reached for the "hard-working folder"? Probably not. One might imagine that you would be inclined to think through your past sensitive and insensitive behaviors and use this opportunity to update your estimate of your sensitivity quotient.

The argument we want to make here has nothing to do with ecological validity of situations or experimental measures. Clearly, both examples given here are extreme. The point is this: There are many times when people are encouraged to make rather quick judgments about their traits, and in such situations it is even reasonable to imagine that latency might be considered relevant data (for those who worry, as we do not, about the ecological validity of this particular measure). But just as clearly there are times when thinking about behavior is useful and important in making self-judgments, and people may be quite slow and reflective in reaching a judgment. We should be wary of generalizing from tasks in which subjects are pressured to make quick and unreflective judgments to those in which they are likely to think more about the basis of their decisions.

We are convinced that behaviors and traits must have a closer relationship than Klein and Loftus would seem to allow. To take their argument to its extreme, once trait judgments are formed and dissociated from their behavioral evidence,

---

[3]Surely readers of this chapter would not answer "no."

it would be hard ever to change one's judgments about one's self. Clearly, such change is neither easy nor commonplace, but it does happen. So the fact that in the paradigm used in this research subjects show relatively little evidence of having made trait judgments by consulting their autobiographical memories does not permit the conclusion that they can never make judgments that way or that behaviors and traits are somehow severed from cognitive contact. The data offered by Klein and Loftus do suggest that the strong form of the exemplar hypothesis—people **must** access behaviors to make trait judgments—is wrong. Their data do not speak to the issue of whether people **can** use such information, or even whether they often or usually do.

Functional Dissociation

There are additional reasons why one cannot maintain anything like a general or strong version of the argument about a lack of functional identity between traits and their supporting behaviors. Perhaps most compelling is the simple fact that one can obviously generate many behavioral instances for and against any particular trait. So at a minimum there must be links from traits to behaviors, although we admit that such informal data do not necessarily prove that such links are frequently operative or that people traverse them in the opposite direction from behavior to trait. However, there are links in the other direction as well. We give you a behavior and ask whether it shows kindness or intelligence. Obviously, this sort of question is an easy one for most people to answer. Ah, but this is surely semantic knowledge at its most personally remote. You are not answering a question about whether this behavior that you performed indicated *your* kindness but a question about the meanings of words or perhaps generalizations based on cultural knowledge. However, it is perfectly reasonable to ask a more personal question as well and to expect an answer: "Were you being kind when you did x?" Such judgments may, of course, continue to have a fairly strong semantic memory component, but they probably also involve considerable self-relevant knowledge.

The Salience Argument.   The fact that reflections on behaviors affect our judgments about our traits is also self-evident from experience and experimental data showing that accessing behavioral data changes the content (if not the speed) of trait judgments. There are several experiments that generally show that thinking about behaviors or otherwise making them salient leads to strong corresponding trait and attitude judgments. Such evidence is potentially quite damaging to the argument of Klein and Loftus, and so they are at some pains to turn these data into support for their argument on pages 36–38. Ultimately they argue that in the most convincing of previous demonstrations (e.g., Fazio, Effrein, & Falender, 1981), the behavioral judgments were actually fairly abstract and far from behavioral exemplars. Thus, Klein and Loftus suggest that the Fazio et al. study really provides no support for behavioral exemplars (as opposed to abstracted summaries) priming trait judgments. They then go on to provide data of their own showing that making such abstracted behavioral judgments does, in fact, facilitate subsequent trait judgments. This makes the latency data and the judgment data line up to salute the Klein–Loftus model. Abstract behavioral summaries facilitate the speed of trait judgments just as they make trait judgments more likely or extreme. These are not, however, the data we require to dispose of the argument that behavior salience affects trait judgments in ways other than latency. Rather, we would like to see subjects placed in the Fazio paradigm with the requirement that they make concrete behavioral judgments and observe the effects on their trait judgments. We expect, but Klein and Loftus presumably do not, that when subjects generate a number of specific instances of kindness they will then rate themselves as kinder. This would show that thinking about even concrete behaviors affects trait judgments but not necessarily the speed with which trait judgments are made.

Amnesics.   The case of amnesics is an interesting one in this regard. For example, patient K. C. studied by Tulving, Hayman, and Macdonald (1991) seems to have a relatively stable self-concept while being unable to remember much of his personal experiences. K. C. is particularly notable in this regard in that he is unable to remember a single incident from his life. Klein and Loftus argue that such loss of autobiographical experiences should produce catastrophic problems in self-identity if exemplar models are correct in suggesting that we make inferences about our own traits by consciously consulting (or recollecting) events of our recent past.

We have two responses. First, that argument applies only to those who would argue that the only way we can make trait judgments is by consulting behaviors. We would agree that the amnesic data diminish the force of the strong exemplar view. On the other hand, we have argued that there may be many ways that people make trait judgments in everyday life, including using stored, already computed summaries of one's behavior. Amnesics may have access to such summaries just as the rest of us do. What we would argue is that the rest of us also have the capacity, which we use at least some of the time, to make trait judgments by recollecting the past behavior of self and others. The fact that amnesics cannot do this does not prove any general statement about functional separations between the behavioral and trait domains.

Second, we also think it possible that Klein and Loftus have drawn the wrong conclusions from observations about amnesics by assuming that exemplar checking must be a conscious process. The great lesson of memory research with amnesics is that although they may be poor on various direct measures of memory such as recall, when their memories are assessed using various implicit memory measures they show performance (priming) just like normal subjects (Shimamura, 1986).

Recently, there has been considerable interest in studying implicit measures of memory (Roediger, 1990; Schacter, 1987) in which retention is expressed as transfer or priming of recent experiences on some other task. Implicit measures of memory often reveal different effects of independent or subject variables from explicit measures of retention such as recall or recognition. Trait judgment tasks can thus function as implicit measures of memory, as pointed out by Smith and Branscombe (1988). In particular, trait judgments (whether of self or others) could be classified as a conceptual (or conceptually driven) implicit memory task because priming is produced on a meaningful dimension. These conceptual tests are contrasted with perceptual implicit memory tasks that are more affected by changes in surface features of materials such as mode of presentation (see Roediger, Weldon, & Challis, 1989, for explicit criteria to distinguish the two types of tests).

To return to amnesics, it is quite possible that they (and the rest of us) use personal experiences in making trait judgments but do so without conscious recollection of these experiences. Implicit memory tests such as trait judgments need not draw on conscious recollection of experiences; remember that amnesics do show normal effects on implicit memory tests in cases where there performance is quite poor on explicit memory tasks. If trait judgments operate as implicit memory measures, then conscious recollection of episodes may not be the basis for such judgments. Episodes from the past may thereby bias the judgment without necessarily being recalled. The test-facilitation paradigm, with its focus on conscious recollection of events, may then not be so critical to the issue as Klein and Loftus assume.

In another comment in this volume, Tulving (chapter 11) reports interesting new data about judgment's of K. C.'s personality before and after his accident. The interesting question is whether K. C.'s self-knowledge of his personality matches his premorbid (outgoing) personality or his new (more introverted) one? If Klein and Loftus are correct that self-knowledge is held in enduring and abstract schemas or even in schema that are occasionally updated by conscious recollection of experiences, then K. C. should not be aware of his personality change. However, Tulving's study shows that his self-descriptive trait judgments agree with his mother's; K. C. judges himself as reserved now. Surely K. C. updated his personality trait judgments via his changed behavior since the accident, even though he cannot consciously recollect the relevant behavioral episodes. This bolsters our contention that judging trait descriptiveness functions as a conceptual implicit memory test: Amnesics show change on the measure (through their experiences) even in the absence of conscious recollection. In short, amnesics (and the rest of us) may use experiences in making trait judgments about ourselves, but not in a way that is necessarily consciously accessible.[4]

---

[4]Our interpretation of these results differ in some ways from Tulving's. He assumes that conceptual priming on semantic memory reflects "abstract" representations; we assume that since judgments are changed on the basis of episodes, they are not so abstract.

Another interesting population that could be used to evaluate Klein and Loftus' ideas are those people with multiple personalities. When there are two or more personalities, will there be priming or transfer of one judgment to the same judgment when the person has shifted to a new personality? If so, will this priming be greater than with repetition priming when the personality has not shifted between occasions of testing? We know that people with multiple personalities show substantial semantic differential differences for their different personalities (Osgood & Luria, 1954; Osgood, Luria, Jeans, & Smith, 1976). Also, in an implicit memory study, a multiple personality case showed priming over occasions when the personality has shifted, but only on perceptual and not conceptual tests (Nissen, Ross, Willingham, Mackenzie, & Schacter, 1988). Thus, we might expect that even direct conceptual priming may not occur in Klein and Loftus' task-facilitation paradigm. One complication is that the same subject may give different responses to the same trait question, making direct comparison problematic. Nonetheless, the natural (if rare) phenomenon of multiple personality cases may serve as an interesting within subject variation for the study of self-judgments. Bipolar disorder may also represent an interesting case to test their ideas.

SELF AND OTHER KNOWLEDGE

Despite our criticisms, we reiterate that we found the methods and data presented in the target chapter provocative and important. Ultimately, however, we think the most important feature of this body of research is the stimulus it provides for collecting data as opposed to speculating about how self-knowledge is encoded, stored, and retrieved. Clearly, Klein and Loftus did not mean to say that self-knowledge consists only of stored, abstract trait attributions. We agree. The relations between traits and behaviors, we would argue, depend on what questions subjects are asked, how reflective they are, and how they choose to access the knowledge base that reflects their self-knowledge. Admittedly, that seems an uninspired summary. Much the same could be said of various other kinds of knowledge. Perhaps one of the lessons learned after 25 years of cognitive psychology is that people can and do access and perhaps represent their knowledge in many ways. There is probably no single way information about trees, George Bush, mothers, and self is stored, and there seem to be many ways we can access and manipulate that information.

The more interesting question at this point is whether different domains of knowledge are structured differently in principle. Klein and Loftus seem to argue that knowledge about self and about others differs only in quantitative ways (i.e., in terms of the amount of relevant experience). When we first acquire behavioral knowledge about a person (self or other), we may generate a trait summary. In time, however, that trait becomes autonomous from the evidence supporting it, and links between the trait and related behaviors are, for all intents and purposes, severed. Thus, the main difference between making judgments about self and others is that these links have been severed in the former because of great use. In principle, however, we may have links between behaviors and traits well preserved for self-knowledge in certain areas. And these same links might be broken for mother or another important figure about which one has much behavioral information as the Klein and Loftus data seem to show in Experiment 5. So, for example, imagine a new father making judgments about his fatherly behaviors and whether he is a good father. We might imagine that such judgments require a good deal of reflection and weighing of behavioral information. On the other hand, as our friend makes judgments about whether his own father was a fatherly sort of person, he might make such a judgment quickly and without much behavioral assessment because he has made that same judgment many times in the past. The point we wish to make, then, is that for Klein and Loftus there seems to be no other way that self and other knowledge differ except in how often trait judgments have been made in the past.

Is there more to the self-other difference? We suspect that there is. Self-theorists, at least in modern social psychology, have developed a strong case of Bemian wariness—a sort of Bem's razor.[5] Bem's (1967) paper would suggest that all trait judgments are generated on the fly, that there is no privileged summary information about traits available to me that is not available to you (given equivalent information), and that we should not assume storage of abstract knowledge about the self unless absolutely necessary. Although Bem (1972) subsequently backed away from the stronger forms of that argument, the legacy has been one of extreme mistrust of our own experience of self in this most phenomenological of domains. One salient virtue of the Klein and Loftus chapter is that it seeks to break the hegemony of the Bemian notion that traits must be inferred from behavior. However, our criticisms of this tradition are along different lines from those of Klein and Loftus.

Autobiographical Memory.   So at the risk of offending Bemians past and present, consider the following question. What do we know about our own behavior that others probably do not know? One answer is that we have more information about situational contingencies and the circumstances of behavior for our own behavior. Indeed, research on autobiographical memory makes this very point.

For example, Reiser, Black, and Abelson (1985) suggest that autobiographical memories are retrieved by accessing the larger (more abstract) knowledge structures used to encode the event. One recalls last Saturday night's concert by thinking about concert-going in general. They note that specific instances of

---

[5]With apologies to William of Ockham.

behavior can also be encoded in terms of generalized behaviors. So applauding a musical performance can be seen as a example of applauding, even perhaps (more generally) showing appreciation or playing out a scene from the concert-going script. They argue that activities (close to what have been called scripts) will provide a more efficient cue for specific behaviors than will general actions, and they showed that activities are more effective than general actions as cues with both latency and successful retrieval measures. Also, when the two cues are presented in combination, giving the activity cue followed by the general action cue is more effective than the reverse order. These data were interpreted as suggesting that there may be tighter links between specific behaviors and the scripts in which they are embedded than between behaviors and more general summaries (such as, taken to the extreme, traits).

Our point here is not to argue on behalf of any particular arrangement of traits, behaviors, contexts, and other autobiographical knowledge. Rather we want to suggest that at our present stage of knowledge about how self-relevant information is organized we are probably well advised to assume that this organization includes more than behaviors and traits and represents a complex set of interrelationships.

Privileged Information About Self.   There is something more. We know (or think we know—which is sufficient for present purposes) why we performed a particular behavior, and we know this not by performing some abstract attributional mental gymnastics but because we were privy to our own intentions and other relevant mental states prior to our performance of the behavior.[6] Moreover, at our best we have a fairly sophisticated knowledge not only about how our behaviors are affected by situational forces but how those relate to our goals and intentions. It seems important that such information be represented in our conceptions of self, but it is not easy to imagine how this might be done.

There are, however, at least two general issues that any such model must be able to address. The first is that although specific behaviors may be well coordinated with specific traits, it is also true that the same specific behavior can reflect many traits. Thus, your remembering that you helped your mother-in-law with her taxes may be, depending on your mental state at the time, an example of kind or snoopy behavior. Therefore, your knowledge that you are kind might, depending on your intentions at the time of the helping behavior, lead you to access that behavior as an exemplar. But the reverse is more problematic. Having accessed the tax behavior does not automatically lead you to any particular trait.

Second, people's trait judgments, at least for themselves, are not so much

---

[6]It is not especially germane to our argument that sometimes we are deluded, that profound unconscious forces may affect our behavior, or that much of the time we have no relevant mental states at all that accompany our behavior. All we require is that sometimes we have such privileged knowledge.

about past behaviors as about goals and intentions (Read, Jones, & Miller, 1990). If that were so, a functional dissociation between behaviors and traits at least for one's self would not be surprising, because those links were never formed explicitly in the first place. The judgments are about intentions, not past behavior. On the other hand, trait judgments of others are much more likely to be summary judgments of their past behaviors because we do not ordinarily have direct information about their intentions and goals.

Our general point is this: Traits and behaviors may be (probably are) linked in many ways. Klein and Loftus rely on what has historically been the most popular and influential of the ways by suggesting that traits are summaries of previous behaviors. We do not wish to dispute the possibility that at least some of the trait knowledge we have about others and ourselves may arise in just this way. We simply propose that there is more. Especially for information about the self, traits may represent summaries of goals and intentions so that in trying to decide whether one is kind or unkind people may access their knowledge of their general goals rather than their past behaviors. There are many ways they may access these goals. If such goals are strong enough, they may be easy to access more or less directly. If not, they may be accessed through a variety of means including situations, usual activities, and contexts.

SUMMARY

The points we have made can be summarized as follows

1. the task-facilitation paradigm can be considered as a conceptual priming paradigm;
2. there is evidence of some indirect priming in this paradigm on (at least) the trait description task;
3. other paradigms for accessing self-knowledge may give rise to quite different conclusions from those of Klein and Loftus;
4. traits and behaviors are likely more tightly linked in most cases than they assume;
5. assessing self-knowledge may be affected by episodes or experiences but in nonconscious ways as in studies of implicit memory; and
6. trait descriptions of oneself may reflect goals and intentions rather than summaries of past behavior.

REFERENCES

Bem, D. J. (1967). Self-perception: An alternative interpretation of cognitive dissonance phenomena. *Psychological Review, 74,* 183–200.

Bem, D. J. (1972). Self-perception theory. In L. Berkowitz (Ed.), *Advances in experimental social psychology* (Vol. 6, pp. 1–62). New York: Academic Press.

Cofer, C. N. (1967). Conditions for the use of verbal associations. *Psychological Bulletin, 68,* 1–12.

Fazio, R. H., Effrein, E. A., & Falender, V. J. (1981). Self-perceptions following social interactions. *Journal of Personality and Social Psychology, 41,* 232–242.

Klein, S. B., Loftus, J., & Burton (1989). Two self-reference effects: The importance of distinguishing between self-descriptiveness judgments and autobiographical retrieval in self-referent encoding. *Journal of Personality and Social Psychology, 56,* 853–865.

Nissen, M. J., Ross, J. L., Willingham, D. B., Mackenzie, T. B., & Schacter, D. L. (1988). Memory and awareness in a patient with multiple personality disorder. *Brain and Cognition, 8,* 117–134.

Osgood, C. E., & Luria, Z. (1954). A blind analysis of a case of multiple personality using the semantic differential. *Journal of Abnormal and Social Psychology, 49,* 579–591.

Osgood, C. E., Luria, Z., Jeans, R. F., & Smith, S. W. (1976). The three faces of Evelyn: A case report. *Journal of Abnormal Psychology, 85,* 247–286.

Read, S. J., Jones, D. K., & Miller, L. C. (1990). Traits as goal-based categories: The importance of goals in the coherence of dispositional categories. *Journal of Personality and Social Psychology, 58,* 1048–1061.

Reiser, B. J., Black, J. B., & Abelson, R. P. (1985). Knowledge structures in the organization and retrieval of autobiographical memories. *Cognitive Psychology, 17,* 89–137.

Roediger, H. L. (1990). Implicit memory: Retention without remembering. *American Psychologist, 45,* 1043–1056.

Roediger, H. L., Weldon, M. S., & Challis, B. H. (1989). Explaining dissociations between implicit and explicit measures of retention: A processing account. In H. L. Roediger & F. I. M. Craik (Eds.), *Varieties of memory and consciousness: Essays in honor of Endel Tulving* (pp. 3–41). Hillsdale, NJ: Lawrence Erlbaum Associates.

Schacter, D. L. (1987). Implicit memory: History and current status. *Journal of Experimental Psychology: Learning, Memory, and Cognition, 13,* 501–518.

Shimamura, A. P. (1986). Priming effects in amnesia: Evidence for a dissociable memory function. *Quarterly Journal of Experimental Psychology, 38A,* 619–644.

Smith, E. E., & Branscombe, N. R. (1988). Category accessibility as implicit memory. *Journal of Experimental Social Psychology, 24,* 490–504.

Tulving, E., Hayman, C. A. G., & Macdonald, C. A. (1991). Long-lasting perceptual priming and semantic learning in amnesia: A case experiment. *Journal of Experimental Psychology: Learning, Memory and Cognition, 17,* 595–617.

10 In Defense of Behavior-Level Accessing and Use of Self-Knowledge

Constantine Sedikides
University of Wisconsin—Madison

The self has been a fascinating area of inquiry for social cognition researchers (Kihlstrom & Cantor, 1984; Markus & Wurf, 1987). One of the persistent trends of the social cognitive perspective is the focus on the mental representation and accessing of self-knowledge.

In their provocative, thorough, and well-documented treatise, Klein and Loftus (chapter 1, this volume) argue for the autonomy of the cognitive store of abstract (i.e., trait) versus specific (i.e., behavior) self-knowledge. Most importantly, they contend that specific self-knowledge plays no critical role in abstract self-descriptiveness judgments.

Klein and Loftus astutely observe that "The findings from any one paradigm . . . are open to multiple interpretations and vulnerable to the charge that they reflect more the idiosyncracies of the methodology than the behavior of the variables of interest" (p. 15). In agreement with the spirit of their observation, this chapter contends that the validity and generalizability of Klein and Loftus' conclusions are somewhat limited by the methodology employed. In that sense, the chapter stands in defense of behavior-level accessing and use of self-knowledge.

POSSIBLE METHODOLOGICAL CONFINES: ON THE RELATION BETWEEN BEHAVIORS AND TRAITS

On the Relation Between Behaviors and Traits

Two of the task combinations that Klein and Loftus' research employed was *Remember-Describes* and *Describes-Remember*. In the *Remember-Describes* case, subjects were asked to (a) recall a specific incident where they manifested a behavior relevant to a trait, and (b) decide whether the trait described them or not. If the *Remember* task led to a reduction in response time (compared to a semantic task), this would indicate support for the exemplar model. However, if the *Remember* task failed to facilitate response times (again, in comparison to a semantic task), this would evidence support for the mixed model.

In the *Describes-Remember* case, subjects were asked to (a) decide whether a trait described them or not, and (b) bring to mind a trait-relevant behavior that they performed. The exemplar model would be supported if performing the *Describes* task first led to reduction in response time compared to a semantic task. On the other hand, the mixed model would be supported if performing the *Describes* task first led to no facilitation compared to a semantic task.

Underlying the use of these two task combinations is the authors' assumption that subjects regard stored single behavioral instances and stored trait knowledge as equally relevant and applicable to trait self-descriptiveness judgments. This assumption is questionable.

Remember-Describes Task Combination

The instruction *Remember* presumably activated a single behavior in subjects' minds. The issue is whether this behavior was used in making a *Describes* judgment.

It is likely that a single behavior is not implicitly regarded by the human respondent as directly relevant to the formation or revision of a trait judgment, because of the unequal specificity level of behaviors and traits. For a trait representation to be formed, the manifestation of multiple behaviors (sharing semantic and even temporal similarities) is necessary. Consequently, a single additional behavior should not be capable of drastically altering a consolidated trait judgment.

Even if the behavioral store is regarded marginally relevant to the trait judgment, it is likely that the application of the store to the judgment is implicitly deemed inappropriate. That is, the plasticity and randomness inherent in any single behavior may render the behavior inappropriate for application to the modification of crystallized trait judgments. It is behavioral summaries, not single behaviors, that are likely to be perceived as appropriate and applicable to trait judgments.[1]

If a single behavior is perceived as irrelevant and/or inappropriate for use in making trait self-descriptiveness judgments, then Klein and Loftus' contention of having empirically backed the mixed model is to be challenged. The results did not necessarily reveal a preference for abstract over concrete stores when making

---

[1]This argument is reminiscent of the attitude–behavior relation. Attitudes best predict behaviors when the two are at an equal specificity level (e.g., Davidson & Jaccard, 1979; Weigel & Newman, 1976).

trait judgments. Concrete stores might not even have entered the cognitive competition. Hence, it is not surprising that the *Remember* task had an equally negligible impact on trait judgments as the semantic task.

This reservation is seemingly contradicted by the results of Experiments 5, 6, and 7. All these experiments showed that single behaviors can affect trait judgments. However, the common theme in all these experiments was the unfamiliarity of the stimulus domain. Single behaviors should be capable of affecting relatively unfounded traits judgments but not consolidated trait judgments.

Describes-Remember Task Combination

According to Klein and Loftus, the instruction *Describes* could activate either a stored behavioral incident or a stored trait judgment. Absence of facilitation regarding the subsequent *Remember* task would imply that a stored trait judgment was activated, a result consistent with the mixed model.

However, it is hard to tell what subjects bring to mind when asked to decide whether a trait describes them. Subjects may indeed bring to mind either a single stored behavior or a stored trait judgment, as Klein and Loftus assume. Equally plausible, subjects may recall multiple concrete behaviors. If so, the match between the recalled multiple concrete behaviors and the target experiment-defined single behavior is likely to be poor or nonexistent. No facilitation would be predicted in that case. The *Describes* judgment would have equally inconsequential effects on the *Remember* task as the semantic task.[2]

A Concluding Note

This section served to raise some doubts about the underlying premises of the Klein and Loftus task (however novel this task may be). Future research will need to specify the cognitive processes through which people make describes judgments.

GENERALIZABILITY CONFINES: THE ACCESSING AND USE OF BEHAVIORS IN SELF-DESCRIPTIONS

Klein and Loftus' conclusions regarding the nonrole of behavioral knowledge in self-description (e.g., pp. 30–36) may not be adequately generalizable to everyday life. Arguably, self-descriptions are rarely communicated as responses to computer-controlled presentation of trait words, and reaction times do not customarily figure in self-descriptions. Self-description occurs in social context and

---

[2]The contention that the *Remember* task is irrelevant or inapplicable to the *Describes* tasks is valid regardless of whether the *Describes* task is assumed to activate trait representations or multiple behavior representations.

serves multiple functions. As Schlenker and Weigold (1991) put it, self-description (which they call self-identification) "is a goal-directed activity in which the self is specified for some purpose to some audience" (p. 246).

In all fairness to Klein and Loftus, their methodology was designed with specific theoretical intentions in mind. However, this chapter is not rasing any objection to using theory-relevant methodological procedures. The claim is rather that the generality of inferences Klein and Loftus drew from their work may be limited in scope.

The discussion in the following section centers on circumstances under which behavioral self-knowledge is likely to be accessed and used in self-description. This discussion entertains the possibility that the accessing and use of behavioral self-knowledge is more prevalent in self-descriptions compared to trait self-knowledge. The exemplar model may present a valid appraisal of the self-description process.

When Is Behavior Knowledge More Likely to be Accessed and Used Than Trait Knowledge?

This section considers characteristics of self-knowledge, the perceiver, and the situation that are likely to render behavioral knowledge more impactful than trait knowledge on self-descriptiveness.

Characteristics of Self-Knowledge

Expertise.   Klein and Loftus' own research (Experiments 6 and 7) establishes expertise with the autobiographical domain (e.g., home vs. school) under consideration as a crucial variable regulating accessing of trait versus behavioral self-knowledge. Trait accessing occurs when subjects are experts on the relevant autobiographical domain; behavior accessing takes place when subjects are novices on the pertinent domain.

Certainty.   Self-knowledge can vary along the certainty–uncertainty dimension (Pelham, 1991). Certainty can be conceptualized independently of expertise and importance. It is likely that people rely on behavior knowledge when forming self-descriptiveness judgments about new low-certainty autobiographical domains, but rely on trait knowledge when forming self-descriptiveness judgments about new high-certainty autobiographical domains.

Structural Properties.   Whether behavior or trait self-knowledge is likely to be brought to bear on self-description may depend on the manner in which relevant information was acquired and structured in autobiographical memory (*the encoding specificity principle*). Obviously, behavior self-knowledge acquisition (as when a person learns by observing his or her behavior) will lead to the use of behaviors in self-descriptions, whereas trait self-knowledge acquisition (as when the person is consistently ascribed particular traits by his or her parents) will lead to the use of traits in self-descriptions.

Characteristics of the Perceiver

Are there any individual differences that might regulate people's inclination to describe themselves in terms of behaviors rather than traits? At least three such individual differences appear likely candidates.

People who are chronically *high in self-consciousness* (Fenigstein, Scheier, & Buss, 1975) will have access to concrete behaviors they performed by virtue of their self-focusing orientation and tendency to ruminate (Ingram, 1990). Self-relevant behaviors will be chronically accessible in their minds, and thus highly likely to be used in self-descriptions either independently of or in conjunction with trait descriptions. Similarly, individuals who are *high in need for cognition* (Cacioppo, Petty, & Kao, 1984) may be more willing than low-in-need-for-cognition individuals to ponder the specifics of the self, search for meaning in their own behaviors, and describe the self in terms of behaviors. Finally, individuals *low in need for closure* (Kruglanski, 1990) may be more likely than individuals high in need for closure to contemplate self-instigated behaviors in detail before making trait inferences. Again, behavioral autobiographical knowledge may be chronically accessible in these people, as will be self-description at the behavioral level.

Characteristics of the Situation

Research demonstrates that adults spontaneously link their abstract self-descriptions to concrete behavioral contexts (Cantor, Mischel, & Schwartz, 1982; Markus, Crane, Bernstein, & Siladi, 1982; Wright & Mischel, 1988). This tendency should be magnified by situational context. Under several situational characteristics, self-descriptions can either be exclusively composed of behavioral knowledge or at least be a mixture of behavioral and trait knowledge. Such situational characteristics are considered here.

Time or Energy Constraints. It is likely that the self be described in abstract terms when the individual is short of time or energy, but be described in specific terms in the absence of time or energy constraints. This thinking is compatible with literature demonstrating use of stereotypic thinking under time constraints, but use of individuating information in the absence of time constraints (Bodenhausen & Lichtenstein, 1987; Fiske & Pavelchak, 1986; Pratto & Bargh, 1991; Rothbart, Fulero, Jensen, Howard, & Birrell, 1978).

Mood Variations. There is empirical support for the notion that, when in a negative mood (as opposed to neutral or positive mood), individuals process information in an analytic, extensive, and detailed manner rather than a global or heuristic manner (Isen & Daubman, 1984; Mackie & Worth, 1989). Further, negative mood has been found to elicit an introverted and reflective orientation (Sedikides, 1992; Wood, Saltzberg, & Goldsamt, 1990). Paralleling these findings, it is likely that negative moods lead to a detailed internal review of the behavioral basis for holding abstract self-descriptions. Negative moods may evoke detailed self-description. (Consistent with this reasoning, Gleicher and Weary, 1991, found that depressed subjects tended to generate more inferences regarding an actor's behavior than nondepressed subjects.)

Major Life Transitions.   Major life transitions, such as relocation, occupational change, or marriage, cause individuals to regroup and rethink their life course. Such transitions are particularly likely to evoke increased levels of self-awareness and self-reflection. In self-reflecting, the individual will attempt to redefine the self or to rearrange the structure of self-conceptions (Zirkel & Cantor, 1990). In order to do so, the individual will be obliged to resort to a consideration of the basis for self-related beliefs. This basis is behavioral evidence.

Communication Demands.   Several situations demand that people describe themselves in terms of specific rather than abstract self-knowledge. One determinant of the specificity level of self-description is the nature of the interpersonal relationship between the sender and the recipient of the communicative message.

Fiske, Haslam, and Fiske (1991) argued for the existence of four relational structures, which "are the cognitive sources for generating social action, for understanding and evaluating others' social behavior, and for coordinating social interaction" (p. 657). The four relational structures are communal sharing (i.e., close or intimate relationships), authority ranking (i.e., superordinate–subordinate relationships), equality matching (i.e., relationships based on equal power), and market pricing (i.e., relationships based on exchange ratios of goods). Fiske et al. provided empirical support for the cognitive representation of relationships in terms of the four elementary structures.

The argument that is made here is that behaviors are unlikely to figure in the communication of self-knowledge to communal relationships, but are highly likely to be a part of self-descriptions transmitted to the remaining three relationship structures.

Members of communal relationships have had repeated exposure to each other's behaviors, and as a result they are likely to have formed abstract trait representations of one another. Due to the high level of interpersonal expertise, specific self-knowledge is redundant. Self-descriptions are likely to be communicated in abstract form. Further, members of communal relationships are held only partially accountable for their actions. Given the collective spirit and warmth that accompanies such relationships, social gaffes, errors, and even minor infractions are likely to be overlooked. Thus, detailed self-description is frequently unnecessary.

A high level of interpersonal expertise may also be present in the case of authority-ranking relationships. However, expertise in this case will be of limited range, as it will exclusively pertain to one side (i.e., the professional) of the interaction partners. Further, accountability is crucial. Subordinates (and to some extent superordinates) are accountable for their behaviors. Accountability has been shown to evoke complex and multidimensional thinking (Tetlock, 1983), and to lead to "preemptive self-criticism," whereby individuals carefully analyze their position and forthcoming argumentation in anticipation of the opposition's counterarguments (Tetlock, Skitka, & Boettger, 1989). When explaining their decisions, biases, errors, social transgressions, or even preferences, low-authority individuals will resort to specific rather than abstract information.

Persuasion processes are applicable to equality-matching relationships. These relationships are characterized by "turn-taking, in-kind reciprocity in which people get back the 'same thing' they give, distributive justice as equality among shares, an-eye-for-eye revenge in which people match harm for harm on a one-to-one basis, and compensation in which people replace a loss with the same thing that was taken away" (Fiske et al., 1991, p. 657). Persuasive communication is likely to be implemented in equality-matching relationships as a tool for smoothing out or resolving differences. Provided that people are motivated and capable to deal with equality matching transactions, their attitudes will be modifiable through the central route to persuasion (Petty & Cacioppo, 1986). Attitude modification through this route will require favorable cognitive responses on the part of the recipient, and such responses will be evoked only if the recipient finds the message arguments to be strong. To the extent that detailed argumentation is perceived as more compelling than global or vague argumentation (Anderson, 1983; Burnkrant & Unnava, 1989), the recipient will be more persuaded by specific rather than abstract self-related arguments.

Self-presentation is also likely to be important in equality-matching relationships. Self-presentation refers to the tactful management of the impression one is creating to an audience. Self-presentational tactics can be either direct (e.g., releasing positive information about the self, making excuses for socially unskillful behavior, self-handicapping; see Baumeister & Jones, 1978; Berglas & Jones, 1978; Godfrey, Jones, & Lord, 1986) or indirect (e.g., basking in the accomplishments of a friend, blasting the achievements of an enemy, boosting the positive qualities of a person with whom one has found the self associated; see: Cialdini & Richardson, 1980; Finch & Cialdini, 1989). In either case, one is releasing detailed rather than global information about the self.

Persuasion and self-presentation are also likely to play a role in market pricing relationships, as when negotiations are under way for setting the system of ratio values to be used.

Nature of Social Settings. The nature of the social setting is an additional determinant of whether specific or abstract information about the self will be communicated. Such settings as criminal trials or job interviews exert powerful demands on the individuals for the release of concrete self-relevant information. Even more mundane settings, such as social gatherings, typically demand the communication of specific knowledge about the self.

CONCLUDING OBSERVATIONS

This chapter raised methodological and generalizability reservations to Klein and Loftus' attempt to understand the relative contribution of stored behavioral and trait information in self-description. The chapter concludes that it may be premature to argue that behaviors do not play a significant role in self-description.

Klein and Loftus' research was exclusively concerned with trait and behavior representations. This focus of their research inadvertently gives off a rather restrictive image of the diversity of the content of the self. In addition to traits and behaviors, the content of the self includes knowledge of one's own activities, physical attributes, demographic characteristics, feelings, thoughts, goals, values, standards, rules for behavioral regulation, significant relationships with individuals or groups, important life events, and possessions (Markus, 1983; McGuire, McGuire, Child, & Fujioka, 1978; McGuire & Padawer-Singer, 1976). Furthermore, these self-conceptions are interrelated. As Rosenberg (1979) said, "One can no more understand the self-concept by studying its traits, physical characteristics, and social identity elements in isolation than one can understand a watch by studying the gears, springs, and cogs that constitute it; it is the arrangement of the parts that constitute the entity" (p. 281).

Self-knowledge need not be confined to traits and behaviors. The content of the self is uniquely rich (Fiedler, 1990) and inhabited by a plethora of elements that can be and are used for self-descriptiveness purposes. The field needs to move beyond behavior and trait representations of the self and toward the study of the role of additional self-conceptions (and their structural properties!) in self-description.

Berkowitz (1992) criticized social psychologists' tendency to preoccupy themselves with picky criticism of isolated replicational experiments rather than looking at the big picture. The big picture in the case of Klein and Loftus' treatise is a series of seven well-conducted experiments that converge toward the same conclusion. Klein and Loftus undertook an admirably ambitious effort toward confronting an important and difficult issue in personality and social psychology. This chapter will, hopefully, complement their effort.

ACKNOWLEDGMENT

I thank Carolin Showers for her comments and suggestions.

REFERENCES

Anderson, C. A. (1983). Abstract and concrete data in the perseverance of social theories: When weak data lead to unshakeable beliefs. *Journal of Experimental Social Psychology, 19*, 93–108.

Baumeister, R. F., & Jones, E. E. (1978). When self-presentation is constrained by the target's knowledge: Consistency and compensation. *Journal of Personality and Social Psychology, 36*, 608–618.

Berglas, S., & Jones, E. E. (1978). Drug choice as a self-handicapping strategy in response to noncontingent success. *Journal of Personality and Social Psychology, 36*, 405–417.

Berkowitz, L. (1992). Some thoughts about conservative evaluations of replications. *Personality and Social Psychology Bulletin, 18*, 319–324.

Bodenhausen, G. V., & Lichtenstein, M. (1987). Social stereotypes and information-processing strategies: The impact of task complexity. *Journal of Personality and Social Psychology, 52*, 871–880.

Burnkrant, R. E., & Unnava, H. R. (1989). Self-referencing: A strategy for increasing processing of message content. *Personality and Social Psychology Bulletin, 15*, 628–638.

Cacioppo, J. T., Petty, R. E., & Kao, F. G. (1984). *Journal of Personality Assessment, 48*, 306–307.

Cantor, N., Mischel, W., & Schwartz, J. (1982). Social knowledge: Structure, content, use, and abuse. In A. M. Isen & A. H. Hastorf (Eds.), *Cognitive social psychology* (pp. 33–72). New York: Elsevier/North-Holland.

Cialdini, R. B., & Richardson, K. D. (1980). Two indirect tactics of impression management: Basking and blasting. *Journal of Personality and Social Psychology, 39*, 406–415.

Davidson, A. R., & Jaccard, J. (1979). Variables that moderate the attitude-behavior relation: Results of a longitudinal survey. *Journal of Personality and Social Psychology, 37*, 1364–1376.

Fenigstein, A., Scheier, M. F., & Buss, A. H. (1975). Public and private self-consciousness: Assessment and theory. *Journal of Consulting and Clinical Psychology, 43*, 522–527.

Fiedler, K. (1990). Mood-dependent selectivity in social cognition. *European Review of Social Psychology, 1*, 1–32.

Finch, J. F., & Cialdini, R. B. (1989). Another indirect tactic of (self-) image management: Boosting. *Personality and Social Psychology Bulletin, 15*, 222–232.

Fiske, A. P., Haslam, N., & Fiske, S. T. (1991). Confusing one person with another: What errors reveal about the elementary forms of social relations. *Journal of Personality and Social Psychology, 60*, 656–674.

Fiske, S. T., & Pavelchak, M. A. (1986). Category-based versus piecemeal-based affective responses: Developments in schema-triggered affect. In R. M. Sorrentino & E. T. Higgins (Eds.), *Handbook of motivation and cognition: Foundations of social behavior* (Vol. 1, pp. 167–203). New York: Guilford Press.

Gleicher, F., & Weary, G. (1991). Effect of depression on quantity and quality of social inferences. *Journal of Personality and Social Psychology, 61*, 105–114.

Godfrey, D. K., Jones, E. E., & Lord, C. G. (1986). Self-promotion is not ingratiating. *Journal of Personality and Social Psychology, 50*, 106–115.

Ingram, R. E. (1990). Self-focused attention in clinical disorders: Review and a conceptual model. *Psychological Bulletin, 107*, 156–176.

Isen, A. M., & Daubman, K. A. (1984). The influence of affect on categorization. *Journal of Personality and Social Psychology, 47*, 1206–1217.

Kihlstrom, J. F., & Cantor, N. (1984). Mental representations of the self. In L. Berkowitz (Ed.), *Advances in experimental social psychology* (Vol. 17, pp. 1–47). New York: Academic Press.

Kruglanski, A. W. (1990). Motivations for judging and knowing: Implications for casual attribution. In E. T. Higgins & R. M. Sorrentino (Eds.), *Handbook of Motivation and Cognition: Foundations of Social Behavior* (pp. 333–368). New York: Guilford Press.

Mackie, D. M., & Worth, L. T. (1989). Processing deficits and the mediation of positive affect in persuasion. *Journal of Personality and Social Psychology, 57,* 27–40.

Markus, H. (1983). Self-knowledge: An expanded view. *Journal of Personality, 51,* 543–565.

Markus, H., Crane, M., Bernstein, S., & Siladi, M. (1982). Self-schemas and gender. *Journal of Personality and Social Psychology, 42,* 38–50.

Markus, H., & Wurf, E. (1987). The dynamic self-concept: A social psychological perspective. *Annual Review of Psychology, 38,* 299–337.

McGuire, W. J., McGuire, C. V., & Cheever, J. (1986). The self in society: Effects of social contexts on the sense of self. *British Journal of Social Psychology, 25,* 259–270.

McGuire, W. J., McGuire, C. V., Child, P., & Fujioka, T. (1978). Salience of ethnicity in the spontaneous self-concept as a function on one's ethnic distinctiveness in the social environment. *Journal of Personality and Social Psychology, 36,* 511–520.

McGuire, W. J., & Padawer-Singer, A. (1976). Trait salience in the spontaneous self-concept. *Journal of Personality and Social Psychology, 33,* 743–754.

Pelham, B. W. (1991). On confidence and consequence: The certainty and importance of self-knowledge. *Journal of Personality and Social Psychology, 60,* 518–530.

Petty, R. E., & Cacioppo, J. T. (1986). *Communication and persuasion: Central and peripheral routes to attitude change.* New York: Springer-Verlag.

Pratto, F., & Bargh, J. A. (1991). Stereotyping based on apparently individuating information: Trait and global components of sex stereotypes under attention overload. *Journal of Experimental Social Psychology, 27,* 26–47.

Rosenberg, M. (1979). *Conceiving the self.* New York: Basic Books.

Rothbart, M., Fulero, S., Jensen, C., Howard, J., & Birrell, P. (1978). From individual to group impressions: Availability heuristic in stereotype formation. *Journal of Experimental Social Psychology, 14,* 237–255.

Schlenker, B. R., & Weigold, M. F. (1991). Goals and the self-identification process: Constructing desired identities. In L. A. Pervin (Ed.), *Goal concepts in personality and social psychology* (pp. 243–290). Hillsdale, NJ: Lawrence Erlbaum Associates.

Sedikides, C. (1992). Mood as a determinant of attentional focus. *Cognition and Emotion, 6,* 129–148.

Tetlock, P. E. (1983). Accountability and complexity of thought. *Journal of Personality and Social Psychology, 45,* 74–83.

Tetlock, P. E., Skitka, L., & Boettger, R. (1989). Social and cognitive strategies for coping with accountability: Conformity, complexity, and bolstering. *Journal of Personality and Social Psychology, 57,* 632–640.

Weigel, R. H., & Newman, L. S. (1976). Increasing attitude-behavior correspondence by broadening the scope of the behavioral measure. *Journal of Personality and Social Psychology, 33,* 793–802.

Wright, J. C., & Mischel, W. (1988). Conditional hedges and the intuitive psychology of traits. *Journal of Personality and Social Psychology, 55,* 454–469.

Wood, J. V., Saltzberg, J. A., & Goldsamt, L. A. (1990). Does affect induce self-focused attention? *Journal of Personality and Social Psychology, 58,* 899–908.

Zirkel, S., & Cantor, N. (1990). Personal construal of life tasks: Those who struggle for independence. *Journal of Personality and Social Psychology, 58,* 172–185.

11

Self-Knowledge of an Amnesic Individual is Represented Abstractly

Endel Tulving
Rotman Research Institute of Baycrest Centre and University of Toronto

At first glance, the problem that Klein and Loftus (chapter 1, this volume) set for themselves seems to be intractable: How can one possibly gain valid knowledge about the nature of representation of information stored in memory solely on the basis of observations of its retrieval? Because retrieval depends on a large number of complexly interacting variables, Klein and Loftus' problem seems analogous to that of seeking a unique solution of a single equation with a number of unknowns. The approach they adopted—relying on the technique of conceptual priming—is ingenious. Their results, consistent across experiments, look convincing; their case tightly argued.

The major conclusion that Klein and Loftus draw from their study is that long-term trait knowledge about the self is represented primarily in abstract, summary form, and that recollection of specific behavioral instances exemplifying traits plays at best only a secondary role in determining a person's trait knowledge of the self. The second conclusion is that behavioral exemplars and abstract trait knowledge are represented in memory independently: Accessibility of one has no implications for the accessibility of the other.

This chapter examines these conclusions in light of observations made about trait self-knowledge of a man who, because of brain injury, cannot remember any specific behaviors in which he has ever engaged, and who therefore does not possess any autobiographical knowledge of the self. What is his trait self-knowledge like?

The answer to the question is relevant to Klein and Loftus' theory. If a person's knowledge of his or her traits is inseparable from, or computed from, specific autobiographical memories, then a person who has no such memories should have a rather different trait conception of him or herself than others have of him or her. In the limiting case the person might have *no* conception of him or herself at all: How could the individual know what his or her traits are, if he or she has no access to any relevant evidence? If, on the other hand, self-knowledge is represented in abstract or summary form, then the person's self trait conception would depend on the extent to which he or she is capable of acquiring, storing, and retrieving such abstract knowledge, even in the absence of any specific autobiographical recollections.

These issues are examined in light of observations of K. C., a 40-year-old man who, in a motorcycle accident in 1981, suffered closed-head injury, which had two consequences relevant to the issues at stake: (a) it rendered him severely amnesic, and (b) it changed his personality.

This chapter consists of four parts: (a) discussion of the distinction between episodic and semantic memory, (b) description of K. C. and his cognitive status, (c) report of a small study of K. C.'s trait knowledge of himself, and (d) discussion of the implications of the results of the study for the issues at hand. The four sections are followed by a summary.

EPISODIC AND SEMANTIC MEMORY

Students of memory distinguish among five major categories of learning and memory, or memory systems. The five are *procedural* memory, perceptual *priming, short-term* memory, *semantic* memory, and *episodic* memory. Each of the five systems is large and complex, comprising a number of subsystems for which evidence at the present stage of our knowledge is of variable quality (Tulving, 1991; Tulving & Schacter, 1992). The ordering of the major systems in the overall classification scheme corresponds roughly to their presumed developmental sequence, with the procedural system the earliest, and the episodic the latest. The ordering of the systems also reflects the conjectured relations among the systems: The operations of the higher ones depend on, and are supported by, the operations of the lower systems, whereas lower systems can operate essentially independently of the higher ones.

The two forms of memory relevant to the present discussion are semantic and episodic. Broadly speaking, semantic memory has to do with knowing, episodic with remembering (Tulving, 1989). Abstract or summary representation of traits can be identified with the semantic system, whereas trait-relevant behavioral memories and autobiographical knowledge about the self can be identified with the operations and functioning of the episodic system.

Semantic memory (also referred to as *generic memory, factual memory,* or *knowledge memory*) is concerned with acquisition, retention, and use of organized information in the broadest sense; its principal function is cognitive modeling of the world. A good deal of the semantic knowledge a person possesses may be about oneself. Such "personal semantic" memory (Cermak & O'Connor,

1983), or the "third-person" knowledge (Olson & Astington, 1987; Velmans, 1991) that one has of oneself is comparable with the third-person knowledge that one possesses about others, and is acquired, stored, and retrieved according to the same principles that govern the processing of all other information mediated by the semantic memory system. Third-person knowledge of oneself, however, is different from "first-person" knowledge of oneself, which is based on episodic, or "true" autobiographical, memory.[1]

Episodic memory shares many properties with semantic memory—and depends on semantic memory for many of its operations—but it also uniquely transcends the range of the capabilities of semantic memory (Tulving, 1987; Tulving, Hayman, & Macdonald, 1991). Episodic memory enables the individual to remember personally experienced events in subjective time as embedded in a matrix of other personal happenings. One's recollections of personal experiences that happened 10 minutes ago, or the day before, or in the more distant past depend critically on episodic memory. Such recollection is expressed in a unique kind of conscious awareness, referred to as autonoetic consciousness (Tulving, 1985, in press).

An important point in the present context is that semantic knowledge can be acquired, stored, and retrieved independently of, or even in the absence of, the episodic memory system, although typically, with normal adults, episodic memory frequently enhances the operations of semantic memory. Evidence in support of this hypothesis is derived from various sources, including studies of amnesic patients such as K. C. (For further discussion, see Tulving, in press, and Tulving et al., 1991).

AMNESIC PATIENT K. C.

K. C. was born in 1951. He grew up in a professional family near Toronto. After graduating from high school, he enrolled in a 3-year business administration course at a community college, graduating at age 25. During this time he lived at home with his parents and younger siblings. Family members and friends describe him from that time as a normal, active, outgoing, and gregarious person. The accident responsible for K. C.'s present condition occurred in 1981, at age 30. While riding his motorcycle home from work he went off the road at high speed, and suffered extensive closed-head injury. He was unconscious for several days, remained in an intensive care unit for 4 weeks, and spent over 6 months in

---

[1]Some writers (e.g., Brewer, 1986) include under the concept of autobiographical memory many things other than recollections of the personal past, things such as "autobiographical facts, generic personal information, and the self-schema" (p. 33). In these accounts, episodic memory is a subcategory of autobiographical memory. Episodic memory mediates recollection of not just specific events, but also "summarized events" and "extended events" (Barsalou, 1988), if such recollection is accompanied by autonoetic awareness of such events (Tulving, 1987).

a rehabilitation hospital. He was discharged home in July 1982, and since that time has remained living at home in the care of his parents.

As a result of the accident, K. C. is densely amnesic. His anterograde amnesia is as severe as that of H. M., the world's most famous and most thoroughly studied amnesic (Corkin, 1984; Milner, 1966), and his retrograde amnesia is even more severe than that of H. M., inasmuch as K. C. does not remember a single thing that has ever happened to him, unlike H. M. who can recollect events from his childhood and early teens (Corkin, 1984).

K. C.'s cognitive functioning, with the exception of long-term memory, is reasonably intact, His IQ is in the normal range, his language comprehension is normal, he can read and write without difficulty, his perceptual abilities are more or less normal, and so are his thought processes: There is no confusion, and he does not confabulate. In keeping with the typical clinical picture of the amnesic syndrome, his short-term memory is also intact: He can recall eight digits forward and five backward. A more complete picture of his neurological and cognitive status is given in Tulving, Schacter, McLachlan, and Moscovitch (1988; Tulving et al., 1991).

In addition to causing dense anterograde and retrograde amnesia, K. C.'s brain damage produced a rather profound change in his personality. Whereas he used to be outgoing, adventurous, and gregarious, he is now passive, cautious, and reticent. In face-to-face situations with others he is attentive and polite. He typically does not initiate any interactions with people around him, although he does ask questions from time to time. He has a good sense of humor, appreciates jokes and banter, and sometimes makes light remarks about things happening around him. He is only vaguely aware of his memory deficits. He admits that he has problems with memory when he is explicitly questioned, but otherwise seems unaware of it.

In describing K. C.'s memory capabilities it is useful to distinguish between two periods in his life. The *premorbid period* covers his life before the accident in 1981. During that time, of course, his ability to learn everything, to retrieve what he had learned, and to remember personal events and happenings was normal. Even today he can still retrieve much of the *semantic* knowledge he had learned premorbidly. Thus, among countless other things, he can name the three kinds of blood vessels in the human body, can explain the difference between stalagmites and stalactites, and can describe, and find on the map, the exact location of his family's summer cottage. However, as already mentioned, he does not remember any personal events or happenings from the premorbid period. The *postmorbid period* covers the time after the accident. It is characterized by K. C.'s normal or near-normal ability to acquire new perceptual–motor skills as well as normal learning and performance on various priming tasks, as is true of all amnesics (e.g., Schacter, 1987; Shimamura, 1989). But the acquisition of new semantic knowledge in the postmorbid era is highly impoverished and patchy, although he can learn new semantic and factual information under special conditions (Tulving et al., 1991). He is no more capable of recollecting personally experienced postmorbid events and happenings than he is capable of doing so for the premorbid period.

In terms of the distinction between episodic and semantic memory, K. C.'s semantic retrieval of information acquired during the premorbid period is good, although not normal; his current (postmorbid) ability to learn new semantic information is impaired, although not totally lacking; and his episodic memory capabilities are essentially totally lost: He is incapable of recollecting any events or happenings from any period of his life once they recede beyond the reach of short-term memory, or an extended short-term memory, a time span measured in a few minutes.[2]

K. C.'S TRAIT SELF-KNOWLEDGE

K. C. was tested for his knowledge of himself and one familiar other, his mother, in two sessions.

In the first session, K. C. rated himself and his mother on 72 traits, and his mother rated K. C. and herself on the same traits.[3] The 72 trait names were listed on three sheets of paper, 24 traits per sheet. Beside each trait were shown four choices: "not at all," "somewhat," "quite a bit," and "definitely." The instructions, specially constructed for the four combinations of rater and referent, were typed at the top of each page. For K. C. rating himself the instructions were as follows: "Please rate YOURSELF on the following personality traits. For each trait indicate to what extent the trait applies to YOU, by circling the appropriate phrase for each trait." Other instructions were appropriately modified.

K. C. had no difficulty with either understanding the task or its execution. He first rated himself, and then, following 45 minutes of activity on another unrelated task, rated his mother. His mother did the two ratings in immediate succession, first rating K. C. and then herself.

The purpose of this exercise was to assess the extent to which K. C. was capable of providing realistic estimates of his own traits, as well as those of his mother. The extent of the validity of his estimates was measured in terms of the agreement between K. C.'s ratings and those of his mother.

K. C.'s mother made use of all four rating scale points in her ratings of both

---

[2]Whether K. C. is capable of storing any episodic information—that is, information about *subjectively experienced* events *as such*—and whether his problem lies only in retrieval, is not known and cannot be known. Given the temporal-logical structure of an act of remembering, simple observation of retrieval failure is always compatible with at least three scenarios: (a) failure of storage or relevant information, (b) adequate storage but subsequent loss of relevant information, and (c) inadequate or inappropriate retrieval cues.

[3]The trait names were the same that Klein and Loftus used in their research. I thank Stanley Klein for making these materials available.

K. C. and herself. But K. C. confined his ratings, with a single exception, to only two categories—"not at all," and "somewhat."[4] To simplify the assessment of K. C.'s ability to provide realistic trait ratings, his mother's ratings were converted to a binary scale similar to that adopted by K. C.: "not at all" ratings were assigned to one category, and all the other higher ratings were assigned to the second category. Analysis of results was thus based on the revised ratings by mother.

Yule's Q was adopted as the measure of association, or dependency, between K. C.'s and Mother's ratings, with chi-square serving as a test of statistical significance of the observed Q values. The association thus measured was positive in both cases. The Q value of the comparison of K. C.'s and Mother's ratings of K. C.'s traits was .77 ($X^2 = 14.55$), and the Q value of the comparison of K. C.'s and Mother's ratings of Mother's traits was .80 ($X^2 = 13.46$).

These data suggest then that K. C.'s judgments of traits are reasonably reliable, regardless of whether he is rating himself or his mother.

Following the initial assessment as just described, a new two-alternative forced-choice trait test was constructed on the basis of K. C.'s and Mother's ratings of K. C.'s traits in the first session. The test consisted of 32 pairs of traits. Both words in every pair had been rated identically by K. C., but differently by Mother, in the first session. Thus, for instance, one of the pairs was "reliable–serious." K. C. had given himself a rating of "somewhat" on both of these traits in Session 1, whereas Mother had rated K. C. as "quite a bit" on "reliable" and "somewhat" on "serious." An attempt was also made to equate the presumed social desirability of the two traits in a pair. Some other examples of the pairs of traits were "ambitious" versus "industrious," "quarrelsome" versus "selfish," and "artistic" versus "musical."

K. C. was given the 32-pair forced-choice test on two separate occasions in Session 2, separated by a 45-minute interval. (By the time he took the test for the second time, he had, of course, no recollection of having done anything like it ever before.) There was satisfactory agreement between the two tests, with 25 choices out of 32 being identical.

Mother was given the same 32-pair forced choice test also twice. The first time she rated K. C. as he is now, and the second time she rated K. C. as he was before his accident. The two tests yielded rather different outcomes. Of the 32 ratings of pairs of traits, 16 were the same for the two time periods, and 16 were different, indicating zero correlation between the tests. These data confirm the family's observations that K. C.'s head injury changed his personality.

With the data available from the tests as described, it was possible to make three comparisons. First, K. C.'s choices on the 32-pair test, pooled over his two

---

[4]He has done so on previous occasions, too, when he has been asked to make numerical scale judgments about presented materials. When asked to explain this behavior, he says that he is following the instructions.

tests, were compared with Mother's ratings of K. C. on the 72-trait test in Session 1. His choices agreed with Mother's ratings 47 times out of 64 possible. That is, when K. C. was asked to choose between two traits for self-descriptiveness that he had rated identically in Session 1, he sided with Mother's choices 73% of the time. Second, K. C.'s own trait judgments on the 32-pair test were compared with Mother's choices for the "postmorbid K. C." on the same test, that is, for K. C. as he is now. The results again showed 73% (47 out of 64) agreement between K. C. and Mother. Third, K. C.'s own trait judgments did not agree at all with Mother's choices for the "premorbid K. C.," that is, K. C. as he was before his accident. The two sets of choices agreed in only 52% of the cases (33 out of 64), an outcome one would expect by chance alone.

As a check on the meaningfulness of the 73% agreement between K. C. and Mother on K. C.'s present traits, two professional women, in K. C.'s age range but without any memory impairment, and their mother, were given the same 32-pair trait test that had been used with K. C. and his mother. Each woman rated herself, and their mother rated each daughter. The agreement between this Other Mother and Number One Daughter, in rating the latter, was 22/32; the agreement between the Other Mother and Number Two Daughter, in rating the latter, was 24/32. These figures are rather similar to those expressing agreement between K. C. and his mother, and suggest that K. C.'s severe episodic memory impairment does not constitute a readily identifiable handicap when he makes judgments about his self.

The findings of the small study of K. C.'s trait self-knowledge can be summarized succinctly: K. C. possesses reasonably realistic trait self-knowledge. It corresponds to his present (postmorbid) self as perceived by others, and is noticeably different from his previous (premorbid) self.

IMPLICATIONS

The findings of the small study reported here must be taken with a grain of salt. They are based on a rather small database derived from observations of a single principal subject and a few others. Both the reliability and generalizability of the data are uncertain, and the tests used may have unknown limitations. Replication and extension of this kind of research is needed before more definite conclusions can be reached.

But within the constraints provided by these caveats, some tentative conclusions can be drawn. One such is suggested by the finding that K. C. seems to have acquired the necessary information about his "new" traits during the years after his accident, during the postmorbid period characterized by profound anterograde amnesia. As K. C. cannot consciously recollect any events or happenings from this period of his life—fleeting or long-lasting, single or repeated, bland or emotionally laden—any more than he can recollect any events or happenings from any other period of his life, the conclusion follows that his current self-knowledge of traits cannot be based on remembering of any relevant behavioral instances.

This conclusion supports Klein and Loftus' theory regarding the representation of self-knowledge in memory. Contrary to the predictions of exemplar models, trait judgments about the self can be made, and in K. C.'s case must have been made, without reference to trait-relevant autobiographical episodes. It follows then that trait knowledge about the self is represented in memory in abstract form.

K. C.'s semantic knowledge of the world at large—knowledge that he can express symbolically—is mostly derived from his premorbid period. Before undertaking the little study of K. C.'s self-trait judgments it was quite possible, and perhaps even reasonable, to entertain the hypothesis that his beliefs concerning his traits would have been based on his life experiences during the premorbid period, and that "relearning" the traits of the "new" K. C. postmorbidly would have been as unlikely as postmorbid acquisition of knowledge about the rest of the world. The data suggest otherwise: K. C. seems to have successfully acquired knowledge about his "new" self despite his profound episodic memory impairment.

The memory system that mediated K. C.'s relearning of his traits is presumably the semantic system. We already know that he is capable of acquiring, and retaining over long periods of time, other kinds of semantic information. K. C. has not only demonstrated semantic priming of premorbidly acquired semantic knowledge (Tulving et al., 1988), he has also shown new semantic learning of collections of facts such as "student withdrew—INNUENDO" (Tulving et al., 1991) and "a civilized custom that ought to be imported to Canada—SIESTA" (Hayman, Macdonald, & Tulving, in preparation). There are reasons to believe that repetition, meaningfulness, and minimization of response-competition interference are important determinants of K. C.'s learning of new factual information. At least one of these factors, repetition, fits well with Klein and Loftus' suggestion, based on their review of the relevant literature, that a person's formation of abstract knowledge of traits, either one's own or a familiar other's, is a function of the extent of relevant experience. The other two relevant conditions—meaningfulness of the to-be-acquired information and minimization of interference—also seem to be reasonably well satisfied in the case of acquisition of trait knowledge from individual instances that are not subsequently remembered.

Thus, it seems reasonable to hypothesize, along with Klein and Loftus, that the abstract representations of traits are held in semantic memory, whereas individual behavioral instances that can also serve as a source of relevant knowledge are maintained in and retrieved from episodic memory. Klein and Loftus' suggestion that the two representational bases of trait knowledge are independent follows directly from this hypothesis, inasmuch as semantic and episodic memory are independent in the sense that once information has been stored, it can be retrieved from either system independently of the existence or retrievability of the same or different information in the other system. (For further discussion see Tulving, 1987, 1992; Tulving et al., 1991).

SUMMARY

Can a person who does not remember a single event or happening from his life, and who does not know how he has behaved in any particular instance, know what kind of a person he is? Can he possess accurate self-knowledge? The observations reported here about K. C., a densely amnesic person, suggest that the answers to both questions are affirmative. Since the accident that caused his profound amnesia and changed his personality K. C. has relearned his trait self-knowledge. He has done so despite the fact that his episodic memory system is severely impaired and that, as a consequence, and as far as we know, he has no access to any behavioral instances from which the traits can be inferred.

The facts of the case suggest that K. C.'s self-knowledge is represented in a memory system other than episodic memory. This other system is presumably semantic memory, because none of the other currently known memory systems could support his performance on the trait judgment tasks. K. C.'s self-knowl-edge belongs to the same category as all his other knowledge about the world.

Thus, the results of the small case study of a single special individual and the implications of these results are in excellent agreement with the theory that Klein and Loftus have constructed on the basis of their own much more sophisticated and extensive study and analysis.

ACKNOWLEDGMENTS

My research is supported by the National Sciences and Engineering Research Council of Canada, Grant A8632. I am grateful to K. C. and his mother, Mrs. Ruth Cochrane, for their cooperation in the study, and to Linda Tulving for editorial assistance.

REFERENCES

Barsalou, L. W. (1988). The content and organization of autobiographical memories. In U. Neisser & E. Winograd (Eds.), *Remembering reconsidered: Ecological and traditional approaches to the study of memory* (pp. 193–243). Cambridge, England: Cambridge University Press.

Brewer, W. (1986). What is autobiographical memory? In D. C. Rubin (Ed.), *Autobiographical memory* (pp. 25–49). Cambridge, England: Cambridge University Press.

Cermak, L. S., & O'Connor, M. (1983). The anterograde and retrograde retrieval ability of a patient with amnesia due to encephalitis. *Neuropsychologia, 21,* 213–234.

Corkin, S. (1984). Lasting consequences of bilateral medial temporal lobectomy: Clinical course and experimental findings in H. M. *Seminars in Neurology, 4,* 249–259.

Hayman, C. A. C., Macdonald, C. A., & Tulving, E. (in preparation). *Repetition and interference as determinants of new semantic learning in amnesia: A case experiment.*

Milner, B. (1966). Amnesia following operation on the temporal lobes. In C. W. M. Whitty & O. L. Zangwill (Eds.), *Amnesia* (pp. 109–133). London: Butterworth.

Olson, D. R., & Astington, J. W. (1987). Seeing and knowing: On the ascription of mental states to young children. *Canadian Journal of Psychology, 41,* 399–411.

Schacter, D. L. (1987). Implicit expressions of memory in organic amnesia: learning of new facts and associations. *Human Neurobiology, 6,* 107–118.

Shimamura, A. P. (1989). Disorders of memory: The cognitive science perspective. In F. Boller & J. Grafman (Eds.), *Handbook of neuropsychology* (pp. 35–73). Amsterdam: Elsevier.

Tulving, E. (1985). Memory and consciousness. *Canadian Psychology, 26,* 1–26.

Tulving, E. (1987). Multiple memory systems and consciousness. *Human Neurobiology, 6,* 67–80.

Tulving, E. (1989). Remembering and knowing the past. *American Scientist, 1989, 77,* 361–367.

Tulving, E. (1991). Concepts of human memory. In L. Squire, G. Lynch, N. M. Weinberger, & J. L. McGaugh (Eds.), *Memory: Organization and locus of change.* New York: Oxford University Press.

Tulving, E. (in press). Varieties of consciousness and levels awareness in memory. In A. Baddeley & L. Weiskrantz (Eds.), *Attention: Selection, awareness and control. A tribute to Donald Broadbent.* London: Oxford University Press.

Tulving, E., Hayman, C. A. G., & Macdonald, C. A. (1991). Long-lasting perceptual priming and semantic learning in amnesia: A case experiment. *Journal of Experimental Psychology: Learning, Memory and Cognition, 17,* 595–617.

Tulving, E., & Schacter, D. L. (1992). Priming and memory systems. In B. Smith & G. Adelman (Eds.), *Neuroscience Year: Supplement 2 to the Encyclopedia of Neuroscience.* Cambridge, MA: Birkhauser Boston.

Tulving, E., Schacter, D. L., McLachlan, D. R., & Moscovitch, M. (1988). Priming of semantic autobiographical knowledge: A case study of retrograde amnesia. *Brain and Cognition, 8,* 3–20.

Velmans, M. (1991). Is human information processing conscious? *Behavioral and Brain Sciences, 14,* 651–726.

12

Exploring the Nature and Implications of Functional Independence: Do Mental Representations of the Self Become Independent of Their Bases?

Jacquie D. Vorauer
Michael Ross
University of Waterloo

Klein and Loftus' (chapter 1, this volume) proposals concerning the bases of mental representations of the self provoked considerable discussion between the two authors of this chapter. We found ourselves disagreeing with each other and with Klein and Loftus on a number of points, but we also discovered that we were intrigued by the theoretical implications of their analysis. Their research led us to think about old issues from different perspectives, as we debated the ramifications of functional independence. We describe some of these considerations in the second half of this chapter; first, however, we question a few of Klein and Loftus' assumptions, and discuss our concerns about the interpretation of their data.

THE SIGNIFICANCE OF BEHAVIOR FOR SELF-JUDGMENTS

In the movie *Annie Hall,* Alvy and his girlfriend Annie talk to their psychiatrists on a split screen. The psychiatrists inquire how often Alvy and Annie make love. Alvy replies: "Hardly ever . . . three times a week." Annie answers: "Constantly . . . three times a week."

Klein and Loftus appear to assume a direct and straightforward relation between trait descriptions and behavior. Woody Allen and social psychologists working in the area of attribution theory would suggest otherwise. Behavior is categorized and interpreted: The same behavior can mean distinct things to different observers, and even to the same observer on separate occasions. Virtually anyone would be able to remember an occasion on which he or she behaved rudely. However, people would not necessarily infer from such behavior that they are either rude or polite; instead, they may attribute their behavior to external factors. If a behavioral episode is assessed to be nondiagnostic of an underlying trait, there is no reason to suppose that priming the episode would facilitate trait judgment.

The research literature on causal attribution suggests that people are likely to view others' behaviors as indicative of traits even when the behaviors could reasonably be attributed to external factors; in contrast, people are apt to deny the diagnosticity of their own behaviors in similar circumstances (Jones, 1990). Because people's judgments of others reflect a stronger connection between specific behaviors and traits, priming memories of past behaviors may be more likely to facilitate trait judgments for another person (e.g., one's mother) than for self. This is exactly what Klein and Loftus find.

Nonbehavioral Influences on Self-Knowledge

Klein and Loftus seem to assume that trait judgments are made primarily on the basis of behavioral evidence. Various psychologists have proposed that self-knowledge is derived from many different types of information, of which autobiographical memories of past behaviors are only a subset. To the extent that trait judgments are made on the basis of information other than past behavior, we would not expect the act of making a trait judgment about self to render autobiographical memories of past behavior more accessible. Thus, Klein and Loftus' failure to obtain facilitation effects does not necessarily indicate that trait ascriptions are made independently of their bases.

Several social psychological theories relevant to self-concept development suggest particular types of nonbehavioral information from which individuals might infer their traits. For example, Cooley (1902) proposed the looking glass self, maintaining that people derive their self-views from others' reactions to them. Festinger (1954) suggested that individuals' self-evaluations are shaped and influenced by social comparison. The picture is further complicated by the fact that potentially self-relevant information is assigned different weights, depending in part on social context. For instance, a boy's self-concept may be dramatically affected by feedback from his father that he is stupid; the same feedback from a classmate might have less impact. The reverse might be true for positive evaluations: Children may judge compliments from their parents to be less diagnostic then compliments from friends. Parents are expected to claim that their children are smart or beautiful. Behavioral exemplars are presumably weighted differentially as well: A woman who defrauds a major bank of $10 may be less likely to view herself as dishonest than a woman who cheats her grandmother out of the same sum.

Individuals' self-views are also influenced by goals and expectations. The goal of viewing oneself positively has been shown to affect self-judgments in a wide variety of contexts. For example, Kunda and Sanitioso (1989) demonstrated that a desire to possess particular traits affects the way individuals describe themselves. Additionally, cognitive factors such as expectations and beliefs can affect individuals' views of themselves. People possess theories about the temporal stability of different traits that influence their current self-views, as well as their recollections of what they were like and how they acted when they were younger (Conway & Ross, 1984; McFarland, Ross, & Giltrow, 1992; M. Ross, 1989). Individuals also hold implicit personality theories that specify which traits "go together," and which do not (Schneider, 1973; Schweder, 1975). Thus, two individuals with identical behavioral histories might draw quite different conclusions from the same information, as a function of their beliefs and expectations. To return to our earlier example, Alvy and Annie's discrepant evaluations of their sex life can be understood as an outcome of their differing wants and expectations in this domain.

Interestingly, Klein and Loftus' own data suggest that self-descriptiveness judgments are made on the basis of information other than behavioral exemplars. The authors report that latencies followed an inverted "U" pattern in the descriptiveness task in the second experiment, with judgments for medium descriptive traits taking longer than judgments for high and low descriptiveness traits. Yet facilitation did not occur, regardless of trait self-descriptiveness. Klein and Loftus interpret this failure to obtain facilitation as evidence that individuals access abstractions without reference to behavioral exemplars for all but the most novel of self-judgments. But their inability to find facilitation led us to question why trait self-descriptiveness affected the latency of subjects' trait judgments: Why did subjects take longer to make self-judgments about medium descriptiveness traits if they made all of their trait judgments by accessing trait abstractions, regardless of how self-descriptive the traits were? One possible explanation is that judgments of medium descriptiveness traits do require more "computation" than judgments of high or low descriptiveness traits, but the information that individuals examine is not predominantly behavioral.

Trait Centrality and Trait-Relevant Experience

Klein and Loftus point to trait-relevant experience as the major determinant of the level of abstraction at which a trait is represented. The results of their second experiment seem to have persuaded them that trait centrality does not play a significant role. However, we question the interpretation of the data from this experiment, and are hesitant to dismiss the importance of centrality. Specifically, we are not certain what their "self-descriptiveness" scale was measuring. The centrality of a trait is not synonymous with its self-descriptiveness. For example, traits can be highly self-descriptive without being central to one's self-concept, or only moderately descriptive yet quite central. Conceivably, differential facilitation would be obtained with a more precise measure of centrality.

We believe that trait centrality will be an important determinant of whether a trait can be accessed independently of its basis for two main reasons. First, trait centrality is likely to influence trait-relevant experience: Because individuals strive to obtain information about themselves along self-defining dimensions, they are more likely to encode events in terms of central traits, to pay attention to experiences relevant to central traits, and to think about past events that are perceived as relevant to such traits (Markus, 1983; Markus & Sentis, 1982). For example, a woman for whom the trait "independent" is self-defining might readily interpret her decision to move to another country for a new job as evidence of how independent she is. In contrast, another woman who places a higher value on a view of herself as someone who is dedicated to her work might interpret the same behavior as evidence of dedication. Thus, subjectively at least, individuals will have "more" experiences relevant to traits that are central rather than peripheral to their self-concepts. Additionally, people probably *access* central traits more often. By definition, central traits are important to the individual, and reflect domains of enduring interest and concern. When people think about themselves or try to convey their personalities to others, then, they seem likely to do so in terms of central traits. Perhaps it becomes increasingly likely that trait representations will be accessed independently of their bases as the number of times that the individual has considered the traits increases.

We suspect that traits vary considerably in terms of the extent to which they can be accessed independently of their foundations. Klein and Loftus' data would seem to indicate, however, that there are few domains in which individuals do not make trait judgments independently of their bases: In their second experiment, trait self-descriptiveness did not affect facilitation. However, as mentioned earlier, we are confused about what the self-descriptiveness measure was designed to assess. At some points in their chapter, Klein and Loftus seem to use self-descriptiveness of an index of centrality (e.g., pp. 7–15) and at other points they appear to use it as an index of trait relevant experience (e.g., pp. 20–29). We believe that the self-descriptiveness measure is an imprecise indicator of both centrality and trait-relevant experience. The number of an individual's experiences that are relevant to a particular trait does not necessarily reflect the self-descriptiveness of the trait. For example, as the result of working 5 years in a field that requires her to deal with tourists, a woman might have a lot of experience relevant to the trait "cheerful." On the basis of this extensive experience, she might decide that the trait "cheerful" is only moderately self-descriptive. Equivalently, an individual could judge a trait to be highly self-descriptive on the basis of a single, particularly salient experience. We suggest, then, that a specification of the characteristics of traits that can be accessed independently of their bases awaits further research.

Although we do believe that trait-relevant experience will be one of the determinants of the level of abstraction at which traits are represented, we have some concerns about the evidence the authors present in support of this claim. In

Experiment 6, Klein and Loftus demonstrated that recall of specific behaviors facilitates own trait judgments when the trait judgments are restricted to a specific context. Freshman who had been on campus for only a short time were asked whether specific traits described themselves since entering college. In this instance, remembering past behaviors first facilitates people's trait judgments. We are not certain, however, how people respond to a request to make a trait judgment in a novel context in which they have little behavioral experience. Do they actually have context-specific traits in memory that they can access, or is their response more equivalent to a behavioral description? If the latter is more accurate, then it is not surprising that behavioral recall facilitates "trait" descriptions. With no trait to access and few behavioral exemplars to draw on, people essentially may be performing the same task twice.

Incidentally, we share Klein and Loftus' concern that the findings in Experiment 6 may reflect qualitative differences in participants' experiences of home and school. We are less sanguine, however, that Experiment 7 unconfounds the type and amount of experience associated with context in Experiment 6. In Experiment 7, participants refer to their experience at home and school during their high school years. The quality of their experience in high school is likely to differ dramatically from that in the early months of university. Many freshmen live away from home for the first time and develop new friends and interests. We consider it likely that high school and university differ in many ways, and therefore that the shift to high school in Experiment 7 involves much more than a shift in amount of experience in a school context. A longitudinal study in which context is held constant would provide more definitive evidence for the role of trait-relevant experience.

Klein and Loftus' research leaves us uncertain as to the kinds of knowledge individuals access when making trait judgments. Part of the difficultly, we believe, is that Klein and Loftus have focused on a limited range of dependent measures. At this stage, it may be appropriate to invoke more diverse techniques to track down an elusive quarry. For example, a "think-aloud" procedure, whereby individuals disclose what goes through their minds as they make trait judgments, might be informative.

Although we have disputed some of Klein and Loftus's assumptions and inferences, we find the notion of functional independence between trait generalizations and behavioral exemplars intriguing. Next, we consider the implications of functional independence for different aspects of self-knowledge and attitudes. Finally, we discuss the nature of functional independence.

SELF-CONCEPT CHANGE

Some of the most intriguing questions raised by Klein and Loftus' research center around the implications of functional independence when the bases of individuals' trait generalizations cease to be relevant or undergo change. What will happen to trait generalizations in such circumstances? Will they change as well? Imagine a law student who believes that extroverts are likely to be more successful lawyers than introverts. If becoming a successful lawyer is an important goal, she might interpret her behavior in a way that allows her to view herself as an extrovert. Suppose, further, that she eventually accesses this extrovert label independently of her beliefs about extroversion and her motivation to view herself as an extrovert. What would happen to her self-view if her career goal changed and her motivation for the extrovert label vanished? Suppose that she decided instead to be an accountant, and possessed no theory about whether extroverts or introverts excel in this occupation. As an accountant, would she continue to perceive herself as an extrovert, even though the label no longer served its purpose?

Research on the perseverance effect in social perception leads us to suspect that the label would persist (e.g., L. Ross, Lepper, & Hubbard, 1975). In the Ross et al. research, people's self-perceptions endured after the initial bases for the perceptions were completely discredited. Note that this finding is highly consistent with Klein and Loftus' notion of functional independence: To the extent that a given abstraction no longer depends on its base, "removing" the base should have little impact. There is, perhaps, even more reason to suppose that an initial self-concept will persist when an individual's original theories and motivations are simply no longer relevant (as when the law student switched to accountancy), as opposed to discredited.

A related question concerns what happens when *new* motivations and theories are introduced that are at odds with current self-views. The issue here seems not to be whether trait generalizations can be accessed independently of behavioral exemplars, but rather whether exemplars can be accessed independently of trait generalizations. Consider, once more, the example of a woman whose goal is to be a successful lawyer. What would happen if, subsequent to labeling herself an extrovert, she learned that introverts were actually more successful lawyers than extroverts? If she does not immediately dismiss the new theory as personally irrelevant (i.e., not applicable to her for some reason), she may well experience cognitive dissonance. She might try to reduce the dissonance by questioning the credibility of the source of the information, or focusing on other traits (such as intelligence) that she believes ensure her success as a lawyer. Another possible means by which she could resolve the inconsistency between her current self-view (extrovert) and her desired self-view (introvert) would be to change her current self-view in the direction of her desired self-view. She could decide that she is more introverted than she initially believed. Research on motivated reasoning suggests that she is likely to change her self-view in this way: Kunda and Sanitioso (1989) found that subjects led to want to view themselves either as extroverted or as introverted shifted their self-views toward the more desirable trait.

Subsequent research revealed that individuals do not feel free to embrace desired self-views unless they are able to convince themselves that they have grounds for doing so (Sanitioso, Kunda, & Fong, 1990). Sanitioso et al. argued that individuals obtain supportive evidence by accessing behavioral episodes in a biased fashion that reflects their current motivation. For example, in her desire to view herself as an introvert, a woman might access behavioral episodes in which she acted in an introverted manner. Memory will be biased to the extent that she overlooks episodes exemplifying extroverted behavior. Recall is always selective, and the individual's motivation and beliefs at the time of retrieval can influence which behavioral episodes she accesses.

Another means by which individuals might attain desired self-views is through interpreting past events in a manner that is consistent with their current motives and beliefs. Instances originally coded as evidence of extroversion, for example, might instead be taken as evidence of introversion. How might such reinterpretation be accomplished? One possibility is that the person could access the instances from another "direction" (e.g., not through the label "extrovert" but through the label "party behavior"). People presumably code their experiences on multiple dimensions, and are capable of retrieving them through different routes. If the person is able to access an "extrovert" instance from another direction, the ease with which she can reinterpret it as evidence of introversion may depend on the extent to which functional independence is *symmetrical:* As it becomes possible to access an abstract trait representation independently of its bases, does it also become possible to access the bases independently of the trait representation? If functional independence is symmetrical, it should be relatively easy for her to reinterpret the instance as evidence of introversion. If functional independence is asymmetrical, such that accessing the instance inevitably invokes the original extrovert label, reinterpretation should be more difficult. An understanding of how closely autobiographical episodes are tied to the traits originally abstracted from them awaits further research.

To the extent that functional independence is symmetrical, an intriguing possibility presents itself. Individuals should have greater flexibility in interpreting autobiographical episodes that are not closely tied to a particular label. Ironically, then, it may be that episodes associated with traits for which the individual accumulates considerable trait-relevant experience are subsequently susceptible to differing interpretation; these episodes are likely to be "divorced" from their corresponding trait abstraction. Perhaps the relation between flexibility in interpretation and trait-relevant experience is U-shaped. Initially, when the individual has had little trait-relevant experience, the few episodes she has noted might be open to a variety of different interpretations. As the information base builds, the number of potential explanations might decrease somewhat, and a trait abstraction should begin to develop. At this stage, the bases and the abstraction should be closely tied. As time goes on, however, if the abstraction and bases come to be accessible independently of one another, the behavioral episodes might once again become liable to a variety of different interpretations.

INCOMPATIBLE ABSTRACTIONS

Klein and Loftus' ideas about functional independence can perhaps help us understand why individuals sometimes maintain a set of inconsistent abstractions, rather than one global abstraction based on all of the information at hand. For example, individuals may claim many, sometimes contradictory, traits (Sande, Goethals, & Radloff, 1988). In some instances, these traits might be context-specific, and hence not necessarily conflict with one another: Jane might declare that she is extroverted with her friends and introverted with strangers. At other times, however, the traits might contradict one another to a certain extent (e.g., Jane might feel that she is friendly but impatient). The concept of attitudinal ambivalence is also compatible with the proposal that individuals' self-concepts can sometimes be inconsistent with one another (Thompson & Zanna, 1991). People sometimes feel torn between different beliefs and feelings about an object, and they do not always abstract an average or compromise position.

There are a variety of reasons why information might not be combined and integrated into one coherent self-view or attitude. One important factor is probably the ease with which the information can be *categorized* (e.g., as relevant to different contexts or different periods in one's life). Mary might feel that she was shy and withdrawn in high school, but became more outgoing when she went to university. Her theory of personal change will presumably prevent her from experiencing any inconsistency. Additionally, information of different types (e.g., affective vs. cognitive bases of attitudes, or behavioral episodes vs. reflected appraisal as sources of self-knowledge) might be more difficult to integrate than information of the same type. Furthermore, as noted earlier, people do not code incoming information in terms of all of the possible relevant dimensions. Individuals might code a behavior in terms of the trait "friendly" and fail to consider its significance for the trait "impatient." As a result of not having simultaneously considered the two contradictory self-concepts, individuals might initially be unaware of the inconsistency between them.

To the extent that people do become aware of inconsistencies, they should be motivated to resolve them (Heider, 1958). Also, a resolution might be impelled by circumstances; for instance, people often need to decide how to act toward an attitude object. People sometimes have difficulty banishing inconsistencies, however. For example, Devine and her associates found that research participants may experience negative affective reactions to members of particular outgroups, even though such reactions are incompatible with the participants' personal beliefs and they are aware of the inconsistency (Devine, Monteith, Zuwerink, & Elliot, 1991).

How can we understand people's difficulty in resolving inconsistencies? Some of the factors that led the conflicting information to be segregated in the first place (e.g., categorization) will probably hinder its integration. Additionally, it seems that functional independence might sometimes contribute to people's failure to combine information. Integration may become increasingly difficult with increasing levels of abstraction: An individual might experience greater difficulty integrating "extrovert" and "introvert" conceptions than extracting a single meaning from an apparently conflicting set of behavioral episodes. Most specific behaviors can be interpreted in a number of plausible ways; as a result, contradictory evidence often can be readily explained away. Perhaps, with increasing trait-basis independence, it becomes more difficult for individuals to access the bases of trait abstractions when they desire to do so. If functional independence is indeed associated with restricted access to the foundations of self-knowledge, it might exacerbate an individual's difficulty in resolving an inconsistency between self-concepts: Functional independence may render the more integratable behavioral bases less accessible. Note that this speculation does not contradict our earlier proposal that episodes associated with traits that are functionally independent of their bases might be susceptible to different interpretations. At that point, we suggested that behavioral episodes could be accessed by different routes. An individual focused on an inconsistency between two trait abstractions will presumably attempt to access the bases through the original abstractions.

MOTIVATIONAL SELF-STRUCTURES AND ATTITUDES

Klein and Loftus restrict their discussion of the mental representation of the self to the question of how past behaviors and their associated self-concepts are stored. Nonetheless, their suggestion that trait abstractions can be accessed independently of their bases has interesting implications for the representation of other structures as well. It is particularly relevant to the substantial literature suggesting the existence of *possible* selves—for example, ideal selves, feared selves, and ought selves (Higgins, 1987; Markus & Nurius, 1986). These motivational self-structures are thought to represent individuals' goals for the future (the selves they want to achieve or avoid), and to play an important role in guiding behavior.

Possible selves may be associated with imagined, future behaviors. For example, a teacher who seeks to become more sensitive to the needs of his students might imagine future scenarios in which he behaves in a manner consistent with this goal. Possible selves might also be derived from past experiences. An individual's memory of an academic or personal failure might contribute to an "incompetent," feared self. Alternatively, a feared self might be founded on the individual's fervent desire to avoid being like another person (e.g., her mother).

These examples depict the individual as very much conscious of the association between the origin of the goal and the goal itself. Conceivably, individuals are sometimes less aware of this link. For example, a man might not be aware of the fact that his older brother has served as a model for his own ideal self.

Are Klein and Loftus' ideas regarding functional independence generalizable to possible selves? Because of the motivational quality of possible selves, functional independence has particularly intriguing implications for these structures. Klein and Loftus suggest that once traits have been abstracted, individuals should be able to make trait judgments even when the information on which the traits were based cannot be recalled (see p. 15). A parallel notion with respect to motivational self-structures is that once an ideal self has developed, individuals might continue their efforts to achieve the goal, while at the same time being incapable of articulating their original reasons for doing so. Ironically, if functional independence is associated with restricted access to the bases of these structures, it may be the case that people are least able to accurately report the reasons that gave rise to behavior patterns in the domains that are most important to them (i.e., where experience is high).

Next consider what occurs when the motivation that originally gave rise to a possible self ceases to exist. Will individuals continue striving toward the goal, even though their initial reason for pursuing it is no longer valid? Suppose a woman loves a man who wants a politically active partner. Being a politically involved person becomes an ideal self for her, and she pursues this goal with vigor. How does the woman's ideal self change if her relationship with the man ends? If the ideal self-structure has become independent of its basis, the woman should continue striving toward political activism despite the absence of her initial motive.

The suggestion that her efforts would continue even after the relationship ended is consistent with Gordon Allport's (1960) theorizing regarding the "functional autonomy of motives." Allport argued that "motivation may be—and in healthy people usually is—autonomous of its origins" (p. 29). Specifically, he suggested that motives are often sustained through their incorporation into the individual's ego-structure; an individual might continue to pursue a goal for new reasons, perhaps because it has become self-defining in some way. In our scenario, then, the woman's "politically active" ideal self might become an integral part of her self-concept.

We can also extend Klein and Loftus' ideas to attitudes. Functional independence would imply that individuals could indicate their overall evaluation of an entity without accessing the beliefs, feelings, and/or behavioral intentions that originally gave rise to the evaluation. Furthermore, to the extent that the bases of attitudes become less accessible with increasing functional independence, individuals might have more difficulty justifying attitudes that are functionally independent of their foundations. If a husband tells his wife that he dislikes her best friend, but cannot explain why, it is possible that he is not just being difficult.

Next, consider what happens when the original basis of an attitude is eliminated. Suppose a man comes to relish Chinese food because someone he admires exhibits such a preference (see Heider, 1958). What will happen if that admiration turns to hatred? The attitude should persist if it has become independent of its foundation. Lee Ross and his associates' explanation of the perseverance effect (L. Ross et al., 1975) and Allport's discussion of functional autonomy imply that beliefs and motives acquire new bases that serve to sustain them. In our attitude example, then, the man's imitation-based preference for Chinese food might become self-sustaining. He might begin to truly crave egg rolls. It seems likely that structures such as possible selves and attitudes often grow their own "legs," such that they no longer depend on the information on which they were founded.

THE NATURE OF FUNCTIONAL INDEPENDENCE

To this point, we have not distinguished explicitly cases in which a given abstraction is independent of its initial basis from those in which it is independent of any basis. A belief in the former type of independence does not necessitate a belief in the latter type. In particular, we think it is interesting to consider whether abstractions can be of a habitual nature. For example, can one have habitual feelings or attitudes? We use the term *habitual* to denote instances where feelings have their own inertia independent of any bases, and persevere indefinitely unless opposing forces are encountered. Consider an analogy between behavioral and attitudinal habits. A man might continue to do his laundry on Sunday afternoons long after there is any good reason for doing it at that particular time. If he stopped to think about it, he might discover a different day that would suit him much better. By the same token, a person might habitually exhibit an attitude without analyzing it or examining other possible reactions to the entity in question. Zajonc (1980, 1984) argued that cognition is not a necessary antecedent of affect. One implication of the current analysis is that cognition is sometimes also unnecessary for the maintenance of affective reactions.

In short, we wonder whether bases of some type (whether or not the individual can articulate them) need to exist for an abstraction to endure. Or can an abstraction survive in the absence of both its original basis and new "legs"? We are intrigued by the possibility that certain abstractions can become entrenched and endure indefinitely, despite the fact that they are currently without basis. We believe that it is useful at least to consider whether such cases are possible—if for no other reason than it should lead to a more precise specification of what is meant by the term *independence*. When abstractions are accessed and expressed independently of their foundations, do they still depend on these or other bases in some way? Or can abstractions sometimes exist independently of any bases? Although we use the label *abstraction* as an umbrella term to include self-concepts, motivational self-structures, attitudes, and so forth, it seems likely that the nature of functional independence varies, in ways that remain to be specified, depending on the type of abstraction.

In this chapter, we have described some of the thoughts that the Klein and Loftus thesis has engendered in us. The concept of functional independence has interesting implications for the mental representation of the self, as well as for a wide variety of previous research and theorizing. We believe that Klein and Loftus' work raises many questions worthy of discussion and debate, and that it suggests directions for potentially important future research. We expect that others will also find their ideas provocative.

REFERENCES

Allport, G. W. (1960). *Personality and social encounter: Selected essays*. Boston: Bacon Press.

Conway, M., & Ross, M. (1984). Getting what you want by revising what you had. *Journal of Personality and Social Psychology, 47*, 738–748.

Cooley, D. H. (1902). *Human nature and the social order*. New York: Scribners.

Devine, P., Monteith, M. J., Zuwerink, J. R., & Elliot, A. J. (1991). Prejudice with and without compunction. *Journal of Personality and Social Psychology, 60*, 817–830.

Festinger, L. (1954). A theory of social comparison processes. *Human Relations, 7*, 117–140.

Heider, F. (1958). *The psychology of interpersonal relations*. New York: Wiley.

Higgins, E. T. (1987). Self-discrepancy theory: A theory relating self and affect. *Psychological Review, 94*, 319–340.

Jones, E. E. (1990). *Interpersonal perception*. New York: W. H. Freeman.

Kunda, Z., & Sanitioso, R. (1989). Motivated changes in the self-concept. *Journal of Experimental Social Psychology, 25*, 272–285.

Markus, H. (1983). Self-knowledge: An expanded view. *Journal of Personality, 51*, 543–565.

Markus, H., & Nurius, P. (1986). Possible selves. *American Psychologist, 41*, 954–969.

Markus, H., & Sentis, K. (1982). The self in social information processing. In J. Suls (Ed.), *Psychological perspectives on the self* (pp. 41–70). Hillsdale, NJ: Lawrence Erlbaum Associates.

McFarland, C., Ross, M., & Giltrow, M. (1992). Biased recollections in older adults: The role of implicit theories of aging. *Journal of Personality and Social Psychology, 62*, 837–850.

Ross, L., Lepper, M. R., & Hubbard, M. (1975). Perseverance in self-perception and social perception: Biased attributional processes in the debriefing paradigm. *Journal of Personality and Social Psychology, 32*, 880–892.

Ross, M. (1989). Relation of implicit theories to the construction of personal histories. *Psychological Review, 96*, 341–357.

Sanitioso, R., Kunda, Z., & Fong, G. T. (1990). Motivated recruitment of autobiographical memories. *Journal of Personality and Social Psychology, 59*, 229–241.

Sande, G. N., Goethals, G. R., & Radloff, C. E. (1988). Perceiving one's own traits and others': The multifaceted self. *Journal of Personality and Social psychology, 54*, 13–20.

Schneider, D. J. (1973). Implicit personality theory: A review. *Psychological Bulletin, 79*, 294–309.

Schweder, R. A. (1975). How relevant is an individual difference theory of personality? *Journal of Personality, 43*, 455–484.

Thompson, M. M., & Zanna, M. P. (1991). *Domain-specific and personality-based antecedents of ambivalent attitudes.* Unpublished manuscript, University of Waterloo, Ontario.

Zajonc, R. B. (1980). Feeling and thinking: Preferences need no inferences. *American Psychologist, 35,* 151–175.

Zajonc, R. B. (1984). On the primacy of affect. *American Psychologist, 39,* 117–123.

13 Some Lingering Self-Doubts: Reply to Commentaries

Stanley B. Klein
Judith Loftus
University of California, Santa Barbara

We thank our commentators for their thoughtful and constructive comments on our work. We are particularly pleased to see such a broad range of theoretical perspectives among the commentaries. The insights offered and issues raised by this diverse group of theoreticians have done much to enhance and broaden our work. It is fortunate that even in this age of increasing specialization in psychology, the mental representation of self-knowledge is a topic wide enough in its appeal to cut across domains.

Our goal in this reply is to address some of the main criticisms of our work that commentators have raised. Specifically, we discuss questions about (a) the role of exemplars in the trait-judgment process, (b) the adequacy of definition generation as a control task for our studies, (c) the interpretation of self-in-context findings, and (d) the scope of our conclusions about self-knowledge.

A PURE-EXEMPLAR ALTERNATIVE TO OUR MIXED MODEL

Keenan (chapter 4) offered an interesting alternative to our model. In contrast to the mixed model view that trait judgments activate behavioral exemplars only under certain conditions, Keenan hypothesizes that trait judgments always activate behavioral exemplars. Keenan argues that an exemplar model of trait judgments not only can better explain our data, but also is more consistent with the literature on the self-reference effect.

Keenan's exemplar-based explanation of our data states that facilitation between *Remember* and *Describes* tasks may be seen as a function of the ratio of the number of behaviors activated by one task to the number of behaviors activated by the other. According to Keenan, performance of a *Remember* task activates just one or perhaps a small number of behaviors, whereas performance of a *Describes* task activates most or all of the relevant behaviors in memory. Thus, when trait-relevant behavioral experience is low, the ratio of the number of behaviors activated by the *Remembers* task ($N = 1$ or few) to the number of behaviors activated by the *Describes* task ($N =$ few) will be large, and considerable facilitation should be observed. However, when trait-relevant behavioral experience is high, the ratio of the number of behaviors activated by the *Remembers* task ($N = 1$ or few) to the number of behaviors activated by the *Describes* task ($N =$ many) will be small, and facilitation should be less.

Thus, Keenan's model contrasts with our own as follows: We predict that a *Describes* task will activate behavioral exemplars only when there is not enough behavioral experience for formation of a summary trait representation. Thus, we predict a dichotomous pattern of facilitation: Facilitation should occur for low and medium descriptive traits, but not for high descriptive traits. Keenan, on the other hand, proposes that a *Describes* task *always* will activate behavioral exemplars, even when summary trait information is available. Thus, she predicts a "continuum of facilitation" (p. 75), along which facilitation decreases as behavioral experience increases.

Can Keenan's Exemplar Model Better Account for the Data from the Task-Facilitation Paradigm?

Keenan sees the data from our *Mother* experiment (Study 5) as pivotal for deciding between a pure-exemplar and a mixed model. She concludes that an exemplar model best describes these data, but we do not agree.

In examining the data in Fig. 1.6, Keenan states "It is my impression that the data. . . . are more amenable to a continuum of facilitation than a dichotomous split of all or none facilitation" (p. 75). However, the data in Fig. 1.6 are in fact not at all compatible with such a continuum. Neither of the target tasks shows a decrease in facilitation with increasing trait descriptiveness: The facilitation functions for both tasks show that medium descriptive traits yield more, not less, facilitation than low descriptive traits (we discuss how a mixed model can account for these findings on pp. 24–25 of our chapter).

Further, the data in Fig. 1.6 show another contradiction to Keenan's model. An exemplar model implies that a *Describes-Mother* target task that has been preceded by a *Remember-Mother* task should be preformed more quickly for low than for high descriptive traits. This is because for low descriptive traits, the ratio of the number of behaviors activated by the *Remember-Mother* initial task to the number of behaviors activated by the *Describes-Mother* target task should be large ("1/small N"), whereas for high descriptive traits the ratio should be small ("1/large N"). Contrary to these predictions, Fig. 1.6 shows that the time taken to perform a *Describes-Mother* task that has been preceded by a *Remember-Mother* task is not faster for low than for high descriptive traits.

In summary, although Keenan's exemplar interpretation of our data may be more parsimonious than the mixed model by virtue of having one less process, it has the disadvantage of being unable to account for a number of features of our data. Keenan's approach does offer a very interesting challenge to our conclusions; however, at this point we continue to prefer the mixed model, as it seems to do the best job of explaining the total pattern of our findings.

Can Keenan's Exemplar Model Better Account for Data from the Self-Reference Paradigm?

Keenan proposes that a mixed model cannot stand in the face of the self-reference effect (SRE)—the finding that information is especially well remembered when it is encoded with respect to the self. Specifically, Keenan argues that by removing a role for behaviors in self-descriptiveness judgments, the mixed model eliminates the only "basis for self-referent encodings being more elaborate and hence more memorable" (p. 72) than other types of encodings. By contrast, because an exemplar model assumes that behaviors are activated in trait judgments, Keenan argues that it—unlike a mixed model—allows elaboration and therefore can account for the SRE.

Unfortunately, Keenan's logic rests on some debatable assumptions. To begin with, it assumes that elaboration must be the mechanism underlying the SRE. However, the processes mediating the SRE are far from agreed upon (recent reviews can be found in Greenwald & Pratkanis, 1984; Higgins & Bargh, 1987; Kihlstrom et al., 1988). Elaboration is just one of many explanations that have been proposed; others include organization (e.g., Klein and Kihlstrom, 1986, evaluation (e.g., Ferguson, Rule, & Carlson, 1983) prototype activation (e.g., Kuiper, 1981), cognitive cueing (e.g., Bellezza, 1984) and distinctiveness (e.g., Friedman & Pullyblank, 1982). So far, none of these theories predominates, and it therefore seems premature to argue against the mixed model on the basis of its failure to conform to the predictions of a model utilizing one of them.

Second, even if elaboration were the undisputed process underlying the SRE, Keenan's position would be problematic because it equates elaboration with the activation of trait-relevant behavioral memories. The term *elaboration* refers to a *process* by which associations are formed between a word and other information in memory; it is mute with respect to the *type* of information used to embellish the encoded representation of a word (e.g., Anderson & Reder, 1979; Bellezza, Cheesman, & Reddy, 1977; Craik & Tulving, 1975; Klein, Loftus, Kihlstrom, & Aseron, 1989).

Keenan assumes that behavioral memories are the only type of self-knowledge that may used to elaborate trait words judged for self-reference; however, there are other types of self-knowledge that could provide a basis for trait elaboration.

Among these are one's goals (e.g., Pervin, 1989; Read, Jones, & Miller, 1990), self-beliefs (e.g., Higgins, 1987), social roles (e.g., Wyer & Gordon, 1984), and personal reputation (e.g., Lord, chapter 6, this volume; Nelson, chapter 8, this volume). There is no reason why these sources of self-knowledge should not be as likely as behavioral memories to serve as a basis for trait elaboration during self-referent encoding.

In fact, there is evidence in the literature against a behavior-based elaboration interpretation of the SRE. Researchers have used two types of self-referent encoding tasks to produce self-reference effects: those requiring subjects to decide if a trait word describes them (descriptive tasks) and those requiring subjects to retrieve a behavioral memory involving the trait (autobiographical tasks). According to Keenan's exemplar model, a descriptive task should activate more trait-relevant behaviors than an autobiographical task, because a descriptive task should activate most of the relevant behaviors in memory, whereas an autobiographical task should activate only one or a small number of behaviors. Thus, a descriptive task should provide a comparatively rich set of behaviors with which to elaborate a trait word, whereas an autobiographical task should provide a comparatively limited basis for trait elaboration. Therefore, Keenan's exemplar model predicts that a descriptive task should promote better memory for trait words than will an autobiographical task. Contrary to this prediction, however, descriptive and autobiographical self-reference tasks yield comparable recall (e.g., Bower & Gilligan, 1979; Klein, Loftus, & Burton, 1989).

Finally, although the activation of behaviors during trait judgments about the self may seem intuitive, we are unaware of any empirical demonstration that it actually occurs. In fact, a number of studies have been unable to obtain evidence in favor of this claim (e.g., Kihlstrom et al., 1988; Klein, Loftus, & Burton, 1989; Klein, Loftus, & Plog, 1992; Klein, Loftus, Trafton, & Fuhrman, 1992).

Thus, Keenan's argument that an exemplar model is more compatible than a mixed model with the literature on the SRE requires a number of accommodations. First, one must accept an unproved basis for the effect; second, one must adopt a restricted view of the process of elaboration; and third, one must choose intuition over empirical findings. Although we applaud Keenan's efforts to connect trait-judgment models with the findings from the self-reference paradigm, we believe that those findings do not support an exemplar model.

IS DEFINITION GENERATION AN APPROPRIATE CONTROL TASK?

Brown (chapter 3) and Keenan both question whether a definition generation task serves as an adequate control in our task-facilitation studies. Keenan argues that subjects may actually retrieve behavioral exemplars when generating definitions. For example, a person asked to define the trait word *kind* may think "*kind* is like when I take care of the neighbors cat, so *kind* means helping out neighbors when they need it" (p. 71). Brown suggests that knowledge of trait meanings may be directly linked with both abstract trait self-knowledge and trait-relevant behavioral memories. Both proposals imply that definition generation activates the same type of information (e.g., trait-relevant behavioral memories) assumed to be activated during performance of self-tasks.

We agree that this is an important issue. If we look only at Studies 1 and 2, our failure to find differential facilitation of self-target tasks as a function of initial task performed might indeed be explained by either of these proposals. However, our acceptance of definition generation as an appropriate control task does not rest exclusively on the results of these two studies. It is based also on our finding that a *Remember* initial task is more facilitating than a *Define* initial task when a *Describes* target task is performed with reference to a context in which subjects have limited experience (Study 6), but not one in which they have extensive experience (Study 7). And it is supported by our finding that for judgments about one's mother, initial *Describes-Mother* and *Remember-Mother* tasks provide greater target task facilitation than does an initial *Define* tasks when traits being judged are medium or low in mother-descriptiveness, but not when they are high in mother-descriptiveness (Study 5).

Given these findings, the hypothesis that definition generation activates self-knowledge would have to incorporate a number of exceptions to the rule. For example, generating a definition would have to: (a) activate behavioral knowledge about the self-in-high school (Study 7), but not about the self-in-college (Study 6), (b) activate behaviors pertaining to traits that are high in mother-descriptiveness, but not those pertaining to traits that are medium or low in mother-descriptiveness, and (c) sometimes activate behavioral exemplars about self (e.g., Studies 1 and 2), sometimes activate behavioral exemplars about mother (Study 5), and sometimes activate no behavioral exemplars (Study 6). By contrast, the mixed model easily accommodates all of these findings within a single explanatory framework.

Additional evidence that definition generation does not activate self-knowledge is found in the initial task latency data reported in Study 2 of our chapter. As we noted, latencies for both *Describes* and *Remember* initial tasks show reliable effects of self-descriptiveness, whereas latencies for the *Define* initial task show no effect. We would like to point out, by the way, that our interpretation of these patterns was based on a post hoc analysis of a significant three-way interaction of initial task and trait-descriptiveness (for details, see Klein, Loftus, Trafton, & Fuhrman, 1992), not, as Keenan suggests, on an acceptance of the null hypothesis.

In summary, our conclusion that definition generation is an appropriate control task for our studies is based on a convergence of findings from a number of sources; given this, we believe it is difficult to argue that definition generation involves self-knowledge.

THE SELF-IN-CONTEXT: QUANTITATIVE VERSUS
QUALITATIVE EXPLANATIONS

The self-in-context study (Study 6) showed that a *Remember School* task facilitated the subsequent performance of a *Describes School* task, whereas a *Remember Home* task failed to facilitate performance of a subsequent *Describes Home* task. We interpreted these findings as evidence that when amount of behavioral experience is manipulated, trait-descriptiveness judgments about the self correspond to the predictions of a mixed model.

This conclusion was based on our belief that the principal difference between self-at-home and self-at-school was a quantitative one—amount of trait-relevant behavioral experience. However, we noted that there also are qualitative differences between these two social contexts that might account for our findings. Consequently, we ran an additional study (Study 7) in an attempt to unconfound the type and the amount of experience associated with these contexts. Specifically, we tried to eliminate the difference in the amount of experience between home and school by specifying the same time period for each (*Home* referred to subjects' experience at home during their 4 years of high school, and *school* referred to subjects' experience at school during the same 4-year period). We reasoned that if quantity of behavioral experience was the critical factor, then eliminating the difference in amount of experience between the home and school contexts should eliminate the differential facilitation we found in Study 6. However, if qualitative differences between the two contexts were responsible for the results of Study 6, then removing the difference in amount of experience should not have an effect—we still should see a difference in facilitation.

The results of Study 7 show no evidence of differential facilitation, thus supporting our contention that the facilitation found in Study 6 reflected quantitative rather than qualitative differences in subjects' experiences of home and school. Vorauer and Ross (chapter 12), however, call attention to an interpretive ambiguity that arises from the fact that what we meant by "school" was altered across studies: In Study 6, *school* referred to college, whereas in Study 7 it referred to high school. As they correctly note, it is likely that there are greater qualitative differences between the home and college contexts than between home and high school. Thus, it is possible in Study 7 that by changing the school context from college to high school, we not only eliminated the difference in amount of experience between the home and school contexts, but we also minimized qualitative differences between the two contexts that may have accounted for the difference in facilitation in Study 6. They conclude that a study in which context was held constant, while experience was varied, would provide more definitive evidence for the role we have claimed for trait-relevant experience.

Fortunately, we have data that suggest that changing the school context to high school did not compromise our findings. As part of a larger study, we (Klein & Loftus, in press) used college as the school context and recorded the time college seniors took to perform a *Describes School* target task when it followed either a *Remember School* or a *Define* initial task. If the facilitation observed in Study 6 is attributable to the type of experience associated with college, then seniors should show facilitation similar to that obtained with first year college students— a *Remember School* task should be more facilitating than a *Define* task to the subsequent performance of a *Describes School* task. By contrast, if the facilitation was due to amount of experience, then seniors should perform similarly to subjects in Study 7—a *Remember School* task should be no more facilitating than a *Define* task to the subsequent performance of a *Describes School* task. Our findings revealed that the time required to perform a *Describes School* target task was not differentially affected by the initial performance of a *Remember School* or a *Define* task [$t(16) = 1.32, p > .10$]. It thus appears that amount, not type, of experience is the critical factor determining whether behavioral exemplars will facilitate trait self-descriptiveness judgments.

IS THERE MORE TO SELF-KNOWLEDGE THAN TRAITS AND BEHAVIORS?

The question of whether trait knowledge is inseparable from memory for behaviors has stirred debate among both philosophers (e.g., Grice, 1941; Hume, 1739/1817; Locke, 1690/1731) and psychologists (e.g., Buss & Craik, 1983; James, 1890; Locksely & Lenauer, 1981) for more than three centuries. Unfortunately, as evidenced by the number of years debate on this topic has persisted, an answer to this question has proven elusive. Our research makes a modest contribution to this debate by showing that the role of specific behavioral exemplars in trait judgments is dependent on the amount of trait-relevant behavioral experience one has with the person being judged.

However, although our work has focused on the role of behavioral experience in the acquisition of abstract trait knowledge, we do not mean to imply that behavioral memories are the only source of knowledge contributing to the formation of abstract trait knowledge about the self and others. As several of the commentators have discussed, nonbehavioral factors also may play a role in the formation of abstract trait knowledge (see especially the chapters by Lord and Nelson). The principal contribution of our research is its demonstration that once abstract trait knowledge is acquired, people tend to rely on these abstractions when making trait judgments.

SOME FINAL THOUGHTS

Clearly, our initial attempts to explore the relation between trait and behavioral knowledge have left many questions unanswered. For example, although we have provided evidence that summary representations typically serve as a basis for making trait-descriptiveness judgments, our research does not directly address how these summaries are represented in memory. Are they represented as prototypes (e.g., Cantor & Mischel, 1979)? As goal-based schemata (e.g., Pervin, 1989)? As generic knowledge structures (e.g., Barsalou, 1988)? Another important question is whether our findings apply to other types of social judgments. For example, do people answer questions about their social preferences (e.g., "Do you like to go to parties?") on the basis of abstract knowledge, behavioral memories, or, perhaps, some other type of personal knowledge? Finally, although our research clearly shows that behavioral exemplars are not *required* for trait judgments, it does not rule out the possibility that behavioral exemplars can, under certain conditions, influence these judgments. Indeed, our research has documented some of these conditions (e.g., judgments of self in a novel context). A full accounting of the conditions under which behaviors will have an influence will likely keep researchers busy for some time.

In conclusion, we want to express our appreciation to the commentators for the issues they have raised and perspectives they have offered. To both Lord and to Maki and Carlson (chapter 7) we extend thanks for showing how our task-facilitation paradigm can be used to address questions in domains beyond the limited realm of our research. At the same time, we appreciate Schneider, Roediger, and Khan's (chapter 9) clear articulation of potential limitations of our paradigm. We thank Kihlstrom (chapter 5) for his thoughtful review of cognitive perspectives on the representation of self-knowledge, and Brown for suggesting an interesting new method for exploring that knowledge. We thank Sedikides for his discussion of conditions under which behavioral exemplars may play a role in dispositional attributions. We are grateful to Bellezza (chapter 2) for his enlightening discussion of the plausibility of pure-exemplar models, and to Nelson for showing that simple dichotomies are unlikely to capture the complexity of human memory. We appreciate Vorauer and Ross' work in bringing to light a number of interesting implications of the idea of functional independence for theory and research in social psychology. We are especially grateful to Tulving (chapter 11) for bringing together the domains of clinical amnesia and personality psychology, thus providing an exciting first look at what a neuropsychology of personality might be like. And finally, we thank Keenan, whose very interesting exemplar-based model provides a serious challenge to our mixed model. Although we believe a mixed model can adequately explain the currently available data, the question of whether this is the *best* model to explain the data awaits future research.

REFERENCES

Anderson, J. R., & Reder, L. M. (1979). An elaborative processing explanation of depth of processing. In L. S. Cermak & F. I. M. Craik (Eds.), *Levels of processing in human memory* (pp. 385–403). Hillsdale, NJ: Lawrence Erlbaum Associates.

Barsalou, L. W. (1988). The content and organization of autobiographical memories. In U. Neisser & E. Winograd (Eds.), *Remembering reconsidered: Ecological and traditional approaches to the study of memory* (pp. 193–243). New York: Cambridge University Press.

Bellezza, F. S. (1984). The self as a mnemonic device: The role of internal cues. *Journal of Personality and Social Psychology, 47,* 506–516.

Bellezza, F. S., Cheesman, F. L., & Reddy, B. G. (1977). Organization and semantic elaboration in fre recall. *Journal of Experimental Psychology: Human Learning and Memory, 3,* 539–550.

Bower, G. H., & Gilligan, S. G. (1979). Remembering information related to one's self. *Journal of Research in Personality, 13,* 420–432.

Buss, D. M., & Craik, K. H. (1983). The act frequency approach to personality. *Psychological Review, 90,* 105–126.

Cantor, N., & Mischel, W. (1979). Prototypes in person perception. In L. Berkowitz (Ed.), *Advances in experimental social psychology* (Vol. 12, pp. 3–52). New York: Academic Press.

Craik, F. I. M., & Tulving, E. (1975). Depth of processing and the retention of words in episodic memory. *Journal of Experimental Psychology: General, 11,* 268–294.

Ferguson, T. J., Rule, G. R., & Carlson, D. (1983). Memory for personally relevant information. *Journal of Personality and Social Psychology, 44,* 251–261.

Friedman, A., & Pullyblank, J. (1982, November). *Remembering information about oneself and others: The role of distinctiveness.* Paper presented at the meeting of the Psychonomic Society, Minneapolis, MN.

Greenwald, A. G., & Pratkanis, A. R. (1984). The self. In R. S. Wyer & T. K. Srull (Eds.), *Handbook of social cognition* (Vol. 3, pp. 129–178). Hillsdale, NJ: Lawrence Erlbaum Associates.

Grice, H. P. (1941). Personal identity. *Mind, 50,* 330–350.

Higgins, E. T. (1987). Self-discrepency: A theory relating self and affect. *Psychological Review, 94,* 319–340.

Higgins, E. T, & Bargh, J. A. (1987). Social cognition and social perception. *Annual Review of Psychology, 38,* 369–425.

Hume, D. A. (1817). *A treatise of human nature.* London: Thomas and Joseph Allman. (Original work published 1739)

James, W. (1890). *The principles of psychology* (Vol. 1). New York: Holt.

Kihlstrom, J. F., Cantor, N., Albright, J. S., Chew, B. R., Klein, S. B., & Niedenthal, P. M. (1988). Information processing and the study of the self. In L. Berkowitz (Ed.), *Advances in experimental social psychology* (Vol. 21, pp. 145–177). New York: Academic Press.

Klein, S. B., & Kihlstrom, J. F. (1986). Elaboration, organization, and the self-reference effect in memory. *Journal of Experimental Psychology: General, 115,* 26–38.

Klein, S. B., & Loftus, J. (in press). Behavioral experience and trait judgments about the self. *Personality and Social Psychology Bulletin.*

Klein, S. B., Loftus, J., Kihlstrom, J. F., & Aseron, R. (1989). Effects of item-specific and relational information on hypermnesic recall. *Journal of Experimental Psychology: Learning, Memory, and Cognition, 15,* 1192–1197.

Klein, S. B., Loftus, J., & Burton, H. A. (1989). Two self-reference effects: The importance of distinguishing between self-descriptiveness judgments and autobiographical retrieval in self-referent encoding. *Journal of Personality and Social Psychology, 56,* 853–865.

Klein, S. B., Loftus, J., & Plog, A. E. (1992). Trait judgments about the self: Evidence from the encoding specificity paradigm. *Personality and Social Psychology Bulletin, 18,* 730–735.

Klein, S. B., Loftus, J., Trafton, J. G., & Fuhrman, R. W. (1992). The use of exemplars and abstractions in trait judgments: A model of trait knowledge about the self and others. *Journal of Personality and Social Psychology, 63,* 739–753.

Kuiper, N. A. (1981). Convergent evidence for the self as prototype: The "inverted-U RT" effect for self and other judgments. *Personality and Social Psychology Bulletin, 35,* 63–78.

Locke, J. (1731). *An essay concerning human understanding*. London: Edmund Parker. (Original work published 1690)

Locksley, A., & Lenauer, M. (1981). Considerations for a theory of self-inference processes. In N. Cantor & J. F. Kihlstrom (Eds.), *Personality, cognition, and social interaction* (pp. 263–277). Hillsdale, NJ: Lawrence Erlbaum Associates.

Pervin, L. A. (Ed.). (1989). *Goal concepts in personality and social psychology*. Hillsdale, NJ: Lawrence Erlbaum Associates.

Read, S. J., Jones, D. K., & Miller, L. C. (1990). Traits as goal-based categories: The importance of goals in the coherence of dispositional categories. *Journal of Personality and Social Psychology, 58*, 1048–1061.

Wyer, R. S., & Gordon, S. E. (1984). The cognitive representation of social information. In R. S. Wyer & T. K. Srull (Eds.), *Handbook of social cognition* (Vol. 2, pp. 73–150). Hillsdale, NJ: Lawrence Erlbaum Associates.

Author Index

Subject Index